Plug and Play System Architecture

MINDSHARE, INC.

TOM SHANLEY

Addison-Wesley Publishing Company

Reading, Massachusetts • Menlo Park, California • New York

Don Mills, Ontario • Wokingham, England • Amsterdam

Bonn • Sydney • Singapore • Tokyo • Madrid • San Juan

Paris • Seoul • Milan • Mexico City • Taipei

Many of the designations used by manufacturers and sellers to distinguish their products are claimed as trademarks. Where those designations appear in this book, and Addison-Wesley was aware of a trademark claim, the designations have been printed in initial capital letters or all capital letters.

The authors and publishers have taken care in preparation of this book, but make no expressed or implied warranty of any kind and assume no responsibility for errors or omissions. No liability is assumed for incidental or consequential damages in connection with or arising out of the use of the information or programs contained herein.

Library of Congress Cataloging-in-Publication Data

Plug and play system architecture / MindShare, Inc., Tom Shanley.
          p.   cm.
    Includes index.
    ISBN 0-201-41013-3 (alk. paper)
    1.   Computer architecture.   I. Shanley, Tom.
  QA76.9.A73P59   1995
  004.6'2 – dc20   95-30802
                                               CIP

Sponsoring Editor: Kathleen Tibbetts
Production Coordinator: Deborah McKenna
Cover design: Barbara T. Atkinson
Set in 10 point Palatino by MindShare, Inc.

2 3 4 5 6 7 8 9 10-MA-0099989796
Second Printing, June 1996

Addison-Wesley books are available for bulk purchases by corporations, institutions, and other organizations. For more information please contact the Corporate, Government, and Special Sales Department at (800) 238-9682.

To Bubba and Belle, my constant companions.

Contents

About This Book

Part One—Evolution

Chapter 1: The Perfect Machine

Chapter 2: ISA, an Imperfect Standard

Contents

Chapter 3: EISA and Micro Channel

Chapter 4: PCI

Contents

Chapter 5: PCMCIA

Part Two—E/ISA Plug and Play

Chapter 6: Intro to E/ISA Plug and Play

Chapter 7: Power Up State of PnP Devices

Contents

Contents

Contents

Chapter 13: Intro to PnP BIOS and OS

Contents

Chapter 14: The PnP POST and Device ROMs

Chapter 15: The PnP BIOS Services

Contents

Contents

Contents

Figures

Tables

Tables

Acknowledgments

To the folks at Frame Technology. This is the first book I've done using Frame-Maker, and I cannot bestow too much praise on the developers of this package. To Don Anderson for keeping MindShare going while I wrote this book. To the folks at Addison-Wesley for their collective patience.

About This Book

The MindShare Architecture Series

The MindShare Architecture book series includes: ISA System Architecture, EISA System Architecture, 80486 System Architecture, PCI System Architecture, Pentium System Architecture, PCMCIA System Architecture, PowerPC System Architecture, and Plug-and-Play System Architecture.

Rather than duplicating common information in each book, the series uses the building-block approach. ISA System Architecture is the core book upon which the others build. The figure below illustrates the relationship of the books to each other.

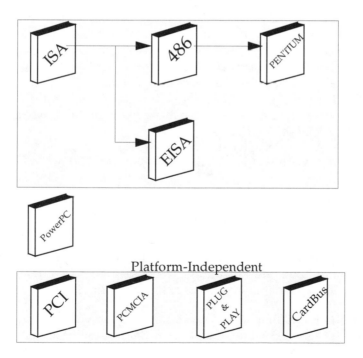

Platform-Independent

Plug and Play System Architecture

Organization of This Book

The author considers this book a companion to the Microsoft Press book entitled *Hardware Design Guide for Microsoft Windows 95*. *Plug and Play System Architecture* is divided into two parts entitled:

- Part One—Evolution
- Part Two—E/ISA Plug and Play.

Part One—Evolution

This part of the book provides an overview of technologies other than E/ISA Plug and Play and how they relate to the realization of PC systems and operating system software that support Plug and Play. This section consists of the following chapters:

- **The Perfect Machine**. This chapter sets the stage by providing a simple portrait of everyone's dream machine and the qualities it would possess.
- **ISA, an Imperfect Standard**. This chapter describes the drawbacks of the ISA machine architecture with regard to system configuration and Plug and Play capability.
- **EISA and Micro Channel**. This chapter describes the configuration methodology used by EISA and Micro Channel devices.
- **PCI**. This chapter describes the automatic configuration achievable with PCI devices. It also discusses the relationship of Windows 95, Windows NT, and PCI devices.
- **PCMCIA**. This chapter describes the relationship of PCMCIA, Plug and Play, and Windows 95, and ends Part One, "Evolution."

Part Two—E/ISA Plug and Play

This part of the book provides a detailed discussion of Plug and Play as defined for ISA and EISA cards. In addition, it includes a detailed description the Plug and Play BIOS. This section consists of the following chapters:

- **Intro to E/ISA Plug and Play**. This chapter provides an introduction to the topic of ISA/EISA Plug and Play. It defines the basic concepts and some basic terminology.
- **Power Up State of PnP Devices**. This chapter describes the state of PnP

cards when the machine is first powered up.

- **Configuration Ports**. This chapter describes the three configuration ports that are used throughout the process of configuring ISA/EISA PnP cards.
- **Configuration States**. This chapter introduces the various configuration states that a PnP device may be in, the relationship of the states to each other, and the purpose of each state.
- **Isolating a Card for Configuration**. This chapter describes the process used to isolate a single PnP device for configuration. This includes the initiation key sequence, the isolation process, and the CSN assignment.
- **Card Resource Requirements**. The next step is to wake up each card, read its resource requirements (memory space, IO space, interrupt request line, DMA channel, etc.), and put it back to sleep. This process is repeated until the resource requirements of all PnP cards have been ascertained. This chapter describes the process of reading the resource data structure and provides a detailed description of its content.
- **The PnP Configuration Registers**. Once the resource requirements of a card have been ascertained, the next step is to program its configuration registers, assigning non-conflicting resources to each logical device residing on the card. A device's configuration registers are programmable address decoders and/or resource selectors. This chapter describes the configuration register set associated with each PnP card and each logical device that resides on the card.
- **Intro to PnP BIOS and OS**. The purpose of this chapter is to provide a basic definition of some of the issues that must be dealt with by a PnP BIOS and a PnP OS. The term "BIOS" is defined, the configuration responsibilities of both the BIOS and the OS are introduced, static and dynamic configuration defined, and the PnP device ROM is introduced.
- **The PnP POST and Device ROMs**. This chapter describes the PnP POST sequence and PnP device (option) ROMs.
- **The PnP BIOS Services**. This chapter provides a detailed description of the PnP BIOS Services.

The Appendices

The book contains the following appendices:

- Appendix A—Device ID Assignments
- Appendix B—Class Code Assignments
- Appendix C—SCSI
- Appendix D—Glossary
- Appendix E—References

Who This Book is For

This book is intended for use by hardware and software design and support personnel. Due to the clear, concise explanatory methods used to describe each subject, personnel outside of the design field may also find the text useful.

Prerequisite Knowledge

It is highly recommended that the reader have a good knowledge of PC architecture prior to reading this book. Knowledge of PCI, PCMCIA, and EISA are also helpful. The MindShare publications entitled *ISA System Architecture*, *EISA System Architecture*, *PCI System Architecture*, and *PCMCIA System Architecture* provide background on these subjects.

Object Size Designations

The following designations are used throughout this book when referring to the size of data objects:

- A byte is an 8-bit object.
- A word is a 16-bit, or two byte, object.
- A doubleword is a 32-bit or four byte, object.
- A quadword is a 64-bit, or eight byte, object.
- A paragraph is a 128-bit, or 16 byte, object.
- A page is a 4K-aligned 4KB area of address space.

Documentation Conventions

This section defines the typographical conventions used throughout this book.

Hex Notation

All hex numbers are followed by an "h." Examples:

```
9A4Eh
0100h
```

Binary Notation

All binary numbers are followed by a "b." Examples:

```
0001 0101b
01b
```

Decimal Notation

Numbers without any suffix are decimal. When required for clarity, decimal numbers are followed by a "d." The following examples each represent a decimal number:

```
16
255
256d
128d
```

Signal Name Representation

Each signal that assumes the logic low state when asserted is followed by a pound sign (#). As an example, the TRDY# signal is asserted low when the target is ready to complete a data transfer.

Signals that are not followed by a pound sign are asserted when they assume the logic high state. As an example, IDSEL is asserted high to indicate that a PCI device's configuration space is being addressed.

Identification of Bit Fields (logical groups of bits or signals)

All bit fields are designated in little-endian bit ordering as follows:

[X:Y],

where "X" is the most-significant bit and "Y" is the least-significant bit of the field. As an example, the PCI address/data bus consists of AD[31:0], where AD31 is the most-significant and AD0 the least-significant bit of the field.

Programming Constants

In the BIOS chapters, all references to labels related to constant values are in all upper case. Some examples follow:

GET_NUM_NODES
SUCCESS
ABORT

Abbreviation for the Term "Plug and Play"

Throughout most of the document, this term is abbreviated as PnP.

We Want Your Feedback

MindShare values your comments and suggestions. You can contact us via mail, phone, fax or internet email.

- Phone: (214) 231-2216
- Fax: (214) 783-4715
- E-mail:mindshar@interserv.com

To request information on our seminars, email your request to:

mindshar@interserv.com.

Mailing Address

MindShare, Inc.
2202 Buttercup Drive
Richardson, Texas 75082

Part One

Evolution

1 *The Perfect Machine*

This Chapter

This chapter sets the stage by providing a simple portrait of everyone's dream machine and the qualities it would possess.

The Next Chapter

The next chapter describes the traditional ISA machine and its less than optimal qualities with regard to autoconfiguration and Plug and Play.

The Perfect Turn-On

You own the perfect PC. In reality, the perfect PC is only a dream at this point in time. Having just received a new card for your PC, you install it in an add-in slot and power up the machine. Will the machine recognize that a new card has been installed? Will the new card work right out of the box, or will the machine go berserk because the new card clashes with other cards previously installed in the machine?

Each time that it is started, the perfect machine automatically scans the machine to determine if any devices have been added or removed. When it senses that a device has been added, it interrogates the device to determine:

- the card's vendor and device ID
- what system resources it requires to perform its task

As an example, a network controller card may require the following resources:

- **A block of IO addresses**. It contains a set of IO registers used to issue commands to it, to check its status, and to write data to and read data from it. The processor communicates with these registers by performing IO read and write transactions. Before the processor can read from or write to these registers, an IO address decoder on the card must be programmed with the system IO address range assigned to the device's register set. The system must ensure that the address range assigned does not conflict with any other IO device in the system. If another device's IO address decoder were set up to respond to some or all of the same IO addresses, a read from an IO address shared between the devices would return the sum of the data returned by the two devices (in other words, trash).

- **Its interrupt line must be routed to a system interrupt request signal line**. This line is used by the card to interrupt the processor when the card completes an operation or incurs an error while attempting to process a command issued to it by the processor. The system must assign it an interrupt request line guaranteed not to conflict with the interrupt line usage of any other device in the system.

- **A block of memory addresses for a memory buffer**. The card contains a read/write memory buffer used to temporarily store data received from the network as well as data received from the processor that must be transmitted over the network. The processor communicates with the buffer by performing memory read and write transactions within the memory range assigned to the buffer. Before the processor can successfully access the buffer, the buffer's memory address decoder must be assigned a memory range guaranteed not to conflict with any other memory in the system.

- **A block of memory addresses for its device ROM**. The card has read-only memory (ROM) containing a start-up program and data used by the device and the processor. The processor reads from the ROM by performing memory read transactions within the memory range assigned to the ROM. Before the processor can access the ROM successfully, the ROM's memory address decoder must be assigned a memory range guaranteed not to conflict with any other memory in the system.

Luckily, the card that you just installed in the perfect machine is a perfect card. It has assignable memory and IO address ranges (in other words, programmable address decoders), and its interrupt line usage is programmable. It also implements a data structure that the configuration program can read to determine its vendor and device ID as well as the resource requirements of the device.

The system maintains a complete list of the resources assigned to other devices previously installed in the system. This list is stored in some form of configuration memory (such as CMOS RAM with a backup battery) that does not lose its contents when the machine is powered down. When the new network controller card is detected, the configuration software consults this list to select address ranges and an interrupt line that are guaranteed not to conflict with the previously installed devices. Once chosen, the resources allocated to the new card are stored in the configuration memory.

The device design must also include a set of predefined configuration registers that are known to the system's configuration program. These registers are used to read the device's vendor and device ID and resource requirement list. Additionally, they are used to assign non-conflicting resources to the device.

In summary, when a perfect card is first installed in the perfect machine, the machine detects its presence and interrogates the device to determine its vendor and device ID and resource requirements. These requirements are compared to the resources already assigned to previously installed devices. A non-conflicting set of resources are allocated to the new device by writing the appropriate values to its configuration registers. In addition, the list of resources allocated to the new card are stored in the system's configuration memory for use in configuring the device each time that the machine is restarted.

Conversely, when a device is removed from the machine, the system detects its absence and deallocates the resources that had been assigned to it.

If the perfect machine has one or more PCMCIA card slots, the system should automatically detect card insertion or removal while the machine is running. The event is reported to the configuration software. The configuration software deallocates its resources (if a device had been removed), or, if a new device is installed, configures the new device with non-conflicting resources and activates it (and load its device driver into memory).

To be truly useful, the perfect machine not only has the ability to detect and configure devices installed inside the machine. It also has the ability to detect the presence of devices connected to the machine by a cables. This includes devices such as printers, modems, mass storage devices, etc. It detects the display type and autoconfigures the display adapter to match the optimal capabilities of the display. The machine has the ability to determine the resource requirements of attached devices and can configure them, if necessary.

A Standard Is Needed

It's already been established that the device designer must implement the following:

- a card detection mechanism
- a vendor and device ID
- a resource list that can be read by the system
- a set of configuration registers (at known locations) that can be read and written

It's also been established that the system designer must supply the following:

- configuration memory to store resource allocation information in
- a configuration program to detect a device, read its resource requirement list and then allocate resources by writing to the device's configuration registers.

If the designer of each device and each system board each devises their own, proprietary variation on these elements, however, the result is a "Tower of Babel" scenario. Only device-specific software written with knowledge of each device's design and each system board's design would know:

- how to detect a device
- where the device's configuration registers are located and how to use them
- where the vendor and device ID are located and their format
- where a device's resource requirement list is located and the format of the list
- where the system board configuration memory is located and the format of the resource allocation lists that it contains

It should be fairly obvious that standard implementation methods must be defined relating to each aspect of the configuration mechanisms.

At Startup, Only Essential Devices Are Enabled

When the machine is started, the majority of the devices in the machine are disabled. The only devices that power up enabled are those devices that must be operational when the machine is first started. As an example, this would include the following devices:

- The keyboard must be responsive at start up.
- The display must be enabled in text mode at start up so that it can be used to display progress and error messages during the start up process.
- The mass storage controller (or possibly the network interface) must be enabled so the operating system can be read into memory and executed (in other words, so the operating system can be booted). This is commonly referred to as the initial program load (IPL) device.

Next, Scan the Machine

The configuration software scans each bus in the system in order to determine the current machine device population. This requires a separate, bus-specific program for each type of bus in the system. As an example, the method used to determine the presence, type, and resource requirements of PCI devices is very different from the method used to acquire the same information for PCMCIA cards. A program specifically written to scan a particular bus type is referred to as a bus enumerator.

In Windows 95, the Configuration Manager (CM) calls each bus enumerator program to determine the community of devices that exist on each bus and their resource requirements. There are three possible cases:

1. **No new devices**. As each device is discovered, the configuration software checks the allocated resource list in configuration memory to determine if the device had been previously detected. No new devices are discovered. In this case, the configuration software doesn't have to check for conflicting resource allocation. It just writes the previously-allocated resource settings from configuration memory to each device's configuration registers.
2. **One or more new devices are discovered**. The configuration software reads each newly detected device's resource requirement list. It compares their requirements to the resources that previously assigned to the devices that were already resident in the machine. It selects non-conflicting resources to be allocated to the newly installed devices. The selected resource settings for the new devices are saved in configuration memory and the software writes the selected resource settings to each device in the system.
3. **One or more devices** that were in the machine **have been removed**. In this case, the configuration software updates configuration memory to indicate that the resources that were previously assigned to the removed devices are now available for future allocation.

Once each device has been configured, the software activates it, thereby making the new resource available for use.

Characteristics of Plug and Play Device Drivers

Plug and play device drivers must support the following features:

- In the event that a device is added or removed during run-time, the driver must be capable of being loaded into or unloaded from memory by the configuration manager.
- The driver must be capable of working with its associated device independent of what system bus it resides on. In other words, the same driver must work with the device whether the device resides on the processor, PCI, EISA, MCA, ISA bus or is installed in a PCMCIA slot. Microsoft refers to this as a "class" driver because it works with a class of devices, rather than a specific implementation of the device.
- The driver must be able to exchange messages with the OS and applications programs if its associated device is installed or removed while the machine is running (so applications programs that require the presence of the device are aware of its presence or absence).

When the OS detects a device, it must have some way to identify the device driver associated with the device. This can be accomplished in one of two ways:

- using the vendor and device ID (and, possibly, the revision). A driver associated with a device in this manner is very device specific.
- using the three-byte class code (as found in PCI and PnP devices). A driver associated with a device in this manner is more generic and can work with a category of device rather than just with a vendor-specific device.

For information about Windows 95 Plug and Play device drivers, refer to "PCMCIA Bus Enumerator and Configuration Manager" on page 45, "The Registry and the Device Installer" on page 46, and "Bus-Independent Plug and Play Device Drivers" on page 47.

Device Driver Configuration

After the machine has completed autoconfiguration and the OS has been loaded into memory and begun execution, the OS loads device drivers associated with the devices that currently populate the machine. As each is loaded into memory, its initialization code is executed. The initialization code communicates either with the configuration program (the preferred method) or directly with its device's configuration registers to determine the resources assigned to its device. This would include:

- IO range assigned to the device's register set
- Memory range assigned to memory on the device
- System interrupt request line used by the device
- DMA channel used by the device

The driver now has the information it needs to communicate with the device. For additional information, see the section entitled "Hot Insertion and Removal" on page 15.

Multiple Instances of a Device

Two or more cards of the same type may be installed in the machine. In this case, each card has the same resource requirements. It is the responsibility of the configuration software to allocate non-conflicting resources to each and to store this information along with the vendor and device IDs in configuration memory. A loadable device driver associated with the device type is subsequently loaded into memory and its initialization code is executed. As discussed in the previous section, the driver issues a request to the configuration software to report any instances of devices that match the vendor and device IDs (and, if the device is a PCI device, possibly the subsystem ID and subsystem vendor ID) supplied as search parameters. In this case, the configuration software supplies the driver with information regarding the number of instances of the device found and the configuration of each. The driver can then communicate with all instances of the device.

Hot Insertion and Removal

The perfect machine may possess the ability to gracefully recognize the insertion or removal of a device while the machine is running. This is typically referred to as hot insertion and removal. Upon detecting one of these events, the machine automatically notifies the configuration software of the event. The configuration software deallocates resources when a device is removed, or, when a device is installed, configures the new device with non-conflicting resources and activates it.

When a device is added, the configuration software locates the device driver associated with the device (using either the vendor/device ID or the class code) and loads it into memory. When the device is removed, the device driver is unloaded from memory.

2 ISA, an Imperfect Standard

The Previous Chapter

The previous chapter introduced some of the more important characteristics of a perfect machine.

This Chapter

This chapter describes the drawbacks of the ISA machine architecture with regard to system configuration and Plug and Play capability.

The Next Chapter

The next chapter describes how EISA and the Micro Channel approach the issue of automatic system configuration.

Introduction

The term "legacy ISA card" was coined to describe old ISA cards that do not implement Plug and Play support. Legacy ISA cards present major impediments to automatic configuration and Plug and Play. The following sections define those impediments.

For a detailed description of the ISA bus architecture, refer to the MindShare book entitled *ISA System Architecture* (Addison-Wesley Publishing Company, 1995).

No Device Detection

There is no reliable way to determine that an ISA card slot is occupied. If it is occupied, there is no reliable way to determine the type of card. Software spe-

cific to a particular card type (i.e., the device driver written specifically to interact with the card), has knowledge of its related card's register set. Using this
knowledge, it can write patterns to specific IO ports associated with its device
and read back from them in an effort to determine if the card is really there.
Generic configuration software cannot reliably probe IO ports to determine the
presence and type of an ISA device. Since this is one of the cornerstones of autoconfiguration and Plug and Play, the lack of a standard card detection mechanism is a serious drawback of the ISA bus architecture.

No Vendor or Device ID (and No Class Code)

Legacy ISA cards do not implement a vendor and device ID (nor a class code)
that can be read by the configuration software. This information is therefore
unavailable to the configuration program and device drivers and cannot be
used by drivers to determine if their associated devices are present in the system.

No Resource List

Legacy ISA cards do not contain a list of resources that can be read by the configuration software. The configuration software therefore has no way to determine the card's:

*   memory space requirements
*   IO space requirements
*   interrupt line requirements
*   DMA channel requirements

No Programmable Configuration Registers

Legacy ISA cards do not implement any standard configuration registers that
configuration software would be aware of. A specific ISA card may utilize one
or more device-specific IO ports as configuration registers, but only software
specific to the device would know of their existence and how to use them.

In lieu of configuration registers, the vast majority of legacy ISA cards use man-
ual switches and jumpers to configure the card. To select IO ranges, memory
ranges, interrupt lines and DMA channels, the end user is required to set the
card's switches and/or jumpers to positions defined by the card designer.

As an example, setting a switch or a group of switches to a specific pattern would condition a memory or IO address decoder to recognize a specific address range as allocated to the card's memory or to its IO register set.

It is the end user's responsibility to set the card's switches to select resources that are not already allocated to other devices installed in the system. This assumes that the end user:

- knows the IO and memory ranges, interrupt lines and DMA channels that are already in use by other add-in cards. This information is used to ensure that the switches select resources that don't conflict with the other cards.
- knows the IO and memory ranges, interrupt lines and DMA channels that are already in use by ISA devices integrated onto the system board. Once again, this information is used to ensure that the switches select resources that don't conflict with the integrated devices.
- not only knows what resources are free, but also sets the switches and/or jumpers correctly (in other words, you're free to make a mistake).

Summary

In summary, legacy ISA devices do not facilitate automatic configuration of a system. They completely lack the characteristics necessary for autoconfiguration and Plug and Play support.

3 EISA and Micro Channel

The Previous Chapter

The previous chapter outlined the inadequacies of the ISA platform and of legacy ISA card design with respect to automatic machine configuration and Plug and Play support.

This Chapter

This chapter describes the configuration methodology used by EISA and Micro Channel devices.

The Next Chapter

The next chapter describes the characteristics that PCI devices possess that support fully automatic device configuration and Plug and Play.

Introduction

Recognizing the inadequacies of the ISA design, IBM later introduced the Micro Channel (MC) Architecture. One of the areas addressed by the Micro Channel specification was the configuration process. The section that follows describes the configuration mechanism used in machines that employ the Micro Channel.

Soon after IBM introduced the Micro Channel definition, a consortium of opposing companies devised the EISA specification to address the same issues. EISA stands for Extension to the **ISA** specification. A later section in this chapter describes the configuration mechanism used in machines that employ the EISA bus.

The two architectures have something in common with reference to the configuration process—both processes are semi-automatic. In other words, they require user intervention to configure a new card into the system.

Plug and Play System Architecture

Micro Channel

General

As described in the sections that follow, Micro Channel cards implement some, but not all, of the features necessary to support automatic configuration. A complete description of the Micro Channel can be found in Tom Shanley's book entitled *The IBM PS/2 from the Inside Out*, Addison-Wesley, 1991. Although this book is now out of print, it can be found in many IBM site technical libraries.

Card Selection

A Micro Channel adapter card installed in a specific add-in connector may be placed into configuration mode by writing the appropriate value to the machine's adapter enable/setup register. In a PS/2 product, the register is implemented at IO port 96h. Using this register, the card is placed into setup (i.e., configuration) mode. The configuration program can then access its configuration registers (described in a subsequent section). After the card is configured, the configuration program writes the appropriate value to the setup register to take the card out of setup mode and enable it for normal operation.

Card Detection

A card is detected by placing it into setup mode and reading its card ID. If the ID returned is FFFFh, the slot is unoccupied. A value other than FFFFh indicates that the slot is occupied.

The configuration software maintains a list (in configuration memory) of the cards installed in each slot and the selected values written to their configuration registers each time that the machine is restarted.

If a slot that was unoccupied now indicates it is occupied, the card must be configured. This process is described in a later section.

Configuration Registers

The Micro Channel specification defines a set of eight configuration registers referred to as programmable option select (POS) registers. They are implemented in the IO address range from 0100h through 0107h and are referred to as POS registers 0 through 7. Each is an 8-bit register. Since every Micro Channel device implements its POS registers at the same locations, there must be a way to select a specific card to respond to POS register accesses. That is the purpose of the adapter enable/setup register described in the previous section.

POS registers 0 and 1 contain the card ID. Since this is a 16-bit number, there are 64K possible card IDs. The IDs are assigned by IBM and the ID for each card type is mutually exclusive.

At a minimum, a card designer must implement POS registers 0 through 2. POS register 2 contains some required card control bits such as the card enable/disable bit. The specification defines the required and optional bits. The card designer uses the POS register bits that are not defined in the specification to implement device-specific configuration features. This includes bit fields to program its address decoders, select an interrupt request line, DMA channel, etc.

Resource Requirement List

An important piece that is missing, however, is the resource requirement list. Micro Channel cards do not implement a resource requirement list that can be read by the configuration software. Instead, the card manufacturer supplies a file on diskette describing the card's POS register bit fields and the resource requirements of the card. When a new card is detected in the system (card ID was FFFFh, but now returns a different value), the configuration software prompts the end user to insert the diskette that came with the card. This diskette contains the card's adapter description file (ADF).

ADF File and the Configuration Process

In addition to the POS registers, the IBM Micro Channel specification also defines the naming convention and format of the adapter description file (ADF). The ADF file is delivered (on diskette) with the card and contains the resource requirement list and the definition of the card-specific configuration register location and usage. When a new card is detected in the system, the end user is prompted to insert the diskette. The content of the ADF file is then read by the configuration program to determine the card's resource requirements and the format and usage of its POS registers. The configuration program selects settings for the card's POS registers that don't conflict with the resource usage of other cards previously installed in the system. These settings are then stored in configuration memory for usage during machine startup.

Each time that the machine is restarted, the configuration program compares the ID for each card installed in the system with the card ID that configuration memory indicates should occupy that slot. If the proper card is in the slot, the values stored in the slot-specific area of configuration memory are written to the card's POS registers to allocate resources to it. The card is then removed from setup mode and enabled for normal operation. This procedure is repeated for each card slot until all of the installed cards have been detected, configured, and enabled for normal operation.

EISA

General

As described in the sections that follow, EISA cards implement some, but not all, of the features necessary to support automatic configuration. For a detailed description of the EISA environment, refer to the MindShare book entitled *EISA System Architecture* (Addison-Wesley Publishing Company, 1995). It should be noted that newly-designed EISA cards can implement the same configuration mechanism as that defined for Plug and Play ISA cards (rather than the traditional EISA configuration mechanism). The PnP mechansim is defined later in this book.

Card Selection

Each card slot in an EISA machine is assigned slot-specific IO space. As an example, a card installed in slot 1 responds to IO accesses within the 1000h through 1FFFh range, while a card installed in slot 2 responds to accesses within the 2000h through 2FFFh range. In other words the most-significant digit of the IO address selects the card slot being addressed.

Within each card's assigned 4KB range (x000h through xFFFh), four ranges of 256 locations each are guaranteed exclusive to the card, while the other 12 ranges of 256 locations each may be recognized by ISA cards. ISA cards occupy the IO address range from 0100h through 03FFh. Because they are often designed to perform an inadequate address decode (they only decode up to address bit 9, ignoring the state of A[15:10]), however, they will recognize any IO address that has address bits [9:8] set to 01b, 10b, or 11b. This problem is discussed in detail in the MindShare book entitled *ISA System Architecture* (Addison-Wesley Publishing Company, 1995). Table 3-1 on page 25 defines the four usable and the 12 unusable ranges within each 4KB of IO space.

The EISA specification defines a subset of each EISA card's IO space as reserved for the implementation of card configuration registers. The reserved range is xC80h through xC84h (where x = the slot the card is installed in). Locations outside of this range are available for the implementation of card-specific configuration registers and IO ports.

Table 3-1: EISA Card IO Space Usage

Start Address	End Address	Usage
x000h	x0FFh	Slot-Specific IO space available to card designer.
x100h	x1FFh	ISA card alias. Do not use.
x200h	x2FFh	ISA card alias. Do not use.
x300h	x3FFh	ISA card alias. Do not use.
x400h	x4FFh	Slot-Specific IO space available to card designer.
x500h	05FFh	ISA card alias. Do not use.
x600h	x6FFh	ISA card alias. Do not use.
x700h	x7FFh	ISA card alias. Do not use.
x800h	x8FFh	Slot-Specific IO space available to card designer.
x900h	x9FFh	ISA card alias. Do not use.
xA00h	xAFFh	ISA card alias. Do not use.
xB00h	xBFFh	ISA card alias. Do not use.
xC00h	xCFFh	Slot-Specific IO space available to card designer.
xD00h	xDFFh	ISA card alias. Do not use.
xE00h	xEFFh	ISA card alias. Do not use.

Table 3-1: EISA Card IO Space Usage (Continued)

Start Address	End Address	Usage
xF00h	XFFFh	ISA card alias. Do not use.

Card Detection

An EISA card is detected by reading the card's EISA device ID from IO ports xC80h through xC83h. A device ID of all hex Fs indicates that the card slot is unoccupied, while a valid product ID consist of a four-byte ID with the following elements:

- The first two bytes (from xC80h and xC81h) contain a three character, compressed (5-bits per character) ASCII manufacturer ID.
- The third byte (from xC82h) contains the 8-bit product ID.
- The fourth byte (from xC83h) contains the 8-bit revision number.

Configuration Registers

As indicated in the previous section, IO ports xC80h through xC83h contain the manufacturer and product IDs and the revision number. IO port xC84h contains some card control bits defined by the specification. The remaining bits in xC84h and any of the other usable IO ports in the card's range may be used to implement card-specific configuration registers.

Resource Requirement List

As with the Micro Channel cards, EISA cards do contain a resource requirement list that can be read by the configuration software. Rather, the card manufacturer must supply the list on diskette as an ASCII file referred to as an EISA configuration file (CFG file). This file contains the list and the definition of the card-specific configuration register location and usage. As stated earlier, a newly-designed EISA card can implement the PnP configuration mechanism. The resource requirement list can then be read from the card, rendering the configuration file unnecessary.

CFG File and the Configuration Process

When a new card is detected in the system, the end user is prompted to insert the diskette. The content of the CFG file is read by the configuration program to determine the card's resource requirements and the format, location, and usage of its configuration registers. The configuration program selects a setting for the card's configuration registers that doesn't conflict with the resources assigned to other cards previously installed in the system. These settings are then stored in configuration memory for usage during machine startup.

Each time that the machine is started, the configuration program compares the ID for each card installed in the system with the card ID that configuration memory indicates should occupy that slot. If the proper card is in the slot, the values stored in the slot-specific area of configuration memory are written to the card's configuration registers to allocate resources to it. The card is then enabled for normal operation. This procedure is repeated for each card slot until all of the installed cards have been detected, configured, and enabled for normal operation.

Summary

In summary, neither EISA nor Micro Channel devices incorporate a resource requirement list. Instead, the list is in a diskette file. Whenever a new card is detected in the system, the end user is prompted to insert the diskette. The configuration program can then access the card's configuration file to determine the resources required and the location and usage of its configuration registers. Although the system configuration software can automatically detect a new card, the necessity of using the diskette renders the process semi-automatic.

Automatic Configuration of EISA Cards

It's important to note that both EISA and ISA cards can be installed on the EISA bus. The mechanism defined by the Plug and Play specification for automatic card detection, resource requirement determination, and configuration can be implemented on both ISA and EISA cards. In other words, EISA cards can be designed as Plug and Play cards.

4 PCI

The Previous Chapter

The previous chapter described the configuration methodology used by EISA and Micro Channel devices.

This Chapter

This chapter describes the automatic configuration achievable with PCI devices. It also discusses the relationship of Windows 95, Windows NT, and PCI devices.

The Next Chapter

The next chapter discusses PCMCIA technology and some of its operational characteristics that impede system Plug and Play. In addition, the manner in which Windows 95 implements PCMCIA Plug and Play is described.

Introduction

A properly designed PCI device provides all of the mechanisms necessary to support fully-automatic device configuration. The following sections provide an introduction to the configuration-related aspects of a PCI device. For a detailed description of the PCI environment, refer to the MindShare book entitled *PCI System Architecture*, *Third Edition* (Addison-Wesley Publishing Company, 1995).

Configuration Address Space

In the PCI environment, each PCI device has 64 doublewords of configuration address space available to be populated with configuration registers. The format and usage of the first 16 doublewords (the configuration header region) are defined by the specification, while the remaining 48 doublewords are available for the implementation of device-specific configuration registers.

Within the first 16 doublewords, a subset of the registers defined by the specification are required. This includes the vendor and the device ID registers. The remaining registers within this group fall into two categories:

- may be required depending on the type of device
- optional (implemented at the discretion of the device designer)

Device Detection

A PCI device may either be embedded on the PCI bus or installed in a PCI add-in connector. In either case, each device is assigned a physical device number, based on its physical position on the bus.

A PCI device is detected by attempting to read from its vendor ID register. This is a required 16-bit register. If the target device is present, a vendor ID other than FFFFh is returned. A vendor ID of FFFFh indicates that the device did not respond and therefore doesn't exist. When a valid vendor ID (a value other than FFFFh) is returned, it indicates that a device occupies that physical device position on the PCI bus (in addition to FFFFh, Windows 95 also interprets a vendor ID of 0000h as a not present indication). The configuration software then proceeds to read from the device's other configuration registers to determine the resources required by the device. A diskette is not necessary.

Each PCI add-in connector implements two card present pins referred to as PRSNT1# and PRSNT2# (the card present 1 and 2 pins). On the system board, these two signal lines are pulled up to a logic 1 by pullup resistors. The card present signals from each card connector can typically be read by software (through a platform-specific IO port). If a card connector is unoccupied, a value of 11b is read from its two card present signals. When a card is installed in a connector, it grounds one, the other, or both of the card present signals. Reading from that connector's card present signals would therefore return a value of 10b, 01b, or 00b. Any of these values indicates that a card is installed in the connector. The exact value indicates the maximum power requirements of the card (when it has been fully configured and enabled).

When the configuration software has determined that a card connector is occupied, it can determine the card type by reading from its vendor and device ID configuration registers.

Configuration Registers and Resource Requirement List

Figure 4-1 on page 32 illustrates the first 16 doublewords of a PCI device's configuration space. This is referred to as the device's configuration header region. The registers indicated in black are required by the specification. Those in white may or may not be optional depending on the device type. A complete description of each register's usage can be found in the MindShare book entitled *PCI System Architecture, Third Edition* (Addison-Wesley Publishing Company, 1995).

The configuration program reads these registers to determine the resources required by the device. Some examples are:

- If the device is a bus master, its MAX_LAT and MIN_GNT registers contain values that indicate how quickly it requires access to the bus and how long it requires the use of the bus when it initiates a transaction. The configuration software uses these two values to determine the bus master's priority and how big a time slice (of bus time) to allocate to it.
- The header type register indicates whether this is a single- or a multi-function device.
- The base address registers indicate how many (and the size of) blocks of memory and IO address space the device requires.
- If the device is a PCMCIA device, the CardBus CIS pointer register indicates where the device's card information structure can be read from.
- For devices based on identical core logic from the same manufacturer, the subsystem ID and the subsystem vendor ID registers allow device differentiation.
- The expansion ROM base address register indicates whether the device has a device ROM, as well as the size of the ROM (that is, the number of memory locations that need to be assigned to it).
- The interrupt pin register indicates if the device generates interrupt requests. If it does, the configuration software uses the interrupt line register to inform its device driver of its assigned system interrupt request line.

Figure 4-1: PCI-Defined Configuration Registers

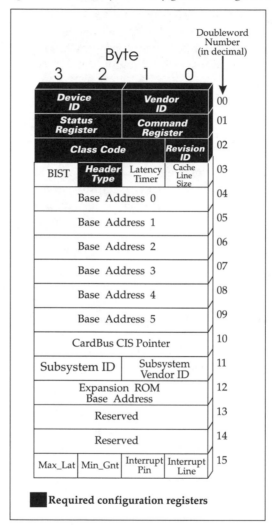

The Configuration Process

Many PCs that incorporate the PCI bus also incorporate the ISA bus. The system has no way of automatically detecting the resources in use by legacy ISA cards residing on this bus. The system must ensure that the resources allocated to the PCI devices do not conflict with the legacy cards. There are three possible solutions to this problem:

- The startup software can perform a series of IO writes and reads throughout the IO range occupied by legacy cards in an attempt to discover which IO locations are currently in use by them. This would include the 0100h through 03FFh range, as well as all IO ranges above 03FFh that alias down to the 0100h through 03FFh range (a detailed discussion of the aliasing problem can be found in the MindShare books entitled *PCI System Architecture* and *EISA System Architecture,* Addison-Wesley Publishing Company, 1995; also refer to Table 3-1 on page 25). This approach yields unreliable results. In addition, there is no mechanism for programmatically determining the IRQ and DMA channels that are used by these cards.
- The system may include a utility program that requires the end user to enter the resources in use by the legacy cards. Alternately, the OS may maintain a list of commonly found legacy ISA cards and the possible resource selections that can be applied to them. This is the approach taken by the Windows 95 Device Installer program. The resources used by the card are then stored in battery backed-up CMOS RAM so that they are available to the system from that point forward. As with the previous approach, this approach can also be unreliable (because the end-user may not enter the information correctly).
- The system may only assign IO addresses (to the PCI devices) that are guaranteed not to conflict with legacy cards—in other words, addresses other than the 0100h through 03FFh range and the ranges above 03FFh that alias down to this range. This approach guarantees that no IO address conflicts will occur. However, as stated earlier, the system can not programmatically determine the IRQ and DMA channels used by the legacy cards.

As described earlier, the configuration software can detect the presence or absence of each PCI device by reading its vendor ID and checking for a value other than FFFFh. Once a device is detected, the configuration program reads from its configuration header registers to determine its resource requirements. The configuration program can then write the appropriate values to these same registers to allocate non-conflicting resources to the device. This process is described in detail in the MindShare book entitled *PCI System Architecture* (Addison-Wesley Publishing Company, 1995). Once resources have been allocated to the device, the configuration program writes the appropriate value to its command register to enable the device for normal operation.

When the operating system begins to read loadable device drivers into memory, the device driver's initialization code calls the PCI BIOS (defined by the PCI specification) requesting a search for its related device using the vendor and device IDs (and possibly the subsystem ID and subsystem vendor ID). A search for the class code can also be requested. The BIOS scans the PCI bus by reading the vendor and device IDs (or the class code) from every device and looking for a match. When a match (or multiple matches) are encountered, the BIOS returns the device number (or numbers) to the driver along with the PCI bus number and the function number (or numbers, if it's a multi-function device). Issuing another call to the PCI BIOS services, the driver then uses that information as input parameters to access its associated device's configuration registers. In this way, the driver can determine the resources allocated to its device. It therefore knows the location of the device's register set in IO space, where its memory buffer is (if it has one), the system interrupt line that it must hook, etc.

It should be noted that Windows 95 device drivers do not interrogate the PCI BIOS to determine the resources allocated to a device. Rather, they interrogate the Configuration Manager program, which in turn searches the Registry to determine the resources allocated to the device. Writing the device driver to call the PCI BIOS would make it implementation specific—in other words, it would only work with a PCI version of the device.

PCI, Windows 95, and Windows NT

Microsoft experienced numerous compatibility problems related to PCI devices. These problems stem from incorrectly implemented interrupt service routines, configuration registers, and PCI BIOS code. In addition, some of the interrupt problems stem from limitations inherent within Windows 95 itself (its inability to handle devices with mixed real and protected mode interrupt service routines sharing the same IRQ line). The following sections briefly discuss the problems and the solutions.

For a complete description of the PCI terminology in this chapter, refer to the MindShare book entitled *PCI System Architecture* (Addison-Wesley Publishing Company, 1995). More information about Windows 95 Plug and Play device drivers can be found in the sections entitled "PCMCIA Bus Enumerator and Configuration Manager" on page 45, "The Registry and the Device Installer" on page 46, and "Bus-Independent Plug and Play Device Drivers" on page 47.

Use of the PCI BIOS

Because Microsoft encountered numerous bugs related to the implementation of the PCI BIOS, Windows 95 does not use the BIOS to access PCI configuration registers. Rather, as its default, the Windows 95 PCI bus enumerator directly accesses the PCI configuration registers. The default can be overridden, forcing the enumerator to use the BIOS. When the BIOS is bypassed, the enumerator attempts to use PCI configuration mechanism #1 first, and, if that fails, attempts to use configuration mechanism #2. The selected mechanism (whichever returns valid PCI device configuration information) is used to access the configuration registers associated with each PCI device.

Windows NT never uses the PCI BIOS. Rather, the NT HAL (hardware abstraction layer) attempts to access PCI configuration registers using the mechanism enabled via the BIOS first, and, if unsuccessful, then uses the opposite mechanism.

Vendor ID

The PCI specification states that the presence of a PCI device is ascertained by reading its vendor ID register. A value of FFFFh indicates the device is not present. Windows 95 considers a device not present if the Vendor ID register returns FFFFh or 0000h.

Class Code Register

Like the PCI specification, Windows 95 requires that the class code register contain a valid value (a value other than 000000h).

Base Address Registers

Base address registers must return 00000000h if they are not implemented. Return of any other value indicates that it is implemented. Microsoft has identified a number of PCI devices that return hardwired, random, non-zero values in the base address registers. This is illegal.

Interrupt Line Register

Windows 95 interprets an interrupt line register value of 00h or FFh as indicating that the device does not use an interrupt line. Some BIOSs return reserved values (10h through FEh; this is an error and should never occur), causing Windows 95 to assume the device does not use an interrupt line.

Subsystem ID and Subsystem Vendor ID

Device designers should implement the newly defined (see rev 2.1 of the PCI spec) subsystem ID and subsystem vendor ID registers. This permits the Windows 95 PCI bus enumerator to recognize two devices that have the same vendor and device IDs as being two different devices based on the same PCI master/target chip set.

Driver Uses Registry to Get Device Configuration

A PnP device driver does not access PCI configuration registers during its initialization process. Rather, it obtains information regarding the current configuration of its device by accessing the Windows 95 Registry (via a call to the Configuration Manager, or CM).

It is the author's belief that Microsoft made this decision for the following reasons:

- The primary reason is that accessing the PCI configuration registers makes the driver PCI-specific and it can only work with a PCI version of the device. This is a direct violation of the architecture of Windows 95 Plug and Play device drivers.
- Some PCI BIOSs are buggy and return incorrect configuration information.
- Any attempt on the part of the device driver to bypass the BIOS and directly access its device's configuration registers using PCI configuration mechanism #1 or #2 makes the driver platform-specific. Non-Intel platforms use mechanisms other than #1 or #2 to stimulate the host/PCI bridge to generate PCI configuration read and write transactions (e.g., in PowerPC platforms, memory-mapped IO is used).

Sharable Interrupts and Changing IRQ Assignment

Windows 95

The PCI spec supports interrupt sharing by PCI devices. Unfortunately, however, Windows 95 does not support interrupt sharing between real and protected mode code. If the device drivers associated with two (or more) devices hook the same interrupt and one of them has a real mode interrupt service routine while the other has a protected mode routine, Windows 95 will experience problems.

From a Windows 95 perspective, the best solution would be for the BIOS configuration code not to configure any two PCI devices to share an interrupt line. Alternatively, only devices with interrupt service routines that operate in the same mode (real or protected) can share an IRQ line.

Another problem that shows up in PCI machines is also related to interrupt sharing. All PCI drivers and interrupt service routines must be written to support sharing. When a driver hooks an interrupt, it first reads and saves the pointer currently occupying the interrupt table entry. It then sets the entry to point to its own routine. Furthermore, when an interrupt occurs and the interrupt service routine begins execution, the routine must check its device's interrupt pending bit before servicing its device. If the bit isn't set, it must execute a far jump to the service routine pointed to by the pointer that was originally in the interrupt table entry. In other words, the service routines must support interrupt chaining. This problem is not peculiar to Windows 95.

The hardware method used on a particular system board to route PCI interrupts to selected system IRQ lines is system design-specific. Windows 95 has no knowledge of how to program the system board logic's interrupt router to select an IRQ line for a PCI device to use. For this reason, it is the responsibility of the system BIOS (at startup time) to program the router and store the routing information in the device's interrupt line register to be read by Windows 95. The BIOS must make this selection and store the routing information even if it doesn't enable the device. This is necessary because Windows 95 may attempt to configure the device (by programming its base address registers) and enable it and it cannot do this if the BIOS hasn't taken care of the interrupt line selection.

Windows NT

Windows NT is compliant with the MPS (multi-processor spec), version 1.1 and supports symmetrical multiprocessing. This means that it supports the Intel APIC and its ability to distribute interrupt requests to any of an array of processors. A well-designed system that implements the Intel APIC IO module can completely segregate the ISA and the PCI interrupts from each other so that each device's interrupt request output has a dedicated line. The ISA IRQs can be handled by an ISA-compatible interrupt controller and the output of this interrupt controller can act as one of the inputs to the APIC IO module. Each of the interrupt request lines from PCI devices can be connected to a separate input of the APIC IO module. Complete segregation of the interrupt lines so that no two devices share the same interrupt line eliminates the problem described in the previous section. In addition, the elimination of interrupt sharing can improve the performance of interrupt driven devices.

A complete discussion of this subject can be found in the chapter on interrupts in the MindShare book entitled *PCI System Architecture*, *Third Edition* (Addison-Wesley Publishing Company, 1995). Additional background information can be found in the chapter on interrupts in the MindShare book entitled *ISA System Architecture* (Addison-Wesley Publishing Company, 1995). The MindShare book entitled *Pentium System Architecture* (Addison-Wesley Publishing Company, 1995) provides a detailed discussion of the APIC operation.

Boot Configuration

At a minimum, the BIOS is responsible for selecting, configuring, and enabling the devices (display controller, keyboard, and the IPL device) to be used during the boot process. It is also responsible for assigning system interrupt lines to interrupt-driven PCI devices.

On startup, Windows 95 examines the three low-order bits in a PCI device's configuration command register to determine if the device has been configured and enabled by the BIOS. These three bits are:

- Memory Enable
- IO Enable
- Enable Bus Mastering

If all three bits are zero, the device has been left disabled by the BIOS. Windows 95 examines the device's base address registers to determine the IO and/or memory requirements of the device. It then programs the base address registers to assign address ranges to the device and performs any other necessary device configuration. It uses the interrupt routing information placed in the interrupt line register by the BIOS to select which interrupt to hook. Finally, it enables the device for normal operation by setting one or more of the first three bits in the command register (and any other bits that must be set to enable it for proper operation).

Consider the case where the device is not enabled and the interrupt pin register indicates (with a value of 01h, 02h, 03h, or 04h) that the device is interrupt driven, but the interrupt line register does not contain a value between 01h and 0Fh. This means that the BIOS has not routed the device's interrupt output to a system IRQ line. Windows 95 does not configure and enable the device.

Time Slice Register

Microsoft found that a number of PCI bus master designers hardwired a value of 00h into the Master Latency Timer (MLT) register. This indicates that the bus master requires a time slice of zero whenever it acquires ownership of the PCI bus! This value doesn't make any sense. Generally, a value of zero in a PCI configuration register indicates that the register isn't implemented and the MLT is a required register.

Dual IDE Adapters

Dual IDE adapters should be built to run in native mode and should be compliant with revision 0.9 (or later) of the PCI IDE Controller specification. When an IDE adapter is enabled, it should be able to tell Windows 95 whether it is programmable in native mode. This permits the OS to move (i.e., reconfigure) the device if necessary. The programming interface byte of the class code register (refer to Table B-1 on page 297 and Table B-2 on page 301) contains the bits to tell the OS if the device is programmable in native mode and whether it is currently in native mode. Bits 0 and 2 of this byte tell the OS if the primary and/or secondary adapters are programmable in native mode, while bits 1 and 3 indicate if the adapter (primary or secondary) is currently in native mode.

Dual IDE adapters must use dual FIFO buffers to permit the OS to write either device asynchronously while in protected mode.

Multifunction PCI Devices

Windows 95 (and the PCI spec) requires that each function in a PCI multifunction device implement its own set of configuration registers.

PCI-to-PCI Bridges

The current implementation of Windows 95 (as of 7/95) does not support PCI-to-PCI bridges. For this reason, it is the responsibility of the BIOS to discover a PCI-to-PCI bridge, scan the secondary PCI bus, configure all devices discovered on the secondary bus, and program the bridge's configuration registers to cover the overall memory-mapped IO, prefetchable memory, and IO ranges for the community of devices that exist behind the bridge. All devices on the secondary bus as well as the bridge itself must be enabled by the BIOS.

PCI Display Devices

If the Windows 95 PCI bus enumerator discovers a PCI device with a class code of 03h (display controller) and a sub-class of 00h (VGA compatible), it automatically assumes that the device consumes the standard VGA resources: IO ranges 03B0h through 03BBh, 03C0h through 03DFh, and memory range 000A0000h through 000BFFFFh (for the video frame buffer). The enumerator only probes the device's base address registers to discover if it requires:

- an additional IO range for any VGA register extensions it may implement
- an additional memory range required for its superset frame buffer.

When it loads, the display driver queries the device's base address registers (note that this approach would make the driver PCI-specific; a better approach is the one used by Windows 95—query the Registry) to determine the addresses assigned to its register extension and the frame buffer. The use of a display interrupt line is not recommended and the interrupt pin register must be hard-wired to 00h. If the device designer requires an interrupt for the device, it should be selected by a jumper or by a vendor-supplied software utility that uses a device-specific configuration register to select the interrupt.

Summary

In summary, PCI devices can be automatically configured without any intervention by the end user. In addition, the OS can identify the driver associated with the device and load it into memory. That's what Plug and Play is all about. There are some unavoidable exceptions. An example would be a network controller card that must know what node it occupies on the network. The end user would have to be prompted for this type of information.

5 PCMCIA

The Previous Chapter

The previous chapter provided a discussion of PCI and its relationship to Plug and Play. Issues related to PCI, Windows 95, and Windows NT were also discussed.

This Chapter

This chapter describes the relationship of PCMCIA, Plug and Play, and Windows 95, and this chapter ends Part One, "Evolution."

The Next Chapter

The next chapter starts Part Two, "ISA/EISA Plug and Play," providing an introduction to E/ISA Plug and Play configuration concepts and related terminology.

Introduction

For a detailed explanation of the PCMCIA hardware and software components, refer to the MindShare book entitled *PCMCIA System Architecture, Second Edition* (Addison-Wesley Publishing Company, 1995).

Relationship of PCMCIA Cards and Plug and Play

The Plug and Play specifications (hardware and software) define the hardware and software necessary to detect the presence of and to configure system board, ISA, and EISA devices. The hardware and software tools necessary to support the detection and configuration of PCMCIA and PCI devices have already been defined by their respective specifications. PCMCIA cards are installed in card slots that interface directly to either:

- a PCMCIA controller or
- a CardBus bridge

The hardware controller interacts with the Socket and Card Services programs to permit the automatic detection and configuration of PCMCIA cards, as well as event notification when a card is installed or removed.

PCMCIA and Windows 95

Microsoft has written a white paper describing the relationship of PCMCIA and Windows 95. This paper is available for download over the Compuserve "Plug-Play" forum.

PCMCIA Problem Areas

Resources Available for Assignation to PCMCIA Cards

The PCMCIA Card Services (CS) program is responsible for determining the pool of resources available for assignment to any PCMCIA cards that may be installed in the system. When the machine is first powered up, CS determines the resources consumed by all system devices other than PCMCIA cards. Any other resources are marked as available for assignment to PCMCIA cards. Consider the following:

1. Sometime after power up, the system (a laptop) is installed in a docking or a convenience station. This station contains additional system devices that consume resources.
2. CS (as defined in the PCMCIA spec) is not capable of recognizing the existence of these new devices and the resources that they consume.
3. Sometime after docking, a PCMCIA card is installed in the laptop system. CS assigns resources to the card based on its out-of-date information regarding the available resources.
4. The card configuration conflicts with one (or more) of the docking station devices.

This is one of the problems that inhibits PCMCIA, as currently defined, from participating in a Plug and Play environment. Windows 95 addresses this problem (see "PCMCIA Bus Enumerator and Configuration Manager" on page 45).

Dynamic Driver Load/Unload Support

When a PCMCIA card is installed in a system that is already powered up (hot installation), the PCMCIA controller generates an interrupt. This interrupt causes the CS program to be executed. Using the Socket Services (SS) program, CS interrogates the PCMCIA controller to determine the event that occurred. When it has determined that a card was installed, CS then sends a message to the device driver (in memory) associated with the device to inform it of the device's presence. The device driver then works with CS to allocate non-conflicting resources to the device and enable it.

One of the basic assumptions in PCMCIA is that the device driver associated with the card is currently in memory. If it isn't, CS issues a missing driver message to the end user and the card will not work. There are two possible solutions to this problem:

- Device drivers for every conceivable PCMCIA card must be resident in system memory at all times. Clearly, this solution is not feasible.
- CS must have the added capability to load the device driver into memory (from disk) if it's currently not in memory. Conversely, it must have the ability to unload the driver from memory automatically when the card is removed (to free up system memory).

Windows 95 addresses this problem (see "PCMCIA Bus Enumerator and Configuration Manager" on page 45).

Support for Event Messaging

PCMCIA doesn't provide a mechanism that permits CS to send messages to any program in the system (other than the PCMCIA device driver) when a card is installed or removed. This capability permits CS to alert the OS and applications programs when devices that they require become available or are removed from the system.

Windows 95 addresses this problem (see "PCMCIA Bus Enumerator and Configuration Manager" on page 45).

PCMCIA Bus Enumerator and Configuration Manager

Windows 95 includes a program referred to as the PCMCIA Bus Enumerator that incorporates the following functions:

- The PCMCIA **CS** program (compliant with revision 2.1 of the PCMCIA specification).
- The PCMCIA **SS** program (compliant with revision 2.1 of the PCMCIA spec).
- The **PCMCIA enumerator** program. This program is responsible for identifying the PCMCIA cards installed in the system.

The CS incorporated in the Windows 95 PCMCIA enumerator implements the 32-bit protected mode binding defined in the 2.1 specification. CS communicates directly with the Windows 95 Configuration Manager (CM) program to ascertain the resources available for assignment to PCMCIA cards. Because CM also keeps track of dynamic changes in the system configuration (e.g., docking and undocking events), the danger of conflicts with docking station devices is eliminated.

The CS also uses messages to inform CM of any changes related to PCMCIA card installation or removal, and the CM communicates these changes to the OS and/or any applications that require this information.

When a PCMCIA card is installed in the system, the enumerator generates a unique Plug and Play ID from information supplied by the card (see "Unique Card Device ID" on page 48). After allocating non-conflicting resources to the device, the CM enables the device and searches the Registry for an entry that matches the unique device ID.

The Registry and the Device Installer

When a device is added to or removed from the system, the CM searches the Registry for the device ID. If a match is found, it reads that Registry entry to ascertain the location of the associated device driver on disk and to determine if the device performance would be enhanced by configuring the device with resource combinations specified in the Registry entry. There are two possible scenarios:

- The Registry indicates that there is no requirement for the assignment of particular resources in order to achieve desired device performance.
- The Registry indicates that the assignment of certain combinations of resources (e.g., a particular IRQ and IO range assignment) to the device will result in the best performance. In this case, the CM will attempt to alter the device's resource assignments to match one of the desired combinations.

Assuming that the device driver information was found in the Registry, the device may be reconfigured based on the (optimized configuration) information supplied from the registry. The device driver identified in the Registry entry is loaded into memory. The driver's initialization code is executed to ready the device for service (e.g., by performing a series of writes to its register set, hooking the interrupt assigned to it, etc.). In order to do this, the driver must know what resources have been assigned to the device. This is accomplished by requesting the information from CM. The driver must not accomplish this by directly interrogating its device's PCMCIA configuration registers. This would make the driver bus specific (i.e., it would only work with a PCMCIA version of the device).

If an entry is not found in the Registry, the CM calls the Device Installer program. This program searches the hard drive for a driver information file (with a .inf extension) with a file name constructed from the device ID. If the inf file is found, the Device Installer program reads the information from the inf file and makes an entry in the Registry. If the inf file is not found, the end user is prompted to insert the floppy that was supplied with the device. The device driver and the inf file are copied to hard disk. An entry is made in the Registry containing the location of the driver on disk and the data from the inf file. Recording this information in the Registry eliminates the need for diskette insertion in the future.

A white paper is available on the Compuserve PlugPlay forum that provides an introduction to inf files. The Windows 95 driver development kit (DDK) contains detailed information.

Bus-Independent Plug and Play Device Drivers

Ideally, all device drivers should be written as dynamically-loadable Windows 95 virtual device drivers (DLVxDs). Unlike a PCMCIA device driver, a VxD leaves the configuration of its device completely up to the CM.

When it receives a message from CS indicating that a card has been added, a PCMCIA device driver (as opposed to a Plug and Play Windows 95 device driver) issues a call directly to CS to ascertain the resources available for assignment to its device. It calls CS with a request to assign selected resources to its device. If the call is successful, the driver issues a request to the CS to enable the device. Now that its device has been configured and enabled, the PCMCIA driver performs the actions necessary (e.g., a series of IO writes to its device's register set, hooking the interrupt assigned to it, etc.) to ready its device for service. In other words, the PCMCIA device driver is directly involved in the configuration of its associated device.

By the time the CM has loaded a VxD, on the other hand, the device has already been configured (by the CM) and the driver may obtain the configuration information from the CM and initialize the device (perform IO writes to its register set, hook its interrupt, etc.). Whereas the PCMCIA device driver is tightly-coupled to the CS and is therefore PCMCIA specific, a VxD assumes that its device has already been configured (by the CM) and is operational. The same VxD will work with any instance of the device, whether it resides on PCMCIA, PCI, ISA, EISA, MCA, etc. In other words, it's universal (as long as the device's IO register set is implemented the same on any instance of the device on any bus).

Because Windows 95 incorporates a fully 2.1-compliant PCMCIA 32-bit CS program, a 32-bit PCMCIA device driver, rather than a VxD, can be used. The CS is present within the CM and the driver can communicate directly with it. However, there are some distinct drawbacks. The driver cannot participate in Windows 95 inter-process message passing. It cannot handle dynamic reallocation of resources by the CM. The driver can only be used with the PCMCIA version of the device. It cannot be used with a compatible version of the device that may reside on another bus (e.g., PCI).

Built-In Drivers and INF files for Common PCMCIA Cards

Windows 95 is delivered with inf files and drivers for a number of PCMCIA devices.

Unique Card Device ID

In order for the CM to find the driver information file associated with a device, the CM must be supplied with a unique card ID. The CM searches the Registry for a match on the ID. When a match is found, the content of that Registry entry is used to locate and load the device driver and, possibly, to alter the device's configuration (i.e., optimize it).

It is the responsibility of the Windows 95 PCMCIA bus enumerator to construct and supply this ID when a PCMCIA card is installed in the system. The two sections that follow define the manner in which the unique device ID is constructed for IO and memory cards.

IO Card Device ID

The PCMCIA bus enumerator constructs a PCMCIA IO card's unique device ID. The ID consists of two elements:

- A manufacturer/product portion of the ID
- A CRC16 portion of the ID

The manufacturer/product portion is constructed from the first two ASCII strings contained in the Level 1 Version/Product Information tuple read from the card. Non-printable characters are removed and spaces are converted to underscores. The white paper does not provide detail regarding the manner in which the ID is constructed.

The CRC16 portion of the ID is calculated mathematically (the exact method is not covered in the white paper) by combining the binary bit patterns that make up the following tuples read from the card:

- Level 1 Version/Product Information tuple
- Manufacturer ID tuple
- Device tuple
- Configuration tuple
- the Configuration Table Entries

Since the Windows 95 PCMCIA bus enumerator must have access to these tuples in order to construct a unique card ID to supply to the CM, it is critical that IO cards implement these tuples. Without them, Plug and Play cannot be achieved for the card in the Windows 95 environment. In addition, because Windows 95 may need to reconfigure the card during run-time, these tuples must not "disappear" after the card is first configured. They must always be available to be read by the enumerator.

Memory Card Device ID

The Windows 95 PCMCIA bus enumerator must also generate a unique ID for PCMCIA memory cards installed in the system. Although the white paper does not provide any detail on the method used to generate this ID, it does identify the tuples that are used to construct it. They are:

- Device tuple
- JEDEC-C tuple
- Device Geometry Information tuple
- Format tuple
- Organization tuple

Since the Windows 95 PCMCIA bus enumerator must have access to these tuples in order to construct a unique card ID for the CM, it is critical that memory cards implement these tuples. Without them, Plug and Play cannot be achieved for the card in the Windows 95 environment. In addition, because Windows 95 may need to reconfigure the card during run-time, these tuples must not "disappear" after the card is first configured. They must always be available to be read by the enumerator.

Socket Services (SS)

The PCMCIA SS program provides the interface between CS and the PCMCIA controller hardware. Windows 95 incorporates SS that support any Intel 365 or Databook compatible PCMCIA controllers. These SSs are implemented as DLVxDs. Both of these SS drivers are compliant with revision 2.1 of the PCMCIA specification.

The SS functions required by the CS contained in the Windows 95 PCMCIA bus enumerator are defined in the Windows 95 driver development kit (DDK).

Memory Card Support

Memory cards are supported in Windows 95 via Memory Technology Drivers (MTDs). The Microsoft Flash File System driver, CARDDRV, uses the CS interface to access memory cards. Memory card designers can supply their own MTDs for their cards, implemented using the PCMCIA 32-bit CS binding.

Part Two

E/ISA
Plug and Play

6 *Intro to E/ISA Plug and Play*

The Previous Chapter

The previous chapter describes the configuration characteristics of PCMCIA devices and Windows 95's relationship with PCMCIA.

This Chapter

This chapter provides an introduction to the topic of ISA/EISA Plug and Play. It defines the basic concepts and some basic terminology.

The Next Chapter

The next chapter describes the state of ISA/EISA Plug and Play cards at power up.

Introduction

There is no way to implement Plug and Play capability on legacy ISA cards without redesigning the card. The ISA Plug and Play specification defines a set of characteristics to be implemented on newly-designed ISA and EISA cards, referred to as Plug and Play ISA/EISA cards. This chapter introduces the mechanisms that enable cards to be Plug and Play capable. For the remainder of the book, Plug and Play is abbreviated as PnP. All instances of the term PnP apply to Plug and Play-capable ISA and EISA cards. It should be stressed that all subsequent references to ISA PnP cards would also be applicable to EISA PnP cards.

Card Detection and Selection

Each individual Micro Channel card can be placed into setup mode, permitting access to its configuration registers. Each EISA card has slot-specific IO space within which its configuration registers reside.

Legacy ISA cards, on the other hand, do not have a mechanism that permits one card to be singled out for configuration. In addition, legacy ISA cards do not have configuration registers that can be read and written. There are no pins on the ISA connector that can be used to place a card into setup (configuration) mode. The PnP specification must therefore define a mechanism for isolating one and only one PnP card for configuration. That mechanism is defined in the chapters that follow.

Resource Requirement List

PnP cards implement a resource requirement list that can be read by the configuration software to determine the resources that the card requires. The specification defines the format and usage of this data structure.

Configuration Registers

The specification defines a configuration register set to be implemented on new cards. These registers are accessed to configure the device once it has been isolated.

Configuration Process

The list that follows defines the typical steps necessary in order to configure PnP cards:

1. Writing a special key sequence to the PnP cards prepares them all to listen.
2. Now that you have their collective attention, performing a special series of reads from the cards causes them to arbitrate amongst themselves to decide which PnP card will enter isolation mode. Once the series of reads has been completed, one PnP card has been isolated.
3. The configuration software assigns a card select number (CSN) to the isolated card. The card leaves the isolation state and enters the configuration state.
4. The software reads the isolated card's resource requirement list to determine its requirements. The card is issued a command to go to sleep.
5. Steps 1 through 4 are repeated until all PnP cards have been isolated, assigned a CSN and their collective resource needs ascertained.

Chapter 6: Intro to E/ISA Plug and Play

6. The configuration software then uses each card's unique CSN to place it back into configuration mode. Its configuration registers are then written to assign non-conflicting resources to the device.
7. The card is then enabled (i.e., activated) for normal operation.
8. Steps 6 and 7 are repeated until all of the PnP cards have been configured and enabled.

In Windows 95, the ISA bus enumerator is called by the CM to perform this function.

Configuration Memory (NV Memory)

The sequence of steps described in the previous section assumes that the machine has never been configured. In other words, configuration memory has no record of the devices installed and the resources allocated to each of them.

The system's configuration memory is used to record the presence, type and current configuration of each device in the system. This information is used to configure each device every time the machine is restarted. After the system has been configured once, the configuration software only has to determine changes that may have occurred in the machine's device population each time the system is started. If any device(s) is removed, configuration memory is updated to reflect the availability of the resources that had been assigned to it. If a device(s) is added, it has a CSN assigned, its resource requirements read, and non-conflicting resources allocated to it. In addition, the information is recorded in configuration memory.

7 Power Up State of PnP Devices

The Previous Chapter

The previous chapter provided an introduction to the topic of EISA/ISA Plug and Play (PnP). It defined the basic concepts and some basic terminology.

This Chapter

This chapter describes the state of PnP cards when the machine is first powered up.

The Next Chapter

The next chapter introduces the configuration ports implemented on all PnP cards.

At Power On

When the machine is first powered on, the voltage outputs of the power supply are not yet at the correct levels. To prevent any devices from operating until the power has stabilized, the power supply keeps its POWERGOOD output deasserted during this period. On the system board, POWERGOOD is inverted to develop the system reset signal. Reset is propagated to all buses in the system, including the ISA bus. It is called RSTDRV on the ISA bus. Reset remains asserted until the power has stabilized. The power supply then asserts POWER-GOOD, causing reset to be deasserted. During the reset assertion period, reset prevents any devices from operating. It also presets all devices to a known state so that they always start operating the same way when reset is removed.

After Power Stabilization

When the power has stabilized and RSTDRV is removed, each PnP card has 2ms to load their resource requirement list from non-volatile storage into their configuration registers. The configuration software must not attempt to access a PnP card's configuration ports until the 2ms interval has elapsed.

The initial assertion of reset causes each PnP card's CSN (card select number) register to be cleared to zero (in other words, its CSN is unassigned). The card's configuration registers cannot be accessed while it is in this state. The card is in a state referred to as the wait for key state. This state is described in a subsequent chapter. Basically, writing a special key sequence to the community of PnP cards prepares them all for isolation and subsequent configuration.

Devices Unnecessary for Initial Startup

PnP devices that are not necessary for the initial startup (boot) process are disabled at startup time. They are in the wait for key state and cannot operate normally until they are configured later in the startup sequence.

Devices Necessary for the Boot Process

The PnP specification states that devices necessary for the initial boot process must come up enabled using default configuration settings. The assertion of reset during the initial power up period loads the device's configuration registers with the default settings. When reset is then deasserted, the device is enabled for normal operation. Examples of devices necessary for the initial boot process are:

- the keyboard
- the display operating in text mode
- the floppy drive interface
- the hard drive controller

8 Configuration Ports

The Previous Chapter

The previous chapter described the state of PnP cards when the machine is first powered up.

This Chapter

This chapter describes the three configuration ports that are used throughout the process of configuring ISA/EISA PnP cards.

The Next Chapter

The next chapter describes the various configuration states a PnP device can be in and the purpose of each state.

Introduction

All configuration activities are performed through three special IO ports: the configuration address port, the configuration write data port, and the configuration read data port. The address and write data ports are implemented at fixed IO addresses, while the read data port can be located anywhere in the IO range from 0203h through 03FFh. These three ports are implemented as 8-bit IO ports on each PnP card. They do not support 16-bit accesses. The address decode logic for the three ports decodes the lower 12 bits of the IO address (in other words, the lower three hex digits of the IO address). The following sections define the three ports.

How Configuration Registers Are Accessed

The three configuration IO ports are used to access a stack of configuration registers that are implemented on each PnP device. The format of these registers is defined in the chapter entitled "The PnP Configuration Registers." The three ports are also used for other configuration-related actions such as accessing the resource requirement list and the serial number. These subjects are covered in subsequent chapters.

Accessing any PnP configuration register is a two-step process:

1. Write the address of the target configuration register to the address port. This identifies the configuration register that will subsequently be read from or written to. The value written to the address port acts as a pointer into a stack of the card's configuration registers.
2. Write data to the targeted configuration register by writing to the write data port or read data from it by reading from the read data port.

Once the address of a particular configuration register has been written into the address port, the target configuration register can be read from or written to any number of times using the read and write data ports. The address port is only written again to select a different configuration register.

Address Port

The configuration address port is implemented as a write-only port at IO address (port) 0279h. This is the same address as the LPT1 printer status port. A read from this address accesses the printer status port, while a write to it writes data into the configuration address port.

Write Data Port

The configuration write data port is implemented as a write-only port at IO address 0A79h. As stated earlier, data written to this port is written to the configuration register targeted by the pointer currently in the address port. The following code fragment illustrates the use of the address and the write data ports:

```
mov  dx,0279h ;dx = IO address of address port
mov  al,03h   ;set al = wake reg pointer
out  dx,al    ;write wake reg pointer to address port
mov  dx,0A79h ;dx = IO address of write data port
mov  al,12h   ;al = 12h (CSN = 12h)
out  dx,al    ;write CSN to write data port (to wake reg)
```

Read Data Port

Selecting the Read Data Port's IO Address

According to the specification, the read data port can be implemented any-where within the range of IO addresses from 0203h through 03FFh (the least-significant two bits of the IO address must be 11b). In reality, however, the address decode logic for the read data port always looks for a 11b in the least-significant two bits of the IO address. This means that IO addresses lacking a 11b in the two lower bits cannot be assigned to the read data port. Examples of addresses that can be assigned are 0203h, 0207h, 020Bh, 020Fh, 0213h, 0217h, etc. The configuration program must find an address within this range (0203h through 03FFh) that doesn't also select a legacy ISA card (all legacy ISA cards reside within the 0100h through 03FFh IO address range). Before attempting to read from the configuration read data port, the configuration software must first tell all of the PnP devices the address of the read data port. In other words, there is a programmable address decoder for this port on all PnP cards.

Location zero in the stack of configuration registers is the **set read data port address configuration register**. In preparation for the configuration process, the programmer must first set the address of the read data port for all PnP devices. This is accomplished in the following manner:

1. The programmer must first write a special byte sequence to the configuration write data port. This sequence is referred to as the initiation key. This subject is covered in the chapter entitled "Isolating a Card for Configuration."
2. Broadcast the wake command to all PnP devices. This is accomplished by writing zero to the wake command configuration register. This subject is covered in detail in the chapter entitled "Isolating a Card for Configuration."
3. Write the pointer value 00h into the address port at IO address 0279h. The address port now points to the **set read data port address configuration register**.

4. Write an 8-bit value to the write data port. The value written supplies the read data port address decoder with address bits A[9:2] of the address to monitor for.

5. When a subsequent IO read is performed from the read data port, the read data port's address decoder compares address bits A[9:2] of the IO address to the 8-bit value that it has been programmed to compare for. On a match, it chip-selects the read data port. The contents of the read data port is then placed on the lower data path of the ISA bus, SD[7:0], to be read by the processor.

The following code sequence sets up the read data port's IO address decoder to recognize IO address 03E4h:

```
mov  dx,0279h    ;address port IO address in dx
mov  al,00h      ;location of set read data port reg in al
out  dx,al       ;set address port = set read port reg.
mov  dx,0A79h    ;dx = IO address of write data port
mov  al,F9h      ;al = bits A[9:2] of read port address
out  dx,al       ;set address
```

This code fragment sets the IO address of the read data port to 03E4h (A[15:10] are zero; A[9:2] are 1111 1001b; A[1:0] are 00b).

How the Read Data Port's Address Decoder Works

At one point, the specification states that all three ports use a 12-bit address decode. At a later point in the specification, however, it states that the read data port's address decoder checks all address bits up to A15. It is the author's opinion that the first statement is correct. The discussion that follows reflects that opinion.

This means that the read data port's address decoder looks at IO address bits A[11:0] during an IO read transaction to determine if the processor is accessing the port. It ignores A[15:12]. Table 8-1 on page 63 describes the address decoder's view of the IO address placed on the bus during an IO read transaction.

As an example, assume that the 8-bit value 1101 0100b (D4h) has been written to the **set read data port address configuration register**. As indicated in the table, this supplies bits A[9:2] of the compare address. The full address the decoder will compare for is xxxx 0011 0101 0011b on A[15:0] (i.e., 0353h). This breaks down as follows:

- xxxx indicates that the address decoder doesn't care what the state of A[15:12] are. It only looks at the lower three hex digits of the address.
- Address bits A[11:10] must be zero.
- Address bits A[9:2] are supplied by the **set read data port address register** and must be 1101 0100b.
- Address bits A[1:0] must be 11b.

Any IO address with 0011b (3h) in the third digit, 0101 (5h) in the second digit, and 0011b in the first digit matches the template and selects the read data port to be read. In other words, addresses that would meet these criteria would be any address with 353h in the lower three digits of the address.

Table 8-1: Read Data Port IO Address Decode

Bit(s)	Description
A[15:12]	The read data port address decoder does not look at these bits.
A[11:10]	The read data port address decoder checks for zeros in these two bits positions. In other words, it's looking for 00b in the upper two bits of the third hex digit of the IO address.
A[9:2]	The address decoder is looking for a match on these address bits with the 8-bit value written to the **set read data port address configuration register.**
A[1:0]	The read data port address decoder looks for a 11b on these two bits.

Checking for Conflict with a Legacy ISA Device

The address chosen for the read data port may conflict with an IO address already used by a legacy ISA device installed in the system. If this is the case, a read from the IO address selects the legacy ISA device as well as the read data port in all PnP devices. In addition to the read data supplied by a PnP device, the legacy device also supplies data on the lower data path. The result is garbled data.

After setting the IO address of the configuration read data port, the configuration program must test its choice to ensure that the selected IO address is only used by the PnP devices. The section entitled "Dealing with Checksum Error or All-Zero Serial Identifier" in the chapter entitled "Isolating a Card for Configuration" defines the mechanism used to ensure that no legacy device shares the IO address. If a conflict is discovered, the configuration software must select a different IO address for the read data port and check again for a conflict. This process is repeated until a conflict-free IO address is found. The configuration process can then proceed.

9 *Configuration States*

The Previous Chapter

The previous chapter introduced the three IO ports used to access the various configuration-related mechanisms defined for PnP devices. These are the configuration address, write data and read data ports.

This Chapter

This chapter introduces the various configuration states that a PnP device may be in, the relationship of the states to each other, and the purpose of each state.

The Next Chapter

The next chapter describes the isolation mechanism used at startup to prepare all PnP devices for configuration.

Introduction

Relative to being configured, a PnP device can be in any one of four possible states at a given moment in time. The four basic states are:

1. The system has just been powered up. None of the PnP cards have been configured. The cards are all in a state awaiting a special key to enable their configuration logic. This is called the **wait for key state**.
2. The key has been received and the community of PnP cards have entered the **sleep state**. They remain in this state until the configuration software awakens them to begin the process of assigning unique card select numbers (CSNs) to each of them.
3. The cards have been awakened and are competing to determine which will be chosen for configuration next. This is referred to as the **isolation state**.

4. The card that wins the competition is assigned a CSN and is ready to be configured. This is called the **configuration state**. The other cards go to sleep to await the next competition.

The Configuration States

During the discussion that follows, keep in mind that the cards all have a CSN of zero at startup (because the assertion of reset clears each card's CSN register to zero). Also remember that the configuration address, write data, and read data ports are implemented at identical IO addresses on all PnP cards. Figure 9-1 on page 68 illustrates the four possible states and the circumstances under which a transition is made from one state to another. The list that follows provides a description of the various situations illustrated.

1. The reset signal has just been deasserted after power up. All PnP cards are in the wait for key state.
2. None of the cards have been isolated, assigned a card select number (CSN), configured, and activated. The community of PnP cards are currently in the wait for key state.
3. The configuration software writes the initiation key sequence to the write data port and it is accepted by all of the PnP cards. When the entire key sequence has been written to the cards, this transitions all of them simultaneously from the wait for key to the sleep state.
4. The configuration software (the Windows 95 E/ISA bus enumerator) sets the pointer in the address port to point to the wake command register and writes a CSN of zero to it. Each card latches the CSN in its wake command register and compares it to its current CSN (CSN register was cleared to zero by reset). The match on the CSN causes all of the cards to transition from the sleep state to the isolation state. In other words, they wake up and prepare to engage in a competition to determine which of them will be isolated and assigned a valid (non-zero) CSN.
5. The competing cards are in the isolation state.
6. During the isolation process, the configuration software causes all of the cards in the isolation state to perform a bit-for-bit comparison of their respective serial identifiers. As the comparison progresses bit-by-bit, the competing cards will drop out of the competition one by one until only one card remains in the isolation state. The cards that lost the competition transition from the isolation state back to the sleep state. A detailed description of the serial identifier and the competition can be found in the chapter entitled "Isolating a Card for Configuration."
7. A card has been isolated, but has not yet been assigned a unique CSN. This is another way of saying it has been isolated for configuration. All of the

other cards (that lost the competition) are in the sleep state. The isolated card remains in the isolation state until a unique CSN is assigned to it.

8. Assigning the CSN transitions the device from the isolation to the configuration state. The isolated card is in the configuration state and all of the other cards (that lost the competition) are in the sleep state.

9. The configuration software now writes a CSN of zero to the wake command register. Since this CSN compares with the CSN of all of the cards that lost the competition and are currently asleep, those cards transition from the sleep state to the isolation state. The card that is in the configuration state has a miscompare on its CSN, however, causing it to transition from the configuration to the sleep state.

10. Steps 6 through 9 are repeated until all cards have been assigned a unique CSN number.

At this point, all of the cards have been assigned CSNs and are currently asleep. The next step is to read the resource requirement lists from all of the cards and prepare for the actual configuration of the cards. This subject is covered in the chapter entitled "Card Resource Requirements." A detailed description of the isolation process can be found in the chapter entitled "Isolating a Card for Configuration."

The list that follows also refers to Figure 9-1 on page 68. It describes additional operations that cause state transitions of a card's PnP configuration logic.

- A card was previously assigned a CSN, configured, and activated for normal operation. It is sent the wait for key command, causing its configuration logic to return to the wait for key state. The target card has been activated, enabling it for normal operation, but it must receive the key sequence and its configuration logic reawakened again in order to access its configuration registers.

- Receipt of the wait for key command causes any device currently in the sleep or isolation state to transition back to the wait for key state.

- Any device currently in the configuration state that receives a wake command with a CSN other than its own transitions to the sleep state.

- Any device that has already had its CSN assigned and is currently in the sleep state, upon receiving a wake command specifying its CSN, transitions to the configure state.

- Any device that is in the isolation state and receives a wake command with a CSN not equal to zero (devices in the isolation state have not yet had a CSN assigned and have a CSN of zero) transitions to the sleep state.

Figure 9-1: The Configuration States

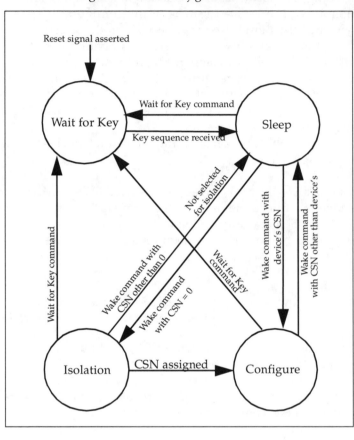

10 *Isolating a Card for Configuration*

The Previous Chapter

The previous chapter introduced the various configuration states that a PnP device may be in, the relationship of the states to each other, and the purpose of each state.

This Chapter

This chapter describes the process used to isolate a single PnP device for configuration. This includes the initiation key sequence, the isolation process, and the CSN assignment.

The Next Chapter

The next step is to wake up each card one at a time, read its resource requirements, and put it back to sleep. This process is repeated until the resource requirements of all PnP cards have been ascertained. The next chapter describes the process of reading the resource data structure and provides a detailed description of its content.

Windows 95 Overview

The CM calls the E/ISA bus enumerator program to discover any E/ISA PnP cards that reside on the E/ISA bus. The enumerator performs the isolation and assigns a unique CSN to each card. It reads the cards' serial numbers and resource requirements and returns them to the CM. The next chapter describes the reading of the resource requirement data and its format.

Plug and Play System Architecture

The Startup State

As described in an earlier chapter, all PnP cards are left in the wait for key state when the reset signal is deasserted. Each of their CSNs has been reset to zero and the cards are deactivated (i.e., they are not enabled to respond to ISA bus transactions to locations other than the three configuration IO ports). When the initiation key sequence is written to them, they transition from the wait for key to the sleep state. The configuration address and write data ports are located at the same fixed IO addresses on all cards, while the IO address of the read data port has not yet been assigned.

The Initiation Key

The configuration software must write a special sequence of characters to the community of PnP cards in order to gain access to their configuration logic. The special character sequence is referred to as the initiation key. Each PnP card must implement a hardware device that generates the special character sequence and compares it to the character sequence written to the cards by the configuration software.

The hardware device responsible for the sequence generation and comparison is referred to as a linear feedback shift register, or LFSR. Before writing the initiation key sequence to the cards, two bytes of 00h must be written to the address port in order to reset each card's LFSR to its initial state. When the second 00h byte is written to the address port, the LFSRs on all cards then contain a start value of 6Ah. The LFSR resets to this initial value (6Ah) any time that the card is in the wait for key state and it receives a byte in the address port that doesn't match the byte currently in the LFSR.

6Ah is the value compared to the first byte of the key sequence that is written to the address port by the configuration software. As each of the 32 bytes that comprise the key sequence are written to the address port, each card's LFSR takes the following steps:

1. The byte in the address port is compared to the byte currently in the LFSR. If it compares, go to step 2. If it miscompares, the LFSRs reset to 6Ah and start over.
2. The LFSR performs an exclusive-OR of bits one and zero of the byte currently in the LFSR. The least-significant two bits of 6Ah are 10b and the exclusive-OR of the two bits yields a 1b.
3. The byte is then shifted right by one bit and the bit resulting from the exclu-

sive-OR becomes bit seven of the newly-created byte. As an example, the exclusive-OR of 10b (bits [1:0] of the 6Ah) results in a 1b. Shifting the 6Ah right one bit results in 35h and adding the 1b as bit seven changes the 35h to B5h.

4. Go to step 1 (the newly-formed byte is compared to the next byte written to the address port by the configuration software).

This sequence is repeated until all 32 bytes of the sequence have been written to the address port and compared correctly. All of the PnP cards then transition from the wait for key state to the sleep state. If any of the 32 characters aren't correct, the LFSR resets its contents to 6Ah and starts over. At the end of the 32 writes, as a result of not having 32 compares, the cards do not transition to the sleep state. In other words—without the right key, you can't configure the cards. It's a security mechanism to ensure that accidental accesses to the wrong locations cannot alter the configuration of a card.

The Wakeup Call

The cards are now all in the sleep state. The next step is to wake them all up collectively and cause them to transition to the isolation state. In the isolation state, the configuration software attempts to isolate one card and assign a CSN to it.

Since the machine has just been powered up, the CSN register on all of the cards contains a value of zero. In other words, all of them have a CSN of zero. In order to wake up all of the cards, the configuration software must write this CSN number into the wake command register on all of the cards. This is accomplished as follows:

1. Write a 03h into the address port. The 03h is latched into the address port on every PnP card. The address port now points to the wake command register (see location 03h in Table 10-3 on page 81). Remember that each card contains a stack of configuration registers that are accessed via the three configuration IO ports. The wake command register occupies location 03h in the stack.

2. The next value written to the write data port is written into the wake command register on every card. In this case, the CSN of 00h is written to the write data port. Because the address port currently points to the wake command register, the data written to the write data port is written into the wake command register. Since this compares with the 00h currently contained in every card's CSN register, all of the cards transition from the sleep state to the isolation state.

Plug and Play System Architecture

All of the cards are now in the isolation state. Internally, the wake command has reset the pointer to each card's serial identifier to point to the first bit of the identifier. The configuration software can now begin to read the serial identifier. Prior to proceeding, however, the IO address for the read data port must be programmed into the **set read data port address register**.

Select Read Data Port Address

In the next step, the configuration software must perform a series of reads from the read data port. Before this, the read data port's address decoder must be set to an IO address in the range from 0203h through 03FFh. A description of the three ports can be found in the chapter entitled "Configuration Ports" on page 59." To set the read data port's IO address, perform the following steps:

1. Write a 00h to the address port. The **set read data port address register** is located at position zero in each card's stack of configuration registers (see Table 10-3 on page 81). The address port now points to the **set read data port address register**.
2. Write a byte to the write data port. That byte is written into the **set read data port address register** on every PnP card. The value written supplies the read data port's address decoder with bits [9:2] of the read data port's IO address. Bits [1:0] of the address decoder are hardwired to 11b, and bits [11:10] are hardwired to 00b. Bits [15:12] are not examined by the address decoder.

As an example, assume that the programmer wishes the read data port to reside at IO address 03F7h. Table 10-1 on page 72 illustrates the bit breakdown. Bits 9:2 are comprised of FDh. This is the value that would be written to the set read data port register. It should be noted that a legacy IO card may also utilize this address. During the isolation process (described in subsequent sections), the programmer can determine if a conflict exists. If it does, the programmer must change the address of the read data port and re-attempt the card isolation procedure described in the sections that follow.

Table 10-1: To Set Read Data Port to IO Address 03F7h

15	14	13	12	11	10	9	8	7	6	5	4	3	2	1	0
0	0	0	0	0	0	1	1	1	1	1	1	0	1	1	1
							F				D				

Chapter 10: Isolating a Card for Configuration

Each Card Has a Unique Serial Identifier

Now that a read data port address has been assigned, the configuration program can proceed with the next step in the configuration process. In this step, the programmer reads the serial identifier from the cards. Before proceeding with this step, however, a description of the serial identifier would be useful.

Each PnP card must implement a 64-bit (eight-byte) unique serial identifier, followed by an 8-bit checksum byte. The first 32-bit field is a vendor ID in the form of an EISA device ID. This 32-bit field has the format indicated in Table 10-2 on page 73. The second 32-bit field of the serial identifier represents a manufacturer-supplied serial number unique to that card. In other words, if two or more cards of the same type from the same manufacturer were installed in the machine, the last 32-bit field of their serial identifiers are different and can be used by the configuration software to determine that there are multiple-instances of the same card present in the machine and to differentiate between them. It is the manufacturer's responsibility to ensure that this rule is adhered to. If a card manufacturer chooses not to support more than one instance of the card in a system, this value (the last 32-bits of the serial identifier) must be set to FFFFFFFFh.

Table 10-2: EISA Device ID Format

Bits	Description
4:0	First character of the three character vendor ID assigned by BCPR services, the administrator of the EISA specification. Represents a compressed ASCII alpha character in the range A through Z. 00001b represents A, while 11010b represents Z (the bits are binarily-weighted; 11010b therefore represents the 26th character in the alphabet).
9:5	Second character of the assigned vendor ID.
14:10	Third character of the assigned vendor ID.
15	Must be zero. The Plug and Play specification doesn't say this, but the EISA specification does.
23:16	Product ID. Supplied by manufacturer.
31:24	Revision ID. Supplied by manufacturer.

Isolating a Card for CSN Assignment

Introduction

All of the cards have been awakened and have transitioned from the sleep to the isolation state. The configuration software now must isolate one of the cards and assign a CSN to it. This process must be repeated until all of the cards have had their CSNs assigned. The description of this process follows.

The Card Game

Consider each card's 72-bit serial identifier (64-bits plus the 8-bit checksum) to be a hand of 72 playing cards, each of which is either a one or a zero. During a round, each player (i.e., each PnP card) plays its 72 cards one at a time in sequence. Each time the next card is played, a one beats a zero. More detail on what occurs during a round is provided in the next section. The winner of a round is assigned a unique CSN and is then put to sleep (and doesn't partici-pate in subsequent hands). Using the same 72 card hand again, the remaining players (the PnP cards that haven't had a CSN assigned yet) play another round. The winner of each round is assigned a unique CSN and is put to sleep. Eventually, all of the players have been assigned a unique CSN and the game is over.

Using its unique CSN, the configuration software (in Windows 95, the CM using the E/ISA bus enumerator program) wakes up one of the cards. The card goes directly from the sleep to the configuration state. The configuration pro-gram reads the card's resource requirement data to ascertain what resources it requires. It then puts the card back to sleep. It wakes up each card in turn, build-ing an overall resource requirement list. It then chooses a non-conflicting set of resources to be assigned to each card. One by one, the cards are awakened again, configured with non-conflicting resources and are then activated for nor-mal operation. Upon completion of the configuration process, all of the cards are commanded to return their configuration logic to the wait for key state. Any time that the configuration software subsequently requires access to a card's configuration registers, it issues the key and then wakes up the target card using its assigned CSN. The card's configuration registers can then be accessed.

Chapter 10: Isolating a Card for Configuration

How the Game Is Played

The card game is initiated by:

1. Issuing the key sequence. This transitions all PnP cards from the wait for key to the sleep state.
2. Issuing a wake command with a CSN of zero. This wakes up all of the cards and transitions them to the isolation state.

When the configuration program tells them to, all of the PnP cards (the players) throw their first card (i.e., the first bit of the serial identifier) on the table. Any player(s) that plays a zero and sees any other player(s) throw out a one drops out of the game. They go back to sleep to await the next game. The player(s) that threw out a one stays in the game and starts another round (when commanded to by the configuration software) by throwing out their next card (bit). If none of them had a one in the first round, they all stay in the game and throw out their next card (bit) when commanded to do so.

A game consists of 72 rounds. As the game progresses, bit by bit, fewer players are participating. The losers of each round go back to sleep to await another game. Eventually, only one player is left in the game. Remember the rule —no two PnP cards can have the same serial identifier and a serial identifier of zero is not permitted. The configuration program writes a unique CSN to the winning player's CSN register. This transitions the player to the configure state. The configuration program then commands the player with the unique CSN to go to sleep and simultaneously commands all players that have not yet been assigned a unique CSN (they still have a CSN of zero) to wake up and re-enter the isolation state to play another game. This process is repeated until all players have been assigned a unique CSN. The configuration program can tell that all players have had their unique CSNs assigned when none of the 72 cards thrown out are a one.

Detailed Description

The description in the preceding section used the metaphor of a card game. This section provides a hardware-level description of the process.

The configuration program must read a 72-bit serial identifier from the cards. In the course of reading the identifier, the PnP cards engage in a competition to determine which of them supplies the entire identifier and accepts the CSN assigned by the configuration program. Issuing the wake command with a CSN of 00h caused all cards without a valid CSN to enter the isolation state and resets their serial identifier pointers to the first bit of the identifier. Before reading the identifier, the programmer sets the address port to point to the serial isolation register. This is accomplished by writing 01h to the address port (see Table 10-3 on page 81). The serial isolation register contains the serial identifier. Any subsequent reads from the read data port access the serial isolation register.

It takes two IO reads from the read data port to ascertain the state of each identifier bit. If the first read returns a 55h and the second returns an AAh, the configuration software interprets this as a 1b. Any other pair of returned values must be interpreted as a 0b. It takes 72 pairs of IO reads, 144 total, to read the 64-bit serial identifier and the checksum byte. The sequence that follows details the procedure.

Figure 10-1 on page 79 provides a flowchart of the process used to read the serial identifier. The first IO read from the read data port causes all of the cards in the isolation state to examine the first bit of their serial identifiers.

- **Actions by card(s) with a one bit in the current bit position of the serial identifier.** The card(s) supply a 55h as the read data during the first read and an AAh during the second read. At the conclusion of the second read, if all 72 bits of the identifier have not yet been read, they shift to the next bit of the serial identifier in preparation for the next pair of reads from the read data port.

- **Actions by cards with a zero bit in the current bit position of the serial identifier.** The cards do not supply data in response to either read. Instead, the cards passively observe the data on the bus during the first read to determine if a 55h is being supplied by any other cards. If not, it is assumed that no other cards have a one bit in the current bit position of the serial identifier. The cards with a zero bit ignore the second read, and wait for the second read to complete. If a card with a zero bit observed a 55h on the data bus during the first read, it observes the second read to determine if any other cards supply an AAh in response to the read. If AAh is detected, one or more other cards have a one bit in the current position. That beats a zero bit, so the cards with a zero bit in the current bit position re-enter the sleep state at the conclusion of the second read. If AAh is not detected during the second read (even if a 55h was detected during the first read), the cards with the zero bit interpret this to mean that no other card had a one bit in that bit position. This means that the cards with the zero bit are still in the game. If all 72 bits of the identifier have not yet been read, they shift to the next bit of the serial identifier in preparation for the next pair of reads from the read data port.

Chapter 10: Isolating a Card for Configuration

When the cards with a zero in the current bit check the pattern on the bus during the first and second reads, they use a minimalist approach. Instead of comparing all 8-bits of the data bus for a 55h or an AAh, they just check the least-significant two bits for a 01b (a 55h is a 0101 0101b) or a 10b (an AAh is a 1010 1010b). This saves on logic cost.

If the configuration program receives a 55h on the first read and an AAh on the second, it interprets this as a one bit. Any other pair of return values is interpreted as a zero bit. The configuration program performs 72 pairs of reads to accumulate an entire serial identifier and its checksum. During the process, cards with zero bits in various bit positions of their identifiers are eliminated and go to sleep. At the conclusion, only one card will be left in the isolation state and the serial identifier read is that card's identifier.

Treatment of Channel Ready Signal

It is a rule that PnP cards must not utilize the CHRDY signal while the configuration software is reading the serial identifier to isolate a card. Normally, a transaction is a two-party affair. The bus master addresses one target, indicates that it is a read transaction, and that target supplies the requested data. If the target requires more time to set up the requested data on the bus, it deasserts CHRDY and keeps it deasserted until it is ready to transfer the data. It then reasserts CHRDY. The deassertion of CHRDY forces the bus master to insert wait states into the transaction to accommodate the slowness of the target device.

During the card isolation process, the bus master (the processor) is reading from multiple cards simultaneously. The specification dictates that none of the cards are permitted to deassert CHRDY during this process. This avoids contention on the CHRDY signal.

Because the CHRDY signal remains asserted during each of the IO reads from the serial isolation register, the ISA system's default ready timer times out after inserting four wait states (125ns per wait state) in the transaction and asserts the processor's ready line. When the processor samples ready asserted, it latches the read data from the bus. This means that each access to the serial isolation register is six BCLK ticks (125ns each) in duration (one address clock, one data clock, and four wait state clocks). If all of this talk of default ready timers, clocks and wait states escapes you, there are two possible reasons for this:

- You are a software person and have no need to know about this hardware stuff. Don't worry about it.

- You are a hardware person and you are not as familiar with ISA system architecture as you need to be. In this case, a detailed discussion of ISA bus transactions and the default ready timer can be found in the MindShare book entitled *ISA System Architecture* (Addison-Wesley Publishing Company, 1995).

Dealing with Checksum Error or All-Zero Serial Identifier

As the first 64-bits are read, a checksum is computed. When the checksum byte (the last byte) has been read, the configuration software compares the computed checksum against the checksum read from the card. If it compares, the serial identifier is good. If there is a checksum error, there are two possible cases:

- If a checksum error occurs during the read of the first serial identifier, this should be interpreted as contention on the read data port. In other words, a legacy ISA card shares the same address that was assigned to the read data port. The programmer should reassign the read data port address and try again.
- If a checksum error occurs during the read of a serial identifier other than the first one, this should be interpreted to mean that there are no more PnP cards to be isolated and assigned a CSN.

There are two possible cases where the 72-bit read yields a serial identifier of all zeros:

- If it occurs during the read of the first serial identifier, this should be interpreted as contention on the read data port. In other words, a legacy ISA card shares the same address that was assigned to the read data port. The programmer should reassign the read data port address and try again.
- If it occurs during the read of a serial identifier other than the first one, this should be interpreted to mean that there are no more PnP cards to be isolated and assigned a CSN.

Figure 10-1: Isolation Flowchart

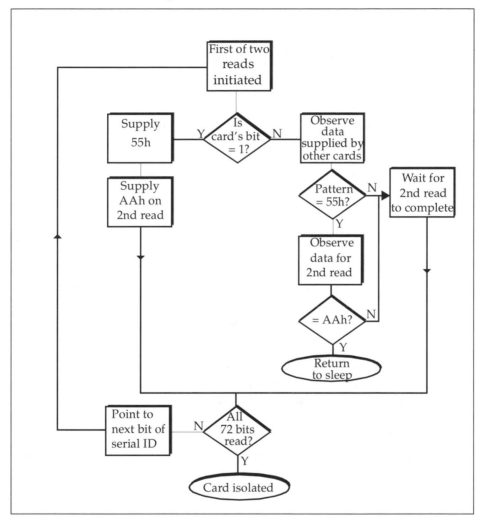

CSN Assignment

Assuming that a good serial identifier is read, the configuration software then assigns a unique CSN to the isolated card. This is accomplished by writing the 8-bit CSN to the card's CSN register. Table 10-3 on page 81 indicates that the CSN register resides at location 06h in the card's configuration register stack.

The value 06h is therefore written to the address port to point it to the CSN register. The unique CSN is then written to the write data port and is latched into the isolated card's CSN register. This causes the card to transition from the isolation to the configure state.

After CSN Assignment, Put Device Back to Sleep

At this time, one card is in the configure state and the rest are in the sleep state (because they lost the game). The configuration software now wakes up all of the cards that still have a CSN of zero and simultaneously puts the card with the CSN to sleep. This is accomplished by issuing the wake command with a CSN of zero. 03h is written to the address port (to point it to the wake command register) and then 00h is written to the write data port (into the wake command register). The card with the unique, non-zero CSN has a miscompare on its CSN register, so it transitions to the sleep state. The cards with a CSN of zero have a compare on their CSN registers and transition from the sleep to the isolation state so the configuration software can begin reading another serial identifier.

Repeat Isolation Process Until CSN Assigned to All Cards

Issuing the wake command automatically resets the bit pointer in the serial isolation register of each awakened card to the first bit. 01h is written to the address port to point it to the serial isolation register. The configuration software plays another "game" by performing 144 reads from the read data port to get another serial identifier. The configuration software (in Windows 95, the CM) builds a list of serial identifiers and the CSNs assigned to each.

Summary

This chapter described the process used to isolate each PnP card and assign it a CSN. Using the CSN, a wake command may be issued to place a specific card into the configure state so that its configuration registers may be accessed. The configuration program can read the resource requirement list associated with a device and assign resources to it by writing the appropriate values to its configuration registers. The next chapter describes the reading and format of the card's resource requirements list.

Chapter 10: Isolating a Card for Configuration

Table 10-3: The Configuration Ports

Register Stack Location	Description
00h	**Set Read Data Port address register.** Used to set bits 9:2 of the port's IO address. Bits 11:10 are hardwired to 00b and bits 1:0 are hardwired to 11b. This is a write-only register and is required. <u>This register is not associated with a specific device on the card. It is associated with the card itself.</u>
01h	**Serial Isolation register.** Used to read the serial identifier during the card isolation process. This is a read-only register and is required. <u>This register is not associated with a specific device on the card. It is associated with the card itself.</u>
02h	**Configuration Control register.** Bits 7:3 are reserved and must be zero. The defined bits are: 0 — **Reset bit.** When set to one, resets all of the card's configuration registers to their default state. The CSN is not affected. 1 — **Return to wait for key state.** When set to one, all cards return to the wait for key state. Their CSNs and configuration registers are not affected. This command is issued after all cards have been configured and activated. 2 — **Reset CSN to zero.** When set to one, all cards reset their CSNs to zero. This is a write-only register and is required. The three bits defined above are required. Any one bits written to this register are automatically cleared by the hardware. <u>This register is not associated with a specific device on the card. It is associated with the card itself.</u>

Table 10-3: The Configuration Ports (Continued)

Register Stack Location	Description
03h	**Wake Command register.** Writing a CSN to this register has the following effects: • If the value written is 00h, cards in the sleep state with a match on the CSN transition to the isolation state. Any card in the configure state (it has a non-zero CSN) transitions to the sleep state. This is done to wake up all of the cards that have not yet had a CSN assigned for another isolation competition. • If the value written is non-zero, any card in the sleep state with a CSN match transitions to the configure state. Any card in the isolation state transitions to the sleep state. Any write to a card's wake command register with a match on its CSN causes the pointer to the serial identifier/resource data to be reset to the first byte of the serial identifier. This is a write-only register and is required. <u>This register is not associated with a specific device on the card. It is associated with the card itself.</u>
04h	**Resource Data register.** This register is used to read the device's resource data. Each time that a read is performed from this register the next byte of the resource data is returned and the resource data pointer is auto-incremented. Prior to reading each byte, the programmer must read from the status register to determine if the next byte is available for reading from the resource data register. The resource data register is read-only and is required. Also see description of the status register in this table. <u>This register is not associated with a specific device on the card. It is associated with the card itself.</u> The card's serial identifier and checksum must be read prior to accessing the resource requirement list via this register.
05h	**Status register.** Prior to reading the next byte of the device's resource data, the programmer must read from the status register and check bit 0 for a one. This is the resource data byte available bit. Bits 7:1 are reserved. This is a read-only register and is required. Also see the description of the resource data register in this table. <u>This register is not associated with a specific device on the card. It is associated with the card itself.</u>

Table 10-3: The Configuration Ports (Continued)

Register Stack Location	Description
06h	**Card Select Number (CSN) register.** This is a read/write register and is required. The configuration software (in Windows 95, the CM) uses the CSN register to assign a unique ID to the card. The CSN is then used to wake up the card's configuration logic whenever the configuration program must access its configuration registers. <u>This register is not associated with a specific device on the card. It is associated with the card itself.</u>
07h	**Logical Device Number register.** The content of the card's resource data list identifies how many logical devices are implemented on this card. To select a logical device's configuration registers, its logical device number must first be written here. A card with only one logical device must hardwire this register to zero. A card with more than one logical device implements this as a read/write register. The register is required. <u>This register is not associated with a specific device on the card. It is associated with the card itself.</u>
08h - 1Fh	**Reserved card-level registers.** Reserved for future use. Do not use. <u>These registers are not associated with a specific device on the card. They are associated with the card itself.</u>
20h - 2Fh	**Vendor-defined card-level registers.** Available to the card vendor for card-specific configuration registers. <u>These registers are not associated with a specific device on the card. They are associated with the card itself.</u>
30h	**Activate register.** Setting bit 0 to a 1 activates the card on the ISA bus. When cleared, the card cannot respond to any ISA bus transactions (other than accesses to its configuration ports). Reset clears bit 0. This bit is required. The register is read/write. Bits 7:1 are reserved and must return zeros when read. <u>This register exists for each logical device on the card. The logical device is selected by writing its number into the card's logical device number register.</u>

Table 10-3: The Configuration Ports (Continued)

Register Stack Location	Description
31h	**IO Range Check register.** The specification does not say if this read/write register is required. It would certainly not be required if the logical device does not use any IO addresses (other than the three configuration ports). If, on the other hand, the logical device does use IO space, it is the author's opinion that it is required. It permits the configuration program to determine if an IO range assigned to the logical device conflicts with that used by a legacy ISA card before enabling the PnP logical device for normal operation. IO range checking is only valid when the logical device is deactivated (see the description of the Activate register in this table). Bit(s) Description 7:2 Reserved and must return zeros when read. 1 When set to one, enables IO range checking and disables it when cleared to zero. When enabled, bit 0 is used to select a pattern for the logical device to return. 0 When set, the logical device returns 55h in response to any read from the logical device's assigned IO space. When cleared, AAh is returned. Also see the description of bit 1 immediately preceding this paragraph. If a legacy ISA card responds to an address that the PnP logical device is programmed to recognize, it drives data onto the data bus (SD[7:0]) at the same time that the PnP device is driving a 55h or an AAh. This will change the pattern so that it will not equal a 55h or an AAh. When the configuration software determines that this is the case, it must then select another IO range to assign to the PnP logical device. The new range is then tested for contention in the same way. This register exists for each logical device on the card. The logical device is selected by writing its number into the card's logical device number register.
32h - 37h	**Reserved for future logical device control registers.** Do not use. These registers may be implemented in the future and are specific to the currently-selected logical device. The logical device is selected by writing its number into the card's logical device number register.

Table 10-3: The Configuration Ports (Continued)

Register Stack Location	Description
38h - 3Fh	**Vendor-defined logical device control registers.** These registers may be implemented for a logical device on the card. The logical device is selected by writing its number into the card's logical device number register.

11 Card Resource Requirements

The Previous Chapter

The previous chapter described the process used to isolate a single PnP card for configuration. This included the initiation key sequence, the isolation process, and the CSN assignment. The card was then put back to sleep, the next card isolated and assigned a CSN, etc. This process is repeated until each of the PnP cards have been identified, assigned a unique CSN and put back to sleep.

This Chapter

The next step is to wake up each card, read its resource requirements (memory space, IO space, interrupt request line, DMA channel, etc.), and put it back to sleep. This process is repeated until the resource requirements of all PnP cards have been ascertained. This chapter describes the process of reading the resource data structure and provides a detailed description of its content.

The Next Chapter

The configuration program's next step is to decide on a conflict-free distribution of the resources requested by the cards. Each card is then reawakened, placed back into the configure state, assigned its resources and activated for normal operation. The resources are allocated to a card by writing the appropriate values to each logical device's configuration register set. When this process is completed, all of the PnP cards are fully enabled for normal operation.

The next chapter describes the configuration register set associated with each PnP card and each logical device residing on the card. The configuration program uses these registers to assign non-conflicting resources to each logical device on a PnP card.

Plug and Play System Architecture

Windows 95 Overview

The Windows 95 CM uses the E/ISA PnP bus enumerator program to isolate PnP cards and assign a unique CSN to each. Using each card's CSN, the cards are awakened (one at a time) and their resource requirement lists are read and supplied to CM. CM uses a resource arbiter program to identify non-conflicting resources to allocate to each card. The process of reading a card's resource requirement list, as well as the format of the list, are covered in this chapter.

When the resource arbiter has identified resources to allocate to a PnP card, the CM calls the PnP bus enumerator to assign these resources to the target card. The process used by the enumerator to program the card's configuration registers is described in the next chapter.

Definition of Logical Device

A PnP card may incorporate more than one device (in other words, it may be a multi-function PnP card). As an example, one card may incorporate a floppy-disk controller, a serial port and a parallel port. The only thing that these three devices have in common is that they reside on the same card. The PnP specification refers to each of these as a logical device.

The card contains a resource requirement list for each device. This list defines the memory, IO, interrupt, and DMA requirements of the device. In addition to its list, each logical device also contains a corresponding set of programmable configuration registers that the configuration software uses to assign the selected resources to the device.

Reading the Resource Data

Each PnP card contains an eight-byte serial identifier, a checksum byte for its identifier, and a resource data structure (i.e., its resource requirement list). The nine-byte serial identifier and the resource data structure must be read as a serial byte stream in one contiguous block. Before attempting to access the resource data structure, the programmer must therefore always read the serial identifier first.

In order to access a card's serial identifier and resource data structure, the card must first be placed in the configure state. Only one card can be in the configure state at a given time. A card can enter the configure state in two ways:

Chapter 11: Card Resource Requirements

1. When a card is first assigned its CSN, it automatically enters the configure state from the isolation state. In this case, the configuration software just completed reading the card's serial identifier and has verified that its checksum is correct. The next read performed from the card's resource data register accesses the first byte of the card's resource requirement list (also referred to as its resource data structure). Each time that a read is performed from the resource data register, the card increments its pointer to the next byte of the resource data structure.

2. Assuming that a card was previously assigned a CSN and then put to sleep, a wake command with a CSN matching the card's CSN transitions the card from the sleep to the configure state. The wake command always resets the card's pointer to the beginning of the serial identifier. For this reason, the programmer must first read the nine-byte serial identifier from the serial isolation register before attempting to read the resource data structure via the resource data register. It should be noted, however, that although the eight-byte identifier is correct (when read in this manner, as opposed to case number one above), the checksum byte is not correct (even though the serial identifier is correct). When the read of the nine-byte serial identifier is completed, the next read performed from the resource data register accesses the first byte of the resource data register.

A card may keep its resource data structure in a slow-access device. After each byte is read from the resource data register, the programmer must not read from the register again until the card has set up the next byte of the resource data structure in the resource data register. This implies that there must be a way for the programmer to know when the next byte is ready to be read from the register. That is the purpose of the card's status register (see the section entitled "Status Register" on page 153). To ensure that the next byte is ready to be read, the programmer must always first check the status register for a ready condition before performing the next read from the resource data register.

The format of the resource data structure is covered in this chapter. The programmer can tell when the end of the structure is reached via a special identifier (the end of list tag). The following code fragment illustrates how the resource data register and the status register are accessed:

```
        mov  dx,0279h      ;dx=io address of address port
        mov  al,05h        ;al= status reg loc.
        out  dx,al         ;address port = status reg.
        mov  dx,0xxxh      ;dx = IO address of read data port
loop:   in   al,dx         ;read from status register
        test al,00000001b  ;
        jz   loop          ;test ready bit,loop if not ready
        mov  dx,0279h      ;
        mov  al,04h        ;
        out  dx,al         ;point to resource data reg
        mov  dx,0xxxh      ;dx=read data port address
        in   al,dx         ;read resource data structure byte
        ...                ;save resource byte
        cmp  al,end        ;end of structure?
        jnz  loop          ;keep reading if not end
        ...                ;analyze card's resource needs
```

What the Resource Data Structure Contains

The resource data structure defines the resources required by each logical
device on the card. A device may require one or a number of resources. Here are
two examples:

1. A device only has an IO register set. It doesn't have any memory, doesn't
    generate any interrupts and doesn't use a DMA channel. The resource
    requirement list for this device would only consist of one IO descriptor that
    defines the lowest and highest IO base address that may be assigned to the
    device and the number of IO addresses it requires. The device only requires
    the implementation of one IO configuration register. It isn't necessary to
    implement any additional IO, memory, interrupt, or DMA configuration
    registers.
2. Another device has two IO register sets, an expansion ROM, a RAM mem-
    ory buffer, generates interrupts to request service, and requires the use of a
    DMA channel to transfer data between it and system memory. The resource
    requirements list for this device consist of two IO, two memory, one inter-
    rupt, and one DMA descriptor. Consequently, this device requires the
    implementation of two IO, two memory, one interrupt, and one DMA con-
    figuration register.

It should be evident that each of a device's resource descriptors is associated
with a corresponding configuration register used by the configuration software
to tell the device what resources (interrupt line, DMA channel, memory range,
etc.) have been assigned to it.

Chapter 11: Card Resource Requirements

Refer to Figure 11-1 on page 91. Each card's resource data structure starts with the Plug and Play version number of the card and an identifier string. The identifier string is used by the OS when displaying configuration and error messages related to the card. The string is followed by a resource requirement list for each logical device on the card. The configuration program ascertains the number of logical devices on the card by scanning through the list. The configuration program determines the logical device number of each device by the position of the device's list within the overall data structure. The device identified by the first list is designated as logical device zero, the second as logical device one, etc. The first list identifies the memory, IO, interrupt and DMA resources required by logical device zero, the second list identifies the resources required by logical device one, etc. The card designer ends the resource data structure with a special end of list tag.

Figure 11-1: Basic Format of Resource Data Structure

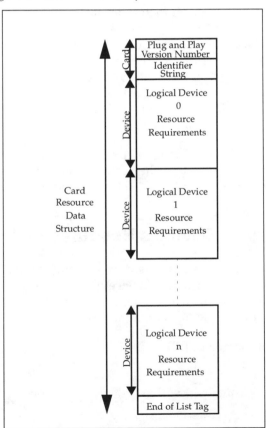

Configuring a Logical Device

Once the number of logical devices and the needs of each have been ascertained, the configuration program writes to the configuration registers associated with each logical device to assign non-conflicting resources to them. A detailed description of the configuration registers can be found in the chapter entitled "The PnP Configuration Registers" on page 143. A target logical device is selected by writing its logical device number to the card's logical device number register. If the card only contains one logical device (device zero), the logical device number register is hardwired to 00h and the device selection step can be skipped.

The card's logical devices do not have to be configured in any particular order. Once selected, the target logical device's configuration registers are programmed to allocate non-conflicting resources to the device. Once configured, the logical device is activated for normal operation by writing the appropriate value to its activate register. The device's configuration logic is put to sleep and another one is awakened for configuration. When all devices on all PnP cards have been configured and activated, the configuration program broadcasts a wait for key command to them (covered in detail in the chapter entitled "The PnP Configuration Registers" on page 143), causing them all to transition from the sleep state to the wait for key state.

The card's logical device number register and the logical device's activate register are described in detail in the sections entitled "Logical Device Number (LDN) Register" on page 154 and "Activate Register" on page 156.

Format of a Logical Device's Resource List

As stated earlier, a card's resource data structure contains a separate resource requirement list for each logical device on the card. Each device's list always starts with the logical device ID. The end of the device's list has been reached when either of the following is encountered:

- another logical device ID
- end of list tag

The information contained within a device's list consists of some or all of the following:

Chapter 11: Card Resource Requirements

- **Compatible device ID(s)**. In addition to the device's own ID, a device's list may also contain one or more compatible device IDs. If the device driver associated with the device cannot be found, the OS can search for a driver associated with one of the compatible device IDs. The OS may interpret the order of the compatible device IDs as indicating highest-to-lowest preference for usage (i.e., if a driver with the first compatible ID can be found, it is loaded and used to control the device; otherwise the OS will search for the second one in the list, etc.).

- **Interrupt descriptor(s)**. A device that generates interrupt requests must implement at least one interrupt request (IRQ) descriptor. If the device must use two separate interrupt lines, a second interrupt descriptor is included in the list. A device may not use more than two interrupt lines. The descriptor identifies which of the 15 system IRQ lines the device's interrupt can be mapped to. In addition, it describes the manner in which the device signals an interrupt request (e.g., positive edge-triggered request).

- **DMA descriptor(s)**. An IO device that uses a DMA channel to perform block transfers between the IO device and memory must implement at least one DMA descriptor. If the device uses two DMA channels, a second DMA descriptor must be included in its list. A device may not use more than two DMA channels. The descriptor identifies which of the seven system DMA channels the device's DMA request and acknowledge lines may be routed to. In addition, it also describes the fastest type of DMA transfer supported (e.g., Type A, or Type F), whether the selected DMA channel should operate in count-by-word or count-by-byte mode, whether the device is an ISA bus master, and whether the device prefers 8- or 16-bit transfers.

- **IO address space descriptor(s)**. The device may implement up to a total of eight separate IO address decoders. Preferably, all of them should be programmable to permit the configuration software maximum flexibility, but some of them may only recognize fixed address ranges. The device designer supplies an IO descriptor for each address decoder. Each descriptor identifies whether the associated decoder performs a full 16-bit decode or only a 10-bit ISA IO decode, how large an IO address range is required, the overall address range within which the device must be located, and the alignment for the base address of the assigned range.

- **Memory descriptor(s)**. Each device may implement up to four separate memory address decoders. A separate memory descriptor must be supplied for each of the decoders. Each descriptor identifies whether the memory is ROM (and, if so, whether it may be shadowed) or RAM, whether it's 8-, 16-, or 32-bit memory (or may be programmed to operate in a selected manner), whether the decoder requires a range length or an end address to be specified, and whether the memory is cacheable (and, if so, whether it requires a write-through policy).

- **Vendor-defined resource descriptors**. The designer may also include device-specific descriptors defined by the designer. These descriptors would define resources to be allocated to the device by programming vendor-defined configuration registers outside the scope of the PnP specification.

The logical device implements a configuration register associated with each of the IO, memory, DMA, and interrupt descriptors found within its list. The association between each resource list item and its associated configuration register is established by the type of resource descriptor and its position in the device's list.

The specification presents an example to highlight the relationship between the resource descriptor list and the implemented configuration registers. Assume that the resource descriptor list (associated with a logical device) is read and that it contains descriptors in the following order:

32-bit Memory descriptor	1
32-bit Memory descriptor	2
IO descriptor	3
IO descriptor	4
Interrupt descriptor	5
DMA descriptor	6
End of logical device's list	7

The author has added line numbers to the right for ease of discussion. The following numbered list explains the correlation between the resource descriptors and the device's implemented configuration registers. The number of the item in the list corresponds to the line numbers above. A complete description of the configuration registers can be found in the next chapter.

1. The first memory descriptor encountered (line 1) is associated with EISA 32-bit memory configuration register 0 at configuration addresses 76h through 7Eh.
2. The second memory descriptor in the list (line 2) is associated with EISA 32-bit memory configuration register 1 at configuration addresses 80h through 87h. Since there are no other 32-bit memory descriptors in the list, this device does not implement 32-bit memory configuration registers 2 and 3. In addition, the fact that there are no ISA 24-bit memory descriptors in the device's list indicates that it doesn't implement any of the 24-bit memory configuration registers (at configuration locations 40h through 5Fh).
3. The first IO descriptor in the list (line 3) is associated with IO configuration register 0 at configuration addresses 60h and 61h.

4. The second IO descriptor in the list (line 4) is associated with IO configuration register 1 at configuration addresses 62h and 63h. The fact that the list doesn't include any additional IO descriptors indicates that the device doesn't implement IO configuration registers 2 through 7 at configuration addresses 64h through 6Fh.

5. The first (and only) interrupt descriptor (line 5) is associated with interrupt configuration register 0 at configuration addresses 70h and 71h. The lack of any additional interrupt descriptor indicates that interrupt configuration register 1 is not implemented at configuration addresses 72h and 73h.

6. The first (and only) DMA descriptor (line 6) is associated with DMA configuration register 0 at configuration address 74h. The lack of any additional DMA descriptor indicates that DMA configuration register 1 is not implemented at configuration address 75h.

The configuration registers are fully-defined in the chapter entitled "The PnP Configuration Registers." The sections that follow provide a detailed explanation of each type of descriptor.

The reader who isn't interested in a detailed discussion of each type of descriptor can skip the remainder of this chapter and proceed to the next chapter, "The PnP Configuration Registers." A detailed example of a device's resource data list can be found at the end of this chapter.

Small vs. Large Descriptors

There are two types of descriptors: small and large. The small descriptors range from two to eight bytes in size, while the large descriptors may range from four to 64K + 3 bytes in size. The first byte of a descriptor indicates its size (small or large) and its type. In addition, a field within a small descriptor indicates the length of the descriptor (in bytes). Table 11-1 on page 96 defines the basic format of a small descriptor. Bit 7 of byte 0 is 0, indicating that this is a small descriptor (1 would indicate that it is a large descriptor). Bits [6:3] encode the descriptor type (Table 11-2 on page 96 lists the possible values), and bits [2:0] define the total number of bytes in the descriptor (not counting byte 0).

Table 11-1: Small Descriptor Format

Byte	Field		
0	Bit 7	Bits [6:3]	Bits [2:0]
	0 = small	Type	Length
1 through n	body of descriptor		

Table 11-2: Small Descriptor Types

Type	Bits[6:3] of byte 0
Plug and Play version number	0001b (1h)
Logical device ID	0010b (2h)
Compatible device ID	0011b (3h)
IRQ descriptor	0100b (4h)
DMA descriptor	0101b (5h)
Start dependent function	0110b (6h)
End dependent function	0111b (7h)
IO port descriptor	1000b (8h)
Fixed IO port descriptor	1001b (9h)
Reserved	1010b - 1101b (Ah - Dh)
Vendor-defined	1110b (Eh)
End Tag	1111b (Fh)

Chapter 11: Card Resource Requirements

Table 11-3 on page 97 defines the basic format of a large descriptor. A one in bit 7 of byte 0 indicates that this is a large descriptor, while the type of large descriptor is defined in bits [6:0] of byte 0 (Table 11-4 on page 97 defines the large descriptor types). Bytes 1 and 2 indicate the length of the descriptor body (in bytes). Since this is a 16-bit field, the maximum length of a large descriptor's body is 64K.

Table 11-3: Large Descriptor Format

Byte	Field	
0	Bit 7	Bits[6:0]
	1 = large	Descriptor type
1	Bits[7:0] of descriptor body length	
2	Bits[15:8] of descriptor body length	
3 through n	Body of descriptor	

Table 11-4: Large Descriptor Types

Type	Bits[6:0] of byte 0
ISA memory range descriptor	0000001b (1h)
ANSI identifier string	0000010b (2h)
Unicode identifier string	0000011b (3h)
Vendor-defined type	0000100b (4h)
Programmable 32-bit memory range descriptor	0000101b (5h)
Fixed 32-bit memory range descriptor	0000110b (6h)
Reserved	0000111b - 1111111b (7h - 7Fh)

The following sections provide an explanation of each type descriptor type and identify each as either a small or a large descriptor.

Plug and Play System Architecture

Descriptors Associated with the Card

Three of the descriptors are associated with the card itself, while the remainder are associated with each logical device on the card. The three associated with the card are:

- Plug and Play version number descriptor
- Identifier string descriptor(s). The card designers may include more than one identifier string if they wish to supply the identifier string in various text formats (ANSI, Unicode, etc.)
- End of list tag

The following sections provide a detailed expanation of these three descriptors.

Plug and Play Version Number

This is typically the first descriptor within the card's resource data structure. The Plug and Play version number descriptor consists of the elements identified in Table 11-5 on page 99. Byte 0 contains 0Ah, indicating that it is a small descriptor (bit 7 is 0), it is the PnP version number descriptor (0001b in bits[6:3]), and the descriptor body length is two bytes (bits[2:0] contain 010b). Byte 1 indicates the PnP version number. As examples, version 1.1 is indicated by a value of 11h, while version 2.7 is indicated by a value of 27h. The card vendor can use byte 2 to indicate the vendor-specified card version number (the content of byte 2 is outside the scope of the PnP specification).

An example PnP version number descriptor would be:

`0A1100h`

0Ah identifies this as a small descriptor, the type is PnP version number, and the descriptor body length is two bytes. The 11h indicates the card is compliant with revision 1.1 of the PnP specification. 00h indicates that the card manufacturer's card version number is revision zero.

Chapter 11: Card Resource Requirements

Table 11-5: Card's PnP Version Number Descriptor

Byte	Description							
	7	6	5	4	3	2	1	0
0	0=small descriptor	0001b=Plug and Play version number descriptor				010b=descriptor body length of 2 bytes		
1	major version				minor version			
2	Vendor-specific card version.							

Identifier Strings

The card designer is required to include at least one card identifier text string. This string is used by the OS when outputting messages related to the card during configuration or when reporting card-specific error messages. As an example, the string might contain the text string "Acme SCSI Host Bus Adapter." The card designer may include more than one string, each using a different text format (e.g., ANSI, Unicode, etc.). Each logical device on the card may optionally include a device-specific text string.

The specification currently defines two types of identifier string descriptors: ANSI and Unicode. Table 11-6 on page 100 and Table 11-7 on page 100 provide the format of these two descriptor types. Both are long descriptors.

An example ANSI string identifier would be:

```
82h  is the type byte
1100h  is the string length (17 bytes)
41434D4520534353492041444150544552h  spells out "ACME SCSI ADAPTER."
```

Plug and Play System Architecture

Table 11-6: ANSI Identifier String Descriptor Format

Byte	Field Description							
	7	6	5	4	3	2	1	0
0	1=lrage descriptor	0000010b = ANSI identifier string descriptor						
1	Defines lower 8 bits of string length. Together with byte 2, defines string length of up to 64K.							
2	Defines upper 8 bits of string length.							
3 through n	ANSI text string (up to 64K in length).							

Table 11-7: Unicode Identifier String Descriptor Format

Byte	Description							
	7	6	5	4	3	2	1	0
0	1=large descriptor	0000011b=Unicode identifier string descriptor						
1	Defines lower 8 bits of string length. Together with byte 2, defines string length plus four (value up to 64K).							
2	Defines upper 8 bits of string length.							

Table 11-7: Unicode Identifier String Descriptor Format (Continued)

Byte	Description							
	7	6	5	4	3	2	1	0
3	Defines lower 8 bits of country (language) identifier. Together with byte 4, defines 16-bit country identifier. The country identifiers will be defined at a later date.							
4	Defines upper 8 bits of country (language) identifier.							
5 through n	Unicode text string.							

End Tag

The last item in the card's resource data structure is always the end of list tag descriptor. It consists of two bytes. The first byte of 79h indicates that it is a small descriptor (a 0 in bit 7), the type is end of list tag (1111b in bits[6:3]), and the descriptor's body length is one byte (bits[2:0] = 001b). The second byte is the checksum of all of the bytes in the resource data structure starting with the first byte. Adding the value in this checksum byte to the checksum computed by adding all of the bytes in the structure must yield a result of zero. If the checksum byte in the descriptor contains a value of 00h, the configuration program assumes that the resource data structure is valid (without performing the checksum test).

Descriptors Associated with a Logical Device

The resource requirement list for each device begins with its logical device ID descriptor and ends with either the next device's logical device ID or the end of list tag. Within the device's list, one or more descriptors identify the device's resource requirements. As stated earlier, the device's descriptors do not have to be in any particular order. The following sections provide a detailed explanation of each descriptor type.

Logical Device ID

Table 11-8 on page 102 defines the format of the logical device ID descriptor. This descriptor is always the first item within a logical device's resource requirement list. The EISA ID "PNP" has been reserved for Microsoft. In addition, Microsoft has assigned 32-bit EISA IDs to many of the devices commonly found in a PC. A list of the standard logical device IDs recognized by Windows 95 can be found in the appendix of this book on page 279. As an example, the logical device ID descriptor might consist of:

```
15h     Descriptor byte, length = 5
0443h   EISA ID = ASCII "ABC"
1234h   Product ID = 1234h
```

Table 11-8: Format of the Logical Device ID Descriptor

Byte	Description							
	7	6	5	4	3	2	1	0
0	0=small descriptor	0010b=Logical device ID descriptor				101b= 5 byte descriptor body length or 110b=6 byte descriptor body length		
1	Bits [7:0] of logical device ID. Has same format as the first 32-bits of the vendor ID field in the card's serial identifier (refer to Table 10-2 on page 73). Note that the device's EISA identifier doesn't have to be the same as the card's.							
2	Bits [15:8] of logical device ID.							
3	Bits [23:16] of logical device ID.							
4	Bits [31:24] of logical device ID.							

Table 11-8: Format of the Logical Device ID Descriptor (Continued)

Byte	Description							
	7	6	5	4	3	2	1	0
5	**Implemented configuration register map.** The bits in [7:1] correspond to the logical device's configuration registers in the range from 31h through 37h, respectively. This includes the device's IO range check register, as well as configuration registers to be defined by the specification at a later date. A one in a bit position indicates that the device implements the associated configuration register. As an example, a value of 02h in this byte indicates that this logical device implements the IO range check register at configuration location 31h, but does not implement the configuration registers at locations 32h through 37h. **Boot-capable device.** Bit 0 indicates whether the device is capable of taking part in the initial boot process. 0 indicates that it is not, while 1 indicates it is. Any device that comes up enabled must set this bit to one, but a device that does not come up enabled may also set this bit to one.								
6	**Implemented configuration register map.** This byte is optional. A value of 6 in the descriptor's size field indicates that it is present, while a value of 5 indicates that it isn't. The bits in [7:0] correspond to the logical device's configuration registers in the range from 38h through 3Fh, respectively. This includes the device's vendor-specific control registers defined by the device designer. A one in a bit position indicates that the device implements the associated configuration register. As an example, a value of 03h in this byte indicates that this logical device implements the vendor-specific device control configuration registers at configuration locations 38h and 39h, but does not implement the configuration registers at locations 3Ah through 3Fh.								

Identifier String

Optionally the designer of a logical device may provide one or more identifier text strings. For more information, refer to the section earlier in this chapter entitled "Identifier Strings" on page 99.

Compatible Device ID

Optionally, the device designer may provide the IDs of one or more devices that are register-compatible with this device. An example usage— if the OS cannot find the device driver for this device, it can search for a device driver associated with one of the listed compatible devices. The order in which the compatible device ID descriptors appear in the list indicates the order of preference (i.e., a device driver associated with the first compatible device ID is preferred by the device designer over the driver associated with an ID that occurs later in the device's list). Table 11-9 on page 104 defines the format of the descriptor. With the exception of the first byte, it is the same as that of the first 32-bits of a card's serial ID. The standard IDs used by Windows 95 are found in "Appendix A— Device ID Assignments" on page 279.

Table 11-9: Format of Compatible Device ID Descriptor

Byte	Description							
	7	6	5	4	3	2	1	0
0	0=small descriptor	0011b=Compatible device ID descriptor				100b=descriptor body size is 4 bytes		
1	Bits [7:0] of logical device ID. Has same format as the first 32-bits of the vendor ID field in the card's serial identifier (refer to Table 10-2 on page 73). Note that the device's EISA identifier doesn't have to be the same as the card's.							

Table 11-9: Format of Compatible Device ID Descriptor (Continued)

Byte	Description							
	7	6	5	4	3	2	1	0
2	Bits [15:8] of logical device ID.							
3	Bits [23:16] of logical device ID.							
4	Bits [31:24] of logical device ID.							

Interrupt Descriptor

For a complete description of interrupt operation in the ISA environment, refer to the interrupt chapter in the MindShare book entitled *ISA System Architecture* (Addison-Wesley Publishing Company, 1995). Refer to the MindShare book entitled *EISA System Architecture* (Addison-Wesley Publishing Company, 1995) for a description of interrupts in the EISA environment.

Background

A device may be interrupt driven—it asserts an interrupt request signal line when it requires servicing by its associated device driver. Some examples of events that may require action by the device driver are:

- Data had been written into the device's buffer by its driver at an earlier point in time, but the device has been extracting data from the buffer to send to another device (e.g., the data is being transmitted over a network) and the buffer is running dry. An interrupt request is generated to have the device driver write additional data into the buffer.
- The device has been receiving data from a third party and loading it into its buffer. The buffer either is full or is approaching the full condition. The device generates an interrupt request to have the driver read data from the buffer before the buffer overflows.
- The device successfully completed an operation requested by the device driver. It generates an interrupt request, requesting that the driver check the device's completion status for a good or a bad completion.
- The device was unsuccessful in performing an action for the driver. It generates an interrupt request, requesting that the driver check the device's completion status for a good or a bad completion.

Plug and Play System Architecture

The designer of a PnP device may not implement any interrupt capability, may implement one interrupt request signal, or may implement two interrupt request signals (two is the maximum number of lines one device may use).

The ISA bus connectors include pins for the following interrupt request signals:

- **IRQ2**. This pin is on the 8-bit portion of the connector and is available for use by 8- and 16-bit cards. It's connected to the IRQ9 (not IRQ2) input of the system board's interrupt controller. This is referred to as IRQ2 redirect and is a peculiarity of the ISA system architecture. For more information, refer to the MindShare book entitled *ISA System Architecture* (Addison-Wesley Publishing Company, 1995) in the interrupt chapter in the section entitled "IRQ2 Redirect."
- **IRQ3**. This pin is on the 8-bit portion of the connector and is therefore available for use by both 8- and 16-bit cards. It is typically used by COM port two.
- **IRQ4**. This pin is on the 8-bit portion of the connector and is therefore available for use by both 8- and 16-bit cards. It is typically used by COM port one.
- **IRQ5**. This pin is on the 8-bit portion of the connector and is therefore available for use by both 8- and 16-bit cards. It is typically used by parallel port two.
- **IRQ6**. This pin is on the 8-bit portion of the connector and is therefore available for use by both 8- and 16-bit cards. It is typically used by the floppy interface.
- **IRQ7**. This pin is on the 8-bit portion of the connector and is therefore available for use by both 8- and 16-bit cards. It is typically used by parallel port one.
- **IRQ10**. This pin is on the 16-bit portion of the connector and is therefore available for use only by 16-bit cards.
- **IRQ11**. This pin is on the 16-bit portion of the connector and is therefore available for use only by 16-bit cards.
- **IRQ12**. This pin is on the 16-bit portion of the connector and is therefore available for use only by 16-bit cards. It is typically used by the mouse.
- **IRQ14**. This pin is on the 16-bit portion of the connector and is therefore available for use only by 16-bit cards. It is typically used by the primary fixed disk controller.
- **IRQ15**. This pin is on the 16-bit portion of the connector and is therefore available for use only by 16-bit cards.

Chapter 11: Card Resource Requirements

The following IRQ signals are dedicated to the indicated system board devices and are not available for use by cards installed in connectors:

- **IRQ0**. Dedicated to the system timer. A request is generated by the timer approximately every 15.09μ seconds.
- **IRQ1**. Dedicated to the keyboard controller. The keyboard controller generates IRQ1 whenever a key is pressed or released and a scan code is ready to be read by the keyboard interrupt service routine.
- **IRQ8**. Dedicated to the alarm output of the real-time clock chip.
- **IRQ13**. Dedicated to the error output of the floating-point processor. Also used by the EISA DMA controller (if the DMA channel was programmed by the host processor rather than an EISA bus master) when buffer chaining is enabled and the current block transfer has completed.

Interrupt Descriptor Format

Assuming that a PnP device generates interrupt requests, the configuration software needs to know the following:

- The system IRQ signal lines the device can be programmed to assert when it has a request. The configuration software selects one of these lines and programs the device's interrupt configuration register to route the request over the selected system IRQ signal line.
- The type of signalling method the device uses to generate an interrupt request. The configuration software uses this information to decide if the device can share a system IRQ line with another device and to program the system interrupt controller to recognize the selected type of signalling as a request on the selected IRQ line.

The interrupt descriptor defines the IRQ lines the device's request can be routed to and its signalling method. Table 11-10 on page 108 defines the format of the interrupt descriptor. The designer can include up to two interrupt descriptors in the device's resource list. The first one corresponds to the device's interrupt configuration register zero and the second to interrupt configuration register one. These registers are described in the chapter entitled "The PnP Configuration Registers." If byte 3 is not included in the descriptor, this must be interpreted as ISA-compatible, positive edge triggered interrupt request signalling. All ISA PnP devices must support positive edge triggered requests.

The Microsoft book entitled *Hardware Design Guide for Windows 95* states that IRQ2 is reserved and cannot be used. It also states that bit 1 in byte 2 (corresponding to IRQ9) must be used in place of IRQ2 (because the ISA IRQ2 connector pin is actually connected to the IRQ9 input of the slave interrupt controller).

The ISA PnP specification includes the same warning in the following form—
"Only IRQs that exists on the ISA bus connectors are valid."

For a detailed discussion of active low, level-sensitive interrupt handling, refer to the interrupt chapter in the MindShare book entitled *EISA System Architecture* (Addison-Wesley Publishing Company, 1995).

Table 11-10: Format of the Interrupt Descriptor

Byte	Description							
	7	6	5	4	3	2	1	0
0	0=small descriptor	0100b=interrupt descriptor				010b=descriptor body size of 2 bytes 011b=descriptor body size of 3 bytes		
1	1=IRQ7 can be used	1= IRQ6 can be used	1=IRQ5 can be used	1=IRQ4 can be used	1=IRQ3 can be used	1=IRQ2 can be used	1=IRQ1 can be used	1=IRQ0 can be used
2	1=IRQ15 can be used	1= IRQ14 can be used	1=IRQ13 can be used	1=IRQ12 can be used	1=IRQ11 can be used	1=IRQ10 can be used	1=IRQ9 can be used	1=IRQ8 can be used
3	This byte of the descriptor is optional. If included, it indicates the type of signalling the device uses on its interrupt request signal. Bits[7:4] are reserved. Bits[3:0] are used to indicate the signalling techniques the device is capable of using (one or more): • A one in bit 3 indicates active low, level-sensitive. • A one in bit 2 indicates active high level-sensitive. • A one in bit 1 indicates negative edge triggered. • A one in bit 0 indicates positive edge triggered. The device is required to support this technique in order to be ISA compatible. If this byte not included, assume that the device uses ISA-compatible, positive edge triggered request signalling.							

Example Interrupt Descriptor

The following represent two example interrupt descriptors:

```
22h    Small descriptor,type=interrupt,size=2 bytes
B8h    Can be mapped to IRQ3,4,5,7
DEh    9,10,11,12,14,and 15
       no byte 3 indicates positive edge triggered
```

```
23h    Small descriptor,type=interrupt,size=3 bytes
38h    Can be mapped to IRQ3,4,5
5Ch    10,11,12,and 14
0Fh    supports all four signalling methods
```

DMA Descriptor

Inclusion of a DMA descriptor in a device's resource list indicates that it uses an ISA DMA channel to handle block transfers between the device and memory. For a complete description of DMA operation in the ISA environment, refer to the DMA chapter in the MindShare book entitled *ISA System Architecture* (Addison-Wesley Publishing Company, 1995). For a complete description of DMA operation in the EISA environment, refer to the DMA chapter in the MindShare book entitled *EISA System Architecture* (Addison-Wesley Publishing Company, 1995).

Background

An ISA system incorporates two 8237A DMA controllers in a master/slave configuration. There are four channels, numbered 0 through 3, available through the slave DMA controller, and three, numbered 5 through 7, through the master. DMA channels 0 through 3 can transfer one byte per transfer, while channels 5 through 7 can transfer two bytes (a word, or 16-bits) per transfer. DMA channel 4 is not available for use because it is used to cascade (i.e., connect) the slave to the master.

Each DMA channel may be connected to and used by only one ISA device. In other words, the DMA channels cannot be shared among two or more devices. When enabled by software, a DMA channel performs a series of bus transactions to transfer a block of data between its associated IO device and memory. When the IO device is ready to transfer the next data item, it asserts its DRQn

(DMA request, where n = its DMA channel number) signal to its associated DMA channel. In response, the DMA channel arbitrates for bus ownership. When it has acquired bus ownership, it:

- Asserts DAKn# (DMA channel *n* acknowledge signal) and IORC# (IO read command line) if it is reading data from the IO device to be written into memory. It also drives the memory address onto the address bus and asserts MWTC# (memory write command line), causing the data supplied by the IO device to be written into addressed memory location.
- DAKn# and IOWC# (IO write command line) to the IO device if it's reading data from memory and writing it to the IO device. It also drives the memory address onto the address bus and asserts MRDC# (memory read command line), causing the data to be read from the currently-addressed memory location and written into the IO device's data buffer.

After the channel has transferred the data object (a byte or a word), it performs housekeeping. It increments the memory address to point to the next location. It also decrements the transfer count and determines if the count has been exhausted. When the count has been exhausted, the DMA controller asserts the TC (transfer complete) ISA signal to instruct the IO device to generate its device-specific interrupt to signal the end of transfer to the device's driver.

DMA Descriptor Format

Assuming that an IO device requires a DMA channel to perform block data transfers, the device designer must include a DMA descriptor in the device's resource list. The Plug and Play specification permits an IO device to use up to two separate DMA channels. If a device uses two channels, two DMA descriptors must be included in the device's resource list. The DMA descriptor defines the following DMA characteristics for the configuration software:

- The ISA bus connector DMA signal pairs that the IO device's request/acknowledge lines may be routed to by the configuration program.
- The fastest type of DMA transfer that the IO device supports.
- Whether the device requires its DMA channel to perform 8- or 16-bit transfers, and, if the device can handle either, which of them it prefers.
- Whether the device is an ISA bus master. If it is, it must be routed to DMA channels 5, 6, or 7, and that channel must be programmed for cascade mode operation. For a detailed discussion of ISA bus masters, refer to the chapter on ISA bus masters in the MindShare book entitled *ISA System Architecture* (Addison-Wesley Publishing Company, 1995).

After examining the device's DMA descriptor(s), the configuration program uses the device's DMA configuration registers to select the DMA channel routing, speed and transfer size (the registers are covered in the chapter entitled "The PnP Configuration Registers" on page 143).

Table 11-11: Format of DMA Descriptor

Byte	Bit Description							
	7	6	5	4	3	2	1	0
0	0 = small descriptor	0101b=DMA descriptor				010b=size of descriptor body is 2 bytes		
1	DMA channels that the device's DRQn/DAKn# can be routed to by the configuration program. Bit 0 corresponds to channel 0 and bit 7 corresponds to channel 7. DMA channel 4 cannot be used. A 1 in a bit position indicates that the configuration program can select that DMA channel.							
2	Reserved	00b=ISA compatible 01b=EISA Type A 10b=EISA Type B 11b=Type F		0=may not use count by word 1=may use count by word	0=may not use count by byte 1=may use count by byte	0=not ISA master 1=ISA master	00b=8-bit only 01b=8- and 16-bit 10b=16-bit only 11b=reserved	

Example DMA Descriptors

Two examples of DMA descriptors follow:

```
2Ah    DMA descriptor
0Fh    Can be routed to DMA channels 0 through 3
08h    Program channel for ISA compatible transfers,
       using count by byte mode. The device is not an ISA
       master and it is only capable of performing 8-bit
       transfers.
```

```
2Ah    DMA descriptor
E0h    Can be routed to channels 5 through 7
32h    Program channel to use Type A transfers,
       count by word mode. The device is not an ISA master
       and can only perform 16-bit transfers.
```

IO Port Descriptors

A logical device may implement one or more blocks of IO registers that are used to control, sense the status of, and feed data to or from the IO device. To provide the configuration program with maximum flexibility in resolving conflicting IO addresses, the PnP device designer must make the IO address decoders programmable via the device's IO configuration registers. The PnP specification permits the device designer to include up to eight IO address decoders per device.

In the case of legacy ISA cards, the IO address decoders are not programmable. Instead, they monitor the bus for transactions that target a fixed address range. Because some IO decoders are programmable and others are fixed, the PnP specification provides two types of IO descriptors: programmable and fixed. The following sections provide a detailed description of each type. The device designer must include an IO descriptor for each decoder and a corresponding IO configuration register used to assign an IO range to that decoder (if it's programmable). The IO configuration registers are described in the chapter entitled "The PnP Configuration Registers."

Programmable IO Port Descriptor

In the case of a programmable IO address decoder, the configuration program must be provided with the following information in order to select an IO range to assign to the decoder:

- Whether the device decodes the full 16-bit IO address or only decodes address bits [9:0] (as is the case with many legacy ISA IO cards). For a detailed description of the problems associated with legacy cards that only decode the lower 10 bits, refer to the section on "The ISA IO Address Space Problem" in the chapter on configuration in the MindShare book entitled *EISA System Architecture* (Addison-Wesley Publishing Company, 1995).
- The minimum base IO address that the decoder may be programmed for.
- The maximum base IO address that the decoder may be programmed for.
- The number of contiguous 8-bit IO ports (i.e., IO locations) that the decoder handles.

Chapter 11: Card Resource Requirements

The programmable IO descriptor in the device's list supplies the configuration program with this information. In addition, the programmable IO descriptor may also be used to describe the decode characteristics of a fixed range legacy IO decoder that performs a full, 16-bit address decode (rather than a 10-bit decode). This can be accomplished by placing equal values in the minimum and maximum base address fields of the descriptor.

Table 11-12 on page 113 describes the format of the programmable IO descriptor.

Table 11-12: Format of Programmable IO Descriptor

Byte	Description							
	7	6	5	4	3	2	1	0
0	0=small descriptor	1000b=Programmable IO descriptor				111b=Descriptor size of 7 bytes		
1	Reserved							0=10-bit decode 1=16-bit decode
2	Bits[7:0] of minimum IO base address for device							
3	Bits[15:8] of minimum IO base address for device							
4	Bits[7:0] of maximum IO base address for device							
5	Bits[15:8] of maximum IO base address for device							
6	Required base address alignment (0 is not a valid value). This is a binary-weighted field. As an example, a value of 10h indicates that the assigned base address must be divisible by 16.							
7	Number of contiguous IO ports required (size of IO range to decode). 0 is not a valid value.							

The following are examples of programmable IO descriptors:

```
47h      Programmable IO Descriptor
01h      Performs full 16-bit IO address decode
00h      Minimum base address = 1000h
10h
00h      Maximum base address = 8000h
80h
10h      Base address must be aligned on 16 byte boundary
10h      Requires 16 IO locations


47h      Programmable IO Descriptor
01h      Performs full 16-bit IO address decode
00h      Minimum base address = 0400h
04h
00h      Maximum base address = 0600h
06h
08h      Base address must be aligned on 8 byte boundary
08h      Requires 8 IO locations
```

Fixed IO Port Descriptor

In the case of a fixed IO address decoder, the configuration program must be provided with the following information in order to define the IO range the decoder is hardwired to detect:

- The base IO address of the range detected
- The number of IO locations in the detected range

The fixed IO descriptor is used with legacy ISA IO cards that only decode the lower 10 bits of the address, [9:0]. Table 11-13 on page 115 defines the format of the fixed IO descriptor. For a detailed description of the problems associated with legacy cards that only decode the lower 10 bits, refer to the section on "The ISA IO Address Space Problem" in the chapter on configuration in the Mind-Share book entitled *EISA System Architecture* (Addison-Wesley Publishing Company, 1995).

Table 11-13: Format of Fixed IO Descriptor

Byte	Description							
	7	6	5	4	3	2	1	0
0	0=small descriptor	1001b=Fixed IO descriptor				011b=descriptor size of 3 bytes		
1	Bits[7:0] of IO base address							
2	Not used						bits [9:8] of IO base address	
3	Number of IO locations in range (0 is not a valid value)							

Memory Descriptors

Memory address decoders fall into two basic categories: 24-bit ISA memory address decoders, and 32-bit EISA memory address decoders. The PnP specification provides two types of memory descriptors that correspond to these two basic categories. It is a rule that the card designer (note that I said card, not logical device) may implement 24-bit ISA memory descriptors or 32-bit memory descriptors, but not both. All of the memory descriptors on a card must be one type or the other. There may be up to four memory descriptors per logical device.

The following sections provide detail on the two descriptor types (24-bit ISA and 32-bit EISA).

24-bit ISA Memory Descriptors

The ISA memory descriptor is used to define the characteristics of an ISA memory address decoder. The descriptor provides the following information to the configuration program:

- **Whether the memory is an expansion ROM**. If it is, the configuration software must map it into the ISA-compatible memory range set aside for expansion ROMs (i.e., the memory range from 0C0000h through 0EFFFFh).
- **If an expansion ROM, whether it can be shadowed** or not. If the ROM can be shadowed, the configuration software can copy it into a block of RAM memory assigned an address range within the expansion ROM area and can then disable the ROM address decoder. The code and data in the shadow RAM can then be fetched significantly faster because the RAM has a faster access time than the ROM and the RAM is also typically a 32-bit device rather than an 8- or 16-bit device (as expansion ROMs typically are). For a detailed discussion of legacy ISA expansion (device) ROMs, refer to the section on device ROMs in the chapter on ROM memory in the Mind-Share book entitled *ISA System Architecture* (Addison-Wesley Publishing Company, 1995).
- **Whether the memory supports 8-, 16-, or both 8- and 16-bit memory addressing**. If the device supports both forms of addressing, then the configuration program has the flexibility to select 8- rather than 16-bit decoding to solve some compatibility problems. For a more detailed description of this subject, refer to the section entitled "A Compatibility Problem" on page 164.
- **Whether the decoder must be programmed with a range length or an end address** (a decoder can be designed either way and the configuration software needs to know which to specify in the device's corresponding memory configuration register).
- **Whether the memory is cacheable or not**. This information is used by the configuration software to tell the processor's internal and external cache (if present) which memory ranges not to cache from. The configuration software can supply this information to the OS so it knows the operational characteristics within the assigned memory range.
- **If the memory is cacheable, a write-through policy must be used** by the cache in handling processor memory writes within this memory device's assigned address range. This information is used by the configuration software to tell the processor's internal and external cache (if present) if a memory range is occupied by memory-mapped IO ports. If the processor and its external cache both use a write-through policy in handling memory writes and if neither incorporates a posted-write buffer, this is not an issue. However, if the processor and/or its external cache use a write-back policy or incorporates a posted-write buffer, memory writes may not be propagated all the way through to the target memory device. Rather, the write data may be buffered up to be written to memory at a later time. When a device driver is performing memory writes to update its device's memory-mapped IO ports, the driver proceeds with the assumption that the device

has already received the data written and is processing it. This would be a false assumption. The device and its device driver are out of step with each other. This can cause severe problems. The solution is to designate the memory range populated by the memory-mapped IO ports as write-through. The configuration software can then configure the caches to always use a write-through policy in handling memory writes within the affected range. The configuration software can also supply this information to the OS so it knows the operational characteristics within the assigned memory range. For a detailed discussion of write-back and write-through caches, refer to the chapter on caches in the MindShare books entitled *ISA System Architecture, 80486 System Architecture, Pentium Process System Architecture*, and *PowerPC System Architecture* (all published by Addison-Wesley Publishing Company, 1995).

- **Whether the memory is read-only or read/writable**. The configuration software can supply this information to the OS so it knows the operational characteristics within the assigned memory range.
- The **minimum base address** that may be assigned to the address decoder.
- The **maximum base address** that may be assigned to the address decoder.
- The **alignment of the assigned base address**.
- The **size** of the memory in increments of 256 bytes.

After examining the descriptor, the configuration program can use the acquired information to program the device's corresponding ISA memory configuration register to assign a memory range that doesn't conflict with other memory devices in the system. Table 11-14 on page 118 provides a detailed description of the ISA memory descriptor. Note that it is a large, rather than a small descriptor. In bytes 4 and 5, and 6 and 7, the memory device designer provides the minimum and maximum permissible base address that may be assigned to the device via its corresponding memory configuration register.

Note that the designer only provides address bits [23:8] of the min and max base address. Address bits [7:0] are assumed to be zero. The 16-bit base alignment field indicates the required alignment of the base address assigned. As an example, a value of 0100h indicates that the assigned base address must be aligned on an address divisible by 256 (the 1 bit in bit 8 has a binary-weighted value of 256). The ISA memory descriptor can be used to define a fixed-address memory decoder by specifying the same value in the min and max base address fields.

Table 11-14: Format of 24-bit ISA Memory Descriptor

Byte	Description							
	7	6	5	4	3	2	1	0
0	1=large descriptor	0000001b = ISA memory descriptor						
1	Bits[7:0] of descriptor length = 00001001b, or 9 bytes							
2	Bits[15:8] of descriptor length = 00000000b							
3	Reserved	1=expansion ROM	1=ROM can be shadowed	00b=8-bit memory only 01b=16-bit memory only 10b=8- or 16-bit selectable 11b=reserved		0=requires range length 1=requires end address	0=non-cacheable 1=cacheable,write-through policy	0=read-only (ROM) 1=read/writeable
4	Bits[15:8] of minimum base address							
5	Bits[23:16] of minimum base address							
6	Bits[15:8] of maximum base address							
7	Bits[23:16] of maximum base address							
8	Bits[7:0] of base address alignment field							
9	Bits[15:8] of base address alignment field							

Table 11-14: Format of 24-bit ISA Memory Descriptor (Continued)

Byte	Description							
	7	6	5	4	3	2	1	0
0Ah	Bits[7:0] of memory size. The 16-bit value in bytes 0Ah and 0Bh indicates the number of memory locations in increments of 256 bytes. The maximum possible value is FFFFh, or 16MB.							
0Bh	Bits[15:8] of memory size (see byte 0Ah).							

32-bit EISA Memory Descriptors

A PnP EISA card may implement 8-, 16- or 32-bit memory devices. An 8-bit device on an EISA card can be implemented as an 8-bit ISA or EISA device. A 16-bit memory device can be implemented as either or an ISA or an EISA memory device. A 32-bit memory device must be implemented as an EISA memory device. If an EISA card only implements 8- and/or 16-bit ISA memory, the designer uses the 24-bit ISA memory descriptors already defined. If, on the other hand, the designer implements 16- or 32-bit EISA memory on the card, the designer must use the 32-bit memory descriptors defined in the sections that follow. The 32-bit memory descriptor can be used to define the characteristics of 8-, 16-, or 32-bit memory decoders.

If the card has any 8-, 16-, or 32-bit EISA memory on it, the card designer would implement 32-bit, rather than 24-bit, memory descriptors. There are two varieties of 32-bit memory descriptor: programmable and fixed. There may be up to four memory descriptors per logical device. The following sections define the programmable and fixed 32-bit memory descriptors.

Programmable 32-bit EISA Memory Descriptor. If a device's memory address decoder is programmable, the device designer must supply a programmable 32-bit memory descriptor that defines the decoder's operational characteristics. A corresponding 32-bit memory configuration register must also be provided. The descriptor provides the configuration program with the following information:

- **Whether the memory is an expansion ROM**. If it is, the configuration software must map it into the ISA-compatible memory range set aside for expansion ROMs (i.e., the memory range from 0C0000h through 0EFFFFh).
- **If an expansion ROM, whether it can be shadowed** or not. If the ROM can be shadowed, the configuration software can copy it into a block of RAM

memory assigned a range within the expansion ROM area and can then disable the ROM address decoder. The code and data in the shadow RAM can be fetched significantly faster because the RAM has a faster access time than the ROM and the RAM is also typically a 32-bit device rather than an 8- or 16-bit device (as expansion ROMs typically are). For a detailed discussion of expansion (device) ROMs, refer to the section on legacy device ROMs in the chapter on ROM memory in the MindShare book entitled *ISA System Architecture* (Addison-Wesley Publishing Company, 1995).

- Whether the memory supports only **8-, only 16-, both 8- and 16-bit, or only 32-bit memory addressing**. If the device supports both 8- and 16-bit addressing, then the configuration program has the flexibility to select 8- rather than 16-bit decoding to solve some compatibility problems. For a more detailed description of this subject, refer to the section entitled "A Compatibility Problem" on page 164.

- Whether the decoder must be programmed with a **range length or an end address** (a decoder can be designed either way and the configuration software needs to know which to specify in the device's memory configuration register).

- Whether the memory is **cacheable** or not. This information is used by the configuration software to tell the processor's internal and external cache (if present) which memory ranges not to cache from. The configuration software can supply this information to the OS so it knows the operational characteristics within the assigned memory range.

- If the memory is **cacheable, a write-through** policy must be used by the cache in handling processor memory writes. This information is used by the configuration software to tell the processor's internal and external cache (if present) if a memory range is occupied by memory-mapped IO ports. If the processor and its external cache both use a write-through policy in handling memory writes and if neither incorporates a posted-write buffer, this is not an issue. However, if the processor and/or its external cache use a write-back policy or incorporates a posted-write buffer, memory writes may not be propagated all the way through to the target memory device. Rather, the write data may be buffered up to be written to memory at a later time. When a device driver is performing memory writes to update its device's memory-mapped IO ports, the driver proceeds with the assumption that the device has already received the data and is processing it. This would be a false assumption. The device and its device driver are out of step with each other. This can cause severe problems. The solution is to designate the memory range populated by the memory-mapped IO ports as write-through. The configuration software can then configure the caches to always use a write-through policy in handling memory writes within the affected range. The configuration software can also supply this information to the OS so it knows the operational characteristics within the assigned memory range. For a detailed discussion of write-back and write-through caches, refer to the chapter on caches in the MindShare books entitled *ISA System Architecture*, *80486 System Architecture*, *Pentium Process System Architecture*, and *PowerPC System Architecture* (all published by Addison-Wesley Publishing Company, 1995).

- Whether the memory is **read-only or read/writable**. The configuration software can supply this information to the OS so it knows the operational characteristics within the assigned memory range.
- The **minimum base address** that may be assigned to the address decoder.
- The **maximum base address** that may be assigned to the address decoder.
- The **alignment of the assigned base address**.
- The **size** of the memory in increments of one byte.

Table 11-15 on page 121 provides a detailed description of the programmable 32-bit memory descriptor.

Table 11-15: Format of Programmable 32-bit EISA Memory Descriptor

Byte	Description							
	7	6	5	4	3	2	1	0
0	1=large descriptor	0000101b = programmable 32-bit memory descriptor						
1	Bits[7:0] of descriptor body length = 00010001b, or 17d bytes							
2	Bits[15:8] of descriptor body length = 00000000b (see byte 1)							

Table 11-15: Format of Programmable 32-bit EISA Memory Descriptor (Continued)

Byte	Description							
	7	6	5	4	3	2	1	0
3	Reserved	1=Expansion ROM	1=may be shadowed	00b=8-bit only 01b=16-bit only 10b=8- and 16-bit 11b=32-bit		0=requires range length 1=requires end address	0=non-cacheable 1=cacheable,write-through	0=read-only (ROM) 1=read/write
4	Bits[7:0] of minimum base address							
5	Bits[15:8] of minimum base address							
6	Bits[23:16] of minimum base address							
7	Bits[31:24] of minimum base address							
8	Bits[7:0] of maximum base address							
9	Bits[15:8] of maximum base address							
10	Bits[23:16] of maximum base address							
11	Bits[31:24] of maximum base address							
12	Bits[7:0] of base address alignment field. This is a binary-weighted field. As an example, a value of 00000100h indicates the assigned base address must be aligned on an address divisible by 256d.							
13	Bits[15:8] of base address alignment field							
14	Bits[23:16] of base address alignment field							
15	Bits[31:24] of base address alignment field							
16	Bits[7:0] of memory size in bytes							

Table 11-15: Format of Programmable 32-bit EISA Memory Descriptor (Continued)

Byte	Description							
	7	6	5	4	3	2	1	0
17	Bits[15:8] of memory size in bytes							
18	Bits[23:16] of memory size in bytes							
19	Bits[31:24] of memory size in bytes							

Fixed 32-bit EISA Memory Descriptor.

If a device's memory address decoder is hardwired to recognize only one address range, the device designer must supply a fixed 32-bit memory descriptor that defines the decoder's operational characteristics. A corresponding 32-bit memory configuration register must also be provided. The descriptor provides the configuration program with the following information:

- **Whether the memory is an expansion ROM.**
- **If an expansion ROM, whether it can be shadowed** or not. If the ROM can be shadowed, the configuration software can copy it into a block of RAM memory assigned a range within the expansion ROM area and can then disable the ROM address decoder. The code and data in the shadow RAM can then be fetched significantly faster because the RAM has a faster access time than the ROM and the RAM is also typically a 32-bit device rather than an 8- or 16-bit device (as expansion ROMs typically are). For a detailed discussion of expansion (device) ROMs, refer to the section on device ROMs in the chapter on ROM memory in the MindShare book entitled *ISA System Architecture* (Addison-Wesley Publishing Company, 1995).
- Whether the memory supports only 8-, **only 16-, both 8- and 16-bit, or only 32-bit memory addressing**. If the device supports both 8- and 16-bit addressing, then the configuration program has the flexibility to select 8- rather than 16-bit decoding to solve some compatibility problems. For a more detailed description of this subject, refer to the section entitled "A Compatibility Problem" on page 164.
- Whether the decoder must be programmed with a **range length or an end address** (a decoder can be designed either way and the configuration software needs to know which to specify in the device's memory configuration register).
- Whether the memory is **cacheable** or not. This information is used by the configuration software to tell the processor's internal and external cache (if

present) which memory ranges not to cache from. The configuration software can supply this information to the OS so it knows the operational characteristics within the assigned memory range.

- If the memory is **cacheable, a write-through policy** must be used by the cache in handling processor memory writes. This information is used by the configuration software to tell the processor's internal and external cache (if present) if a memory range is occupied by memory-mapped IO ports. If the processor and its external cache both use a write-through policy in handling memory writes and if neither incorporates a posted-write buffer, this is not an issue. However, if the processor and/or its external cache use a write-back policy or incorporates a posted-write buffer, memory writes may not be propagated all the way through to the target memory device. Rather, the write data may be buffered up to be written to memory at a later time. When a device driver is performing memory writes to update its device's memory-mapped IO ports, the driver proceeds with the assumption that the device has already received the data and is processing it. This would be a false assumption. The device and the device driver are out of step with each other. This can cause severe problems. The solution is to designate the memory range populated by the memory-mapped IO ports as write-through. The configuration software can then configure the caches to always use a write-through policy in handling memory writes within the affected range. The configuration software can also supply this information to the OS so it knows the operational characteristics within the assigned memory range. For a detailed discussion of write-back and write-through caches, refer to the chapter on caches in the MindShare books entitled *ISA System Architecture*, *80486 System Architecture*, *Pentium Process System Architecture*, and *PowerPC System Architecture* (all published by Addison-Wesley Publishing Company, 1995).
- Whether the memory is **read-only or read/writable**. The configuration software can supply this information to the OS so it knows the operational characteristics within the assigned memory range.
- The **hardwired base address** that the device's address decoder recognizes.
- The **size** of the memory in increments of one byte.

Table 11-16 on page 125 provides a detailed description of the fixed 32-bit memory descriptor.

Table 11-16: Format of Fixed 32-bit EISA Memory Descriptor

Byte	Description							
	7	6	5	4	3	2	1	0
0	1=large descriptor	0000101b = fixed 32-bit memory descriptor						
1	Bits[7:0] of descriptor body size = 0000101b, or 9 bytes							
2	Bits[15:8] of descriptor body size = 00000000b (see byte 1)							
3	Reserved	1=Expansion ROM	1=may be shadowed	00b=8-bit only 01b=16-bit only 10b=8- and 16-bit 11b=32-bit		0=requires range length 1=requires end address	0=non-cacheable 1=cacheable,write-through	0=read-only (ROM) 1=read/write
4	Hardwired base address, bit[7:0]							
5	Hardwired base address, bit[15:8]							
6	Hardwired base address, bit[23:16]							
7	Hardwired base address, bit[31:24]							
8	Memory Size, bits[7:0]							
9	Memory Size, bits[15:8]							
10	Memory Size, bits[23:16]							
11	Memory Size, bits[31:24]							

Vendor-Defined Descriptors

The PnP specification also provides both small and large descriptors that a vendor may define themselves. The small vendor-defined descriptor takes the form defined in Table 11-17 on page 126, while the large vendor-defined descriptor takes the form defined in Table 11-18 on page 126. The body of the small descriptor may be from one to seven bytes in size, while the body of the large descriptor may range from one to 64K bytes in size. In both cases, the information contained in the descriptor body is defined by the vendor and is outside the scope of the PnP specification.

Table 11-17: Format of the Small Vendor-Defined Descriptor

Byte	Description							
	7	6	5	4	3	2	1	0
0	0=small descriptor	1110b=vendor-defined descriptor				descriptor body size = value between 1 and 7 (000b through 111b)		
1 through 7	Descriptor body—Vendor-defined							

Table 11-18: Format of the Large Vendor-Defined Descriptor

Byte	Description							
	7	6	5	4	3	2	1	0
0	1=large descriptor	0000100b = vendor-defined descriptor						

Table 11-18: Format of the Large Vendor-Defined Descriptor (Continued)

Byte	Description							
	7	6	5	4	3	2	1	0
1	Bits[7:0] of descriptor body size							
2	Bits[15:8] of descriptor body size							
3 through 64K	Descriptor body—Vendor-defined							

Dependent Functions

Some devices (especially legacy devices) require the allocation of specific groups of related resources. Assume that a device can be configured in any of the following manners:

- 16 contiguous IO ports starting at base IO address 01F0h, using IRQ10
- 16 contiguous IO ports starting at base IO address 02F0h, using IRQ11
- 16 contiguous IO ports starting at base IO address 03F0h, using IRQ15

In other words, the IRQ used is associated with a specific IO address range. As an example, if the configuration software assigns the IO range from 02F0h through 02FFh via one of the device's IO configuration registers, it must also select IRQ11 as the interrupt request line used by the device. The choice of interrupt line "depends" on the IO range selected (and vice versa). If either the IO range or its associated IRQ line has already been allocated to another device, the configuration program has to select one of the other dependent combinations that is currently not allocated to another device.

Each dependent combination included in a device's resource list starts with a start dependent function descriptor. The last combination is immediately followed by an end dependent function descriptor. As an example (using the example device cited earlier):

```
Start Dependent Function Descriptor
  Fixed IO descriptor, 16 Ports starting at 01F0h
  Interrupt Descriptor for IRQ10
Start Dependent Function Descriptor
  Fixed IO descriptor, 16 Ports starting at 02F0h
  Interrupt Descriptor for IRQ11
Start Dependent Function Descriptor
  Fixed IO descriptor, 16 Ports starting at 03F0h
  Interrupt Descriptor for IRQ15
End Dependent Function Descriptor
```

The configuration software must choose one of the above combinations. Each of the start dependent function descriptors may include a priority indicator indicating the order of desirability of the choices. For instance, in the previous example, the device designer could indicate that the 01F0h/IRQ10 combination is the highest priority, followed by the 02F0h/IRQ11 and the 03F0h/IRQ15 combinations. If the start dependent function descriptors do not contain priority information, or if they have the same priority, the groups are prioritized by the order in which they appear in the list (the earlier in the list, the higher the priority). The specification recommends that dependent function descriptors appear at the end of the device's resource list. Table 11-19 on page 128 and Table 11-20 on page 129 provide a detailed definition of the start and end dependent function descriptors.

Table 11-19: Format of the Start Dependent Function Descriptor

Byte	Description							
	7	6	5	4	3	2	1	0
0	0=small descriptor	0110b=start dependent function descriptor				000b=no priority byte 001b=priority byte follows in byte 1		
1	Priority Byte: • 00h = Highest priority and preferred configuration • 01h = Lower priority, but acceptable configuration • 02h = Functional configuration, but not optimal • 03h - FFh = reserved							

Table 11-20: Format of the End Dependent Function Descriptor

Byte	Description							
	7	6	5	4	3	2	1	0
0	0=small descriptor	0111b=end dependent function descriptor				000b, no additional bytes		

Example Card Resource Data Structure

The following is an example of a card resource data structure. This card has three devices on it. The first device is a network controller with the following characteristics:

1. A 16-bit (ISA memory) RAM buffer that needs to be mapped into system memory space. The RAM buffer is 64KB in size. It is not cacheable.
2. An 8KB, 8-bit expansion ROM that can be shadowed and must be mapped into the device ROM area in the first 1MB of memory space.
3. An IO register set eight locations long that must be mapped into IO space. The selected start address must be either 1F0h, 2F0h, or 3F0h. The address selected is dependent on the IRQ line to be used (see the next item).
4. An interrupt request line that can be routed to IRQ2, 10, or 11. The interrupt line routing is dependent on which IO range is selected. The interrupt line uses ISA-compatible, positive edge triggered signalling.
5. It requires the use of one of the 16-bit DMA channels and the device can handle ISA-compatible or Type A DMA transfer timing.
6. It can use the device driver for a compatible network controller.

The second device is a parallel port with the following characteristics:

1. May be set up as LPT1, LPT2,or LPT3.
2. It can use either IRQ5 or 7 using ISA-compatible request signalling.
3. It requires a four-location IO range starting at either 0378h, 0278h, or 03BCh.

Plug and Play System Architecture

The third device is an ISA bus master with the following characteristics:

1. Uses DMA channel 5, 6, or 7.
2. Has a four-location IO register set that may be mapped into IO space any-
   where within the range from IO address 0100h through 03FCh, starting on
   any address divisible-by-four (doubleword-aligned).

The card's resource data structure has the following form:

```
Plug and Play Version Number
Card identifier string (required)
Logical Device ID of network adapter
  Identifier String (optional)
  Compatible Device ID
  ISA memory descriptor for 64KB, non-cacheable, 16-bit RAM buffer
  ISA memory descriptor for Expansion ROM
  Requires 16-bit DMA channel, ISA-compatible
  Start Dependent Function
        8-byte IO block at location 01F0h
        IRQ2, positive edge triggered
  Start Dependent Function
        8-byte IO block at location 02F0h
        IRQ10, positive edge triggered
  Start Dependent Function
        8-byte IO block at location 03F0h
        IRQ11, positive edge triggered
  End Dependent Function
Logical Device ID for parallel port
  IRQ5 or 7, positive edge triggered
  Start Dependent Function
        4-byte IO block at location 0378h
  Start Dependent Function
        4-byte IO block at location 0278h
  Start Dependent Function
        4-byte IO block at location 03BCh
  End Dependent Function
Logical Device ID for ISA Bus Master
  DMA 5, 6, or 7; Bus Master,16-bit
  4 byte IO block, doubleword-aligned, in range from 0100h through 03FFh
End of list
```

The card's data structure is listed in Table 11-21 on page 131. Note that the Byte
column contains the decimal offset of each item. Each of the card's devices must
also implement a corresponding set of configuration registers used to assign
selected resources to it. The example card's devices must implement the following configuration registers:

Chapter 11: Card Resource Requirements

- The network adapter must implement ISA memory configuration registers 0 and 1, DMA configuration register 1, IO configuration register 0, and interrupt configuration register 0. It does not have to implement ISA memory configuration registers 2 and 3, EISA memory configuration registers 0 through 3, IO configuration registers 1 through 7, interrupt configuration register 1, or DMA configuration registers 0 and 1.
- The parallel port must implement interrupt configuration register 0 and IO configuration register 0. It does not have to implement ISA memory configuration registers 0 through 3, EISA memory configuration registers 0 through 3, IO configuration registers 1 through 7, interrupt configuration register 1, or DMA configuration registers 0 and 1.
- The ISA bus master must implement DMA configuration register 0 and IO configuration register 0. It does not have to implement ISA memory configuration registers 0 through 3, EISA memory configuration registers 0 through 3, IO configuration registers 1 through 7, interrupt configuration registers 0 and 1, or DMA configuration register 1.

The location and usage of the configuration registers are covered in the next chapter.

Table 11-21: Sample Card's Resource Data Structure

Byte (dec)	Contents	Description							
		7	6	5	4	3	2	1	0
0	0Ah	Plug and Play Version Number descriptor							
1	10h	Version 1.0							
2	00h	Vendor-specific version number 0.0							
3	82h	Card's ANSI Identifier String descriptor							
4	16h	string is 22d bytes long							
5	00h								
6-27	-	Card's identifier string is "ACME Coyote Combo Card"							
28	15h	Logical Device ID descriptor, length of 5 bytes. **This is the beginning of the network adapter's resource list.**							

Table 11-21: Sample Card's Resource Data Structure (Continued)

Byte (dec)	Contents	Description							
		7	6	5	4	3	2	1	0
29	04h	EISA ID is "ACM", product number is 123h, and revision number is 1h.							
30	6Dh								
31	12h								
32	31h								
33	02h	000000b=configuration registers 32h-37h not implemented						1=IO range check register implemented at location 31h	0=device does not take part in boot
34	82h	Network adapter ANSI Identifier string descriptor. This descriptor is mandatory for the card, but optional for a logical device.							
35	1Fh	ANSI identifier string is 31d bytes long							
36	00h								
37-67		Network adapter's identifier string is "ACME Roadrunner Network Adapter"							
68	1Ch	Network adapter's compatible device ID descriptor							
69	04h	EISA ID is "ABC", product number is 678h, and revision number is 0h.							
70	43h								
71	67h								
72	80h								

Table 11-21: Sample Card's Resource Data Structure (Continued)

Byte (dec)	Contents	Description							
		7	6	5	4	3	2	1	0
73	81h	ISA memory descriptor for the network adapter's 64KB RAM buffer. This is the first memory descriptor for this device. It therefore corresponds to memory configuration register 0 (locations 40h through 44h in the device's configuration space).							
74	09h	Descriptor body length is 9 bytes							
75	00h								
76	09h	Reserved	0b=not ROM	0b=n/a	01b=16-bit memory only		0b=requires range length	0b=non-cacheable	1b=writeable
77	00h	Minimum acceptable base address is 100000h							
78	10h								
79	00h	Maximum acceptable base address is F00000h							
80	F0h								
81	00h	Must start on an address divisible by 64KB							
82	00h								
83	00h	Memory size is 256 x 256 bytes per block = 64KB							
84	01h								

Plug and Play System Architecture

Table 11-21: Sample Card's Resource Data Structure (Continued)

Byte (dec)	Contents	Description							
		7	6	5	4	3	2	1	0
85	81h	ISA memory descriptor for the network adapter's expansion ROM. This is the second and last memory descriptor for this device. It therefore corresponds to the memory configuration register 1 (locations 48h through 4Ch in the device's configuration space). Since the device has no more ISA memory descriptors, the memory configuration registers in locations 4Dh through 5F are not implemented. In addition, since there aren't any 32-bit memory descriptors, locations 76h through A8h are not implemented.							
86	09h	Descriptor body size is 9 bytes							
87	00h								
88	60h	Reserved	1b=Expansion ROM	1b=can be shadowed	00b=8-bit memory only		0b=requires range length	0b=non-cacheable	0b=read-only
89	00h	Minimum acceptable base address is 0C0000h							
90	0Ch								
91	E0h	Maximum acceptable base address is 0DE000h							
92	0Dh								
93	00h	Must start on an address divisible by 8KB							
94	20h								
95	20h	ROM size is 32 x 256 bytes per block = 8KB							
96	00h								

Table 11-21: Sample Card's Resource Data Structure (Continued)

Byte (dec)	Contents	Description							
		7	6	5	4	3	2	1	0
97	2Ah	DMA descriptor for the network adapter. This is the only DMA descriptor associated with the device. It corresponds to the device's DMA configuration register 0 (location 74h in the device's configuration space). Since the device doesn't use any additional DMA channels, it does not implement DMA configuration register 1 at location 75h.							
98	E0h	1b=Can use channel 7	1b=Can use channel 6	1b=Can use channel 5	0b=cannot use channel 4	0b=cannot use channel 3	0b=cannot use channel 2	0b=cannot use channel 1	0b=cannot use channel 0
99	12h	Reserved	00b=ISA compatible transfers		1b=may use count by word mode	0b=may not use count by byte mode	0b=not a bus master	10b=16-bit transfers only	
100	31h	Start Dependent Function descriptor (includes optional priority byte (see byte 101).							
101	00h	Highest priority, preferred configuration							
102	4Bh	Fixed IO port descriptor. If selected by the configuration program, this information is used to program IO configuration register 0 (locations 60h and 61h in the device's configuration space).							
103	F0h	Base IO address = 01F0h							
104	01h								
105	01h	8 IO ports required							

Table 11-21: Sample Card's Resource Data Structure (Continued)

Byte (dec)	Contents	Description							
		7	6	5	4	3	2	1	0
106	23h	Interrupt descriptor with optional signalling method byte. If selected by the configuration program, this information is used to program interrupt configuration register 0 (locations 70h and 71h in the device's configuration space).							
107	00h	0=can't use IRQ7	0=can't use IRQ6	0=can't use IRQ5	0=can't use IRQ4	0=can't use IRQ3	0=can't use IRQ2	0=can't use IRQ1	0=can't use IRQ0
108	02h	0=can't use IRQ15	0=can't use IRQ14	0=can't use IRQ13	0=can't use IRQ12	0=can't use IRQ11	0=can't use IRQ10	1=use IRQ2 (IRQ9)	0=can't use IRQ8
109	01h	reserved				0=can't use active low level sensitive	0=can't use active high level sensitive	0=can't use negative edge triggered	1=can use positive edge triggered
110	31h	Start Dependent Function descriptor (includes optional priority byte (see byte 111).							
111	01h	Lower priority, but acceptable							
112	4Bh	Fixed IO port descriptor. If selected by the configuration program, this information is used to program IO configuration register 0 (locations 60h and 61h in the device's configuration space).							
113	F0h	Base IO address = 02F0h							
114	02h								
115	01h	8 IO ports required							

Table 11-21: Sample Card's Resource Data Structure (Continued)

Byte (dec)	Contents	Description							
		7	6	5	4	3	2	1	0
116	23h	Interrupt descriptor with optional signalling method byte. If selected by the configuration program, this information is used to program interrupt configuration register 0 (locations 70h and 71h in the device's configuration space).							
117	00h	0=can't use IRQ7	0=can't use IRQ6	0=can't use IRQ5	0=can't use IRQ4	0=can't use IRQ3	0=can't use IRQ2	0=can't use IRQ1	0=can't use IRQ0
118	04h	0=can't use IRQ15	0=can't use IRQ14	0=can't use IRQ13	0=can't use IRQ12	0=can't use IRQ11	1=use IRQ10	0=can't use IRQ2 (IRQ9)	0=can't use IRQ8
119	01h	reserved				0=can't use active low level sensitive	0=can't use active high level sensitive	0=can't use negative edge triggered	1=can use positive edge triggered
120	31h	Start Dependent Function descriptor (includes optional priority byte (see byte 121).							
121	01h	Lower priority, but acceptable							
122	4Bh	Fixed IO port descriptor. If selected by the configuration program, this information is used to program IO configuration register 0 (locations 60h and 61h in the device's configuration space).							
123	F0h	Base IO address = 03F0h							
124	03h								

Table 11-21: Sample Card's Resource Data Structure (Continued)

Byte (dec)	Contents	Description							
		7	6	5	4	3	2	1	0
125	01h	8 IO ports required							
126	23h	Interrupt descriptor with optional signalling method byte. If selected by the configuration program, this information is used to program interrupt configuration register 0 (locations 70h and 71h in the device's configuration space).							
127	00h	0=can't use IRQ7	0=can't use IRQ6	0=can't use IRQ5	0=can't use IRQ4	0=can't use IRQ3	0=can't use IRQ2	0=can't use IRQ1	0=can't use IRQ0
128	08h	0=can't use IRQ15	0=can't use IRQ14	0=can't use IRQ13	0=can't use IRQ12	1=use IRQ11	0=can't use IRQ10	0=can't use IRQ2 (IRQ9)	0=can't use IRQ8
129	01h	reserved				0=can't use active low level sensitive	0=can't use active high level sensitive	0=can't use negative edge triggered	1=can use positive edge triggered
130	38h	End dependent function descriptor (end of network adapter's dependent function structure).							
131	15h	Logical device ID descriptor for parallel port							
132	04h	EISA ID is "ACM", product number is 987h, and revision number is 0h.							
133	6Dh								
134	98h								
135	70h								

Table 11-21: Sample Card's Resource Data Structure (Continued)

Byte (dec)	Contents	Description							
		7	6	5	4	3	2	1	0
136	02h	000000b=configuration registers 32h-37h not implemented						1=IO range check configuration register implemented at location 31h	0=device does not take part in boot
137	22h	Interrupt descriptor without optional signalling byte. If selected by the configuration program, this information is used to program interrupt configuration register 0 (locations 70h and 71h in the device's configuration space).							
138	A0h	1=IRQ7 can be used	0=IRQ6 can't be used	1=IRQ5 can be used	0=IRQ4 can't be used	0=IRQ3 can't be used	0=IRQ2 can't be used	0=IRQ1 can't be used	0=IRQ0 can't be used
139	00h	0=IRQ15 can't be used	0=IRQ14 can't be used	0=IRQ13 can't be used	0=IRQ12 can't be used	0=IRQ11 can't be used	0=IRQ10 can't be used	0=IRQ9 can't be used	0=IRQ8 can't be used
140	30h	Start dependent function descriptor without optional priority byte							

Table 11-21: Sample Card's Resource Data Structure (Continued)

Byte (dec)	Contents	Description							
		7	6	5	4	3	2	1	0
141	4Bh	Fixed IO port descriptor. If selected by the configuration program, this information is used to program IO configuration register 0 (locations 60h and 61h in the device's configuration space).							
142	78h	IO port 0378h							
143	03h								
144	04h	requires 4 IO locations							
145	30h	Start dependent function descriptor without optional priority byte							
146	4Bh	Fixed IO port descriptor. If selected by the configuration program, this information is used to program IO configuration register 0 (locations 60h and 61h in the device's configuration space).							
147	78h	IO port 0278h							
148	02h								
149	04h	requires 4 IO locations							
150	30h	Start dependent function descriptor without optional priority byte							
151	4Bh	Fixed IO port descriptor. If selected by the configuration program, this information is used to program IO configuration register 0 (locations 60h and 61h in the device's configuration space).							
152	BCh	IO port 03BCh							
153	03h								
154	04h	requires 4 IO locations							
155	38h	End dependent function descriptor (end of the parallel port's dependent function structure).							

Table 11-21: Sample Card's Resource Data Structure (Continued)

Byte (dec)	Contents	Description							
		7	6	5	4	3	2	1	0
156	15h	Logical device ID descriptor for the ISA bus master.							
157	04h	EISA ID is "ACM", product number is 345h, and revision number is 9h.							
158	6Dh								
159	34h								
160	59h								
161	02h	000000b=configuration registers 32h-37h not implemented						1=IO range check configuration register implemented at location 31h	0=device does not take part in boot
162	2Ah	DMA descriptor. This information is used to program DMA configuration register 0 (location 74h in the device's configuration space). Location 75h (DMA configurgation register 1) is not implemented (because the device doesn't use a second DMA channel).							
163	E0h	111b=can use channel 5,6, or 7			00000b=can't use channels 0-4				

Table 11-21: Sample Card's Resource Data Structure (Continued)

Byte (dec)	Contents	Description							
		7	6	5	4	3	2	1	0
164	06h	Reserved	00b=ISA compatible transfers		0=can not use count by word mode	0=can not use count by byte mode	1=Bus master	10b=16-bit only	
165	47h	Programmable IO port descriptor. This information is used to program IO configuration register 0 (locations 60h and 61h in the device's configuration space).							
166	01h	Reserved							1=decodes all 16 bits
167	00h	minimum base address is 0100h							
168	01h								
169	FCh	maximum base address is 03FCh							
170	03h								
171	04h	base address must be doubleword-aligned							
172	04h	IO range size is 4 bytes							
173	79h	End of card's resource data structure							
174	00h	Checksum. 00h indicates checksum should not be performed and resource data structure should be accepted as is.							

12 *The PnP Configuration Registers*

The Previous Chapter

The previous chapter described the process of reading the resource data structure and provided a detailed description of its content.

This Chapter

Once the resource requirements of a card have been ascertained, the next step is to program its configuration registers, assigning non-conflicting resources to each logical device residing on the card. A device's configuration registers are programmable address decoders and/or resource selectors. This chapter describes the configuration register set associated with each PnP card and each logical device that resides on the card.

The Next Chapter

The next chapter provides an introduction to the PnP BIOS. The term "BIOS" is defined, the typical configuration responsibilities of both the BIOS and the OS are described, static and dynamic configuration are defined, and the PnP device ROM is introduced.

Windows 95 Overview

The Windows 95 CM has no knowledge of the mechanisms used to access configuration registers associated with devices residing on various system buses. Rather, it depends on the bus-specific enumerator programs to perform this function. The PnP bus enumerator is responsible for accessing the configuration registers on E/ISA PnP devices. When the CM needs to access a PnP device's configuration registers, it calls the PnP enumerator. The enumerator accesses the specified target device's configuration registers.

The Wake Up Call

Each of the PnP cards has been isolated, assigned a unique CSN number, its resource data structure has been read, and it has been put back to sleep. At this point, the configuration program (e.g., the CM in Windows 95) has accumulated a list of the resources requested by each logical device on each card. In the next step, the cards are awakened one at a time, and the configuration registers associated with the card itself and each of its logical devices are programmed to assign non-conflicting resources to each device.

In order to place a card into the configure state, the configuration program must write its CSN number into the wake command register. The wake command register is implemented on every PnP card, so every card accepts the CSN number written. Each then compares its assigned CSN number to the CSN number written into its wake command register. The card that has a compare exits the sleep state and enters the configure state.

The Configuration Register Set

After waking up a card's configuration logic, the target logical device on the card is selected by writing its logical device number (LDN) into the LDN register. The target device configuration register is then selected by writing its pointer into the PnP configuration address port at IO address 0279h. Any subsequent access to the read data or write data port access the register the address port is currently pointing to.

Refer to Figure 12-1 on page 147. Configuration locations 00h through 2Fh are used to configure the card, while locations 30h through FFh are used to configure a selected logical device on the card. Since these registers are duplicated for each logical device on the card, the programmer must first use one of the card-level registers to select the target logical device. The target logical device's configuration registers may then be accessed. This process is described in the section in this chapter entitled "Logical Device Number (LDN) Register."

The designer of a logical device only implements the configuration registers necessary for the card's operation. Simply put, the device's configuration registers are comprised of programmable memory and/or IO address decoders, and selectors that are used to select which interrupt or DMA channel that the device is to use.

Chapter 12: The PnP Configuration Registers

The specification sets the following limits for each type of resource a device device may implement:

- Up to four memory configuration registers, numbered 0 through 3
- Up to eight IO configuration registers, numbered 0 through 7
- Up to two interrupt request lines, each with an associated configuration register (numbered 0 and 1)
- Up to two DMA channels, each with an associated configuration register (numbered 0 and 1)

It isn't necessary to implement all of these configuration registers. Only the ones corresponding to resources implemented on the device must be implemented. The example of the network controller used in the previous chapter (see Table 11-21 on page 131) used two memory decoders, one DMA channel, one IO block and one interrupt request line. It is therefore only necessary to implement:

- Memory configuration registers 0 and 1. Memory configuration registers 2 and 3 do not need to be implemented.
- DMA configuration register 0. DMA configuration register 1 does not need to be implemented.
- IO configuration register 0. IO configuration registers 1 through 7 do not need to be implemented.
- Interrupt configuration register 0. Interrupt configuration register 1 does not need to be implemented.

The memory, IO, DMA and interrupt descriptors found within a device's resource data list define which configuration registers of each type are implemented. The order in which each descriptor type is encountered identifies which of the configuration registers is associated with the descriptor. As an example, the network adapter's list contained the following resource descriptors:

- The first memory descriptor in the list defines its 64KB RAM buffer and is associated with ISA memory configuration register 0.
- The second memory descriptor in the list defines its expansion ROM and is associated with ISA memory configuration register 1. Since there are no more memory descriptors in the device's list, ISA memory configuration registers 2 and 3 are not implemented (and there are no 32-bit EISA memory configuration registers implemented).
- The first and only DMA descriptor in the list describes the device's need for a DMA channel and is associated with DMA configuration register 0. Since there are no more DMA descriptors in the device's list, DMA configuration register 1 is not implemented.

- The device's list indicates (via its dependent function list) that the configuration program can choose from one of three fixed IO base addresses and one of three associated interrupt lines. The configuration program uses IO configuration register 0 to set the selected IO address and interrupt configuration register 0 to assign the selected interrupt line to the device. Since there are no additional IO descriptors in the list, IO configuration registers 1 through 7 are not implemented. Likewise, the lack of additional interrupt descriptors in the list indicates that interrupt configuration register 1 is not implemented.

Chapter 12: The PnP Configuration Registers

Figure 12-1: The Configuration Register Set

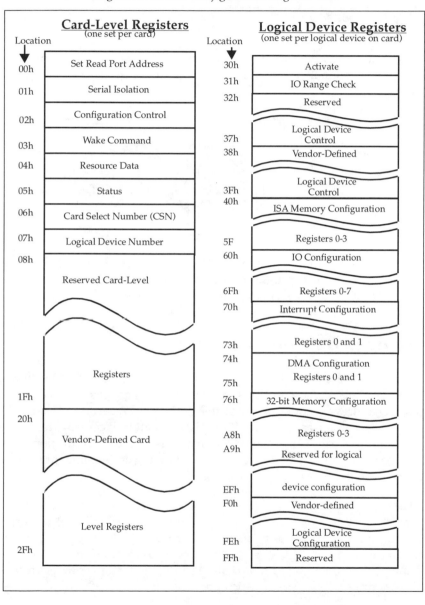

Card-Oriented Registers

General

As stated earlier, the card's configuration registers occupy configuration locations 00h through 2Fh. Figure 12-1 on page 147 illustrates the configuration register set.

The sections that follow provide a detailed description of each of the card-level registers. Some code (programming) fragments are included as examples. The non-programmer may wish to skip these examples.

Set Read Data Port Register

The set read data port address register resides at configuration location 00h. The configuration software uses this register to assign an IO address to the read data port IO address decoder on all of the PnP cards. A write to this configuration address is a broadcast write to this register on all PnP cards. After the read data port's address has been assigned via this register, the configuration registers can then be read via the read data port. The following code fragment illustrates how the set read data port register is accessed:

```
mov  dx,0279h    ;address port IO address in dx
mov  al,00h      ;location of set read data port reg in al
out  dx,al       ;set address port = set read port reg.
mov  dx,0A79h    ;dx = IO address of write data port
mov  al,F9h      ;al = bits A[9:2] of read port address
out  dx,al       ;set address
```

This code fragment sets the IO address of the read data port to 03E4h (A[15:10] are zero; A[9:2] are 1111 1001b; A[1:0] are 00b). A description of how to detect

Chapter 12: The PnP Configuration Registers

read data port conflicts with legacy ISA devices can be found in the section entitled "Dealing with Checksum Error or All-Zero Serial Identifier" on page 78.

Serial Isolation Register

The serial isolation register resides at configuration location 01h. There is one serial isolation register per card. During the card isolation process, the configuration software reads the serial identifier and its checksum from this register. Assuming that the read data port address has already been set (refer to the previous section), the serial isolation register is pointed to by placing its location number into the address port. Any subsequent reads from the read data port access the serial isolation register. The following code fragment illustrates how it is accessed:

```
mov  dx,0279h   ;address port IO address in dx
mov  al,01h     ;location of serial isolation reg in al
out  dx,al      ;set address port = serial isolation reg.
mov  dx,0xxxh   ;dx = IO address of read data port
in   al,dx      ;read from serial isolation register
```

Information on the usage of the serial isolation register during the card isolation process can be found in the chapter entitled "Isolating a Card for Configuration."

Configuration Control Register

There is one configuration control register per card. It resides at configuration location 02h. Table 12-1 on page 150 and Figure 12-2 on page 151 illustrate the bit assignment of this register. A write to this register is a broadcast write to this register on all PnP cards. The register is write-only.

Writing a 07h (the three lower bits are set to one) to this register clears all CSNs, resets all logical devices to their startup state, and returns the configuration logic on all cards to the wait for key state. In other words, the configuration program must go through the isolation process and assign CSN numbers to the cards again. It must then read the resource requirement list from each card and then reconfigure the devices.

Assuming that all devices have already been configured, writing an 02h to this register permits all configured devices to retain their CSN and configuration, but returns their configuration logic to the wait for key state. After this, the configuration software can access any card's configuration registers by issuing the key to transition all cards to the sleep state and then issuing a wake command with a particular card's CSN. The following code fragment illustrates how the configuration control register is accessed:

```
mov  dx,0279h    ;address port IO address in dx
mov  al,02h      ;location of config control reg in al
out  dx,al       ;set address port = config control reg.
mov  al,07h      ;set lower three bits in al
mov  dx,0A79h    ;set dx = write data port address
out  dx,al       ;write to config control reg.
```

Table 12-1: Card Configuration Control Register

Bit(s)	Description
7:3	Reserved.
2	**Reset CSN**. When set to one, the CSN registers on all PnP cards are cleared to zero. Each card then automatically clears bit two in its configuration control register.
1	**Wait for Key**. When set to one, the configuration logic on all of the cards returns to the wait for key state. Each card then automatically clears bit one in its configuration control register. The CSN register on each card retains its assigned CSN number and all of the logical devices on each card retain their configuration information.
0	**Reset**. When set to one, the logical devices on all cards are reset to their default state. Their configuration registers return to their startup state. Each card then automatically clears bit zero in its configuration control register.

Chapter 12: The PnP Configuration Registers

Figure 12-2: Card Configuration Control Register

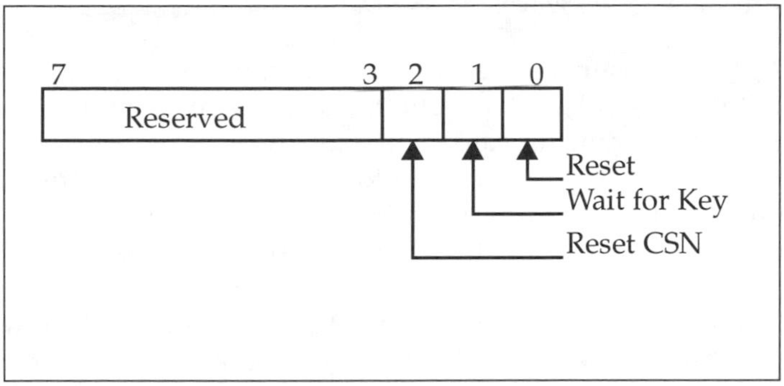

Wake Command Register

The wake command register is write-only and resides at configuration location 03h. A write to this register is a broadcast write to this register on all PnP cards. The 8-bit value written to this register is the CSN of the card(s) to be awakened from the sleep state. A non-zero CSN value causes only the card with that number in its CSN register to transition from the sleep to the configure state. A zero CSN value causes all cards with zero in their CSN registers (in other words, they have not yet been isolated and assigned a CSN) to transition from the sleep to the isolation state. The following code fragment illustrates how the wake command register is accessed:

```
mov  dx,0279h   ;address port IO address in dx
mov  al,03h     ;location of wake reg in al
out  dx,al      ;set address port = wake reg.
mov  al,42h     ;place CSN in al (42 is an example CSN)
mov  dx,0A79h   ;set dx = write data port address
out  dx,al      ;write to wake reg.
```

Resource Data Register

Each PnP card contains an eight byte serial identifier, a checksum byte for its identifier, and a resource data structure (i.e., its resource requirement list). The card considers the nine byte serial identifier and the resource data structure to be one contiguous block of data. Before attempting to access the resource data structure, the programmer must always read the serial identifier first.

Plug and Play System Architecture

Only one card can be in the configure state at a given time. A card can enter the configure state in two ways:

1. When a card is first assigned its CSN, it automatically enters the configure state from the isolation state. In this case, the configuration software has just completed reading the card's serial identifier and has verified that its checksum is correct. The next read performed from the card's resource data register (at configuration location 04h) accesses the first byte of the card's resource requirement list (also referred to as its resource data structure). Each time that a read is performed from the resource data register, the card increments its pointer to the next byte of the resource data structure.
2. Assuming that a card was previously assigned a CSN and then put to sleep, a wake command with a CSN matching the card's CSN transitions the card from the sleep to the configure state. The wake command always resets the card's pointer to the beginning of its serial identifier. For this reason, the programmer must first read the nine-byte serial identifier from the serial isolation register before attempting to read the resource data structure via the resource data register. It should be noted, however, that although the eight-byte identifier is correct when read in this manner, the checksum byte isn't correct (even though the serial identifier is correct). When the nine-byte serial identifier has been read, the next read performed from the resource data register accesses the first byte of the resource data register.

A card may store its resource data structure in a slow-access device. After each byte is read from the resource data register, the programmer must not read from the register again until the card has set up the next byte of the resource data structure in the resource data register. This implies that there must be a way for the programmer to know when the next byte is ready to be read from the register. That is the purpose of the card's status register (see the next section). To ensure that the next byte is ready to be read, the programmer must always first check the status register for a ready condition (bit 0 is set to one) before performing the next read from the resource data register.

The format of the resource data structure is covered in the chapter entitled "Card Resource Requirements." The programmer can tell when the end of the structure has been reached via a special identifier (the end of list tag, discussed in the resource data structure chapter). The following code fragment illustrates how the resource data register and the status register are accessed:

```
            mov  dx,0279h      ;address port IO address in dx
            mov  al,05h        ;location of status reg in al
            out  dx,al         ;set address port = status reg.
            mov  dx,0xxxh      ;dx = IO address of read data port
loop:  in   al,dx         ;read from status register
            test al,00000001b  ;
            jz   loop          ;test for bit 0 set
            mov  dx,0279h      ;
            mov  al,04h        ;
            out  dx,al         ;point to resource data reg
            mov  dx,0xxxh      ;dx=read data port address
            in   al,dx         ;read resource data structure byte
```

Status Register

The status register resides at configuration location 05h and is read-only. It is illustrated in Figure 12-3 on page 153. When a card with an assigned CSN enters the configuration state and its serial identifier has already been read, the resource data structure is then read via the resource data register. Before reading each byte of the resource data structure through the resource data register, the programmer must first ensure that bit zero of the status register is set to one. This indicates that a valid data byte is ready to be read from the resource data register. If bit zero is cleared, the program must spin (i.e., loop) until the bit is set to one. This indicates the presence of a valid byte in the resource data register. This process is described in the previous section. The content of the resource data structure is defined in the chapter entitled "Card Resource Requirements."

Figure 12-3: Status Register

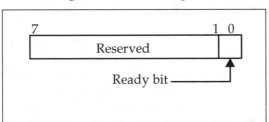

Card Select Number (CSN) Register

The CSN register resides at location 06h and is a read/write register. After a card is isolated, the configuration software assigns it a unique CSN by writing the CSN into its CSN register. The CSN of 00h is reserved to indicate that a CSN has not yet been assigned to the card, while any value between 01h and FFh (255 possibilities) may be used as a unique CSN for the card. Whenever a wake command is issued, the card's CSN register is compared against the CSN number written to the card's wake command register. There are three possible cases:

1. If the CSN register contains zero and zero is written to the wake register, the card transitions from the sleep to the isolation state.
2. If the CSN register contains zero, and a non-zero value is written to the card's wake register, it transitions to the sleep state.
3. If the CSN register contains a valid CSN and a non-zero value is written to the card's wake register, the card goes to sleep if the number doesn't match its CSN. It goes to the configure state if there is a match, and also resets its pointer to the start byte of its serial identifier.

The following code fragment illustrates how the CSN register is accessed:

```
mov  dx,0279h   ;address port IO address in dx
mov  al,06h     ;location of CSN reg in al
out  dx,al      ;set address port = CSN reg.
mov  al,42h     ;place CSN in al (42 is an example CSN)
mov  dx,0A79h   ;set dx = write data port address
out  dx,al      ;write to CSN reg.
```

Logical Device Number (LDN) Register

As stated earlier in this chapter, a PnP card may contain more than one logical device. During the configuration process, the number of logical devices on a card is ascertained by reading the card's resource data structure. The programmer can select a specific logical device to configure on the card by writing its logical device number into the card's logical device number register. After this has been accomplished, subsequent accesses to configuration registers in the 30h through FEh range access the selected device's configuration registers.

The logical device number register is an 8-bit, read/write register. It can indicate any device number between 00h and FFh, permitting a maximum of 256 logical devices per card. Any card that only implements one logical device on the card

Chapter 12: The PnP Configuration Registers

must hardwire 00h into this register (in other words, a card with one device must make it device zero). In this one case, the register is read-only. A detailed description of the resource data structure can be found in the chapter entitled "Card Resource Requirements." A detailed description of the configuration registers associated with each logical device can be found later in this chapter. The following code fragment illustrates how the logical device number register is accessed:

```
mov  dx,0279h   ;address port IO address in dx
mov  al,07h     ;location of LDN register in al
out  dx,al      ;set address port = LDN register
mov  al,01h     ;place LDN in al (example LDN)
mov  dx,0A79h   ;set dx = write data port address
out  dx,al      ;write to LDN reg.
```

Reserved Card-Level Registers

Configuration locations 08h through 1Fh are reserved by the specification for the future implementation of additional configuration registers associated with each card. They must not be used.

Vendor-Defined Card-Level Registers

Configuration locations 20h through 2Fh may be used by a card manufacturer for card-specific configuration registers. Any of these registers that are implemented effect the entire card (in other words, they are not associated with a specific logical device on the card). The definition of these registers and the bits within them is outside the scope of the specification.

Device-Oriented Registers

General

Configuration locations 30h through FFh are duplicated for each logical device that resides on a card. To access a specific logical device's configuration registers, the logical device number is first written into the card's logical device number register (see earlier section in this chapter entitled "Logical Device Number (LDN) Register" on page 154). Any subsequent accesses to registers that reside above location 2Fh access the targeted device's registers.

Each logical device's registers are divided into two groups:

- device control registers
- device configuration registers

The device control registers control some fundamental aspect of the device's operation. As an example, the activate register is used to activate or deactivate the device. The device configuration registers, on the other hand, are used to configure the device's address decoders, interrupt logic, DMA logic, etc. In other words, they are used to assign resources to the device.

Device Control Registers

Activate Register

There is one activate register associated with each logical device. The activate register is read/write and resides at configuration location 30h. It is illustrated in Figure 12-4 on page 157. Bit zero is used to activate or deactivate the card (0 = deactivate, 1 = activate). The default state of this bit after reset or after a one is written to the reset bit in the card's configuration control bit is zero. An exception is a device that must start up in the active state to be used during the startup process (e.g., the keyboard and the display controller). When deactivated, a device can only respond to configuration accesses. It cannot respond to other ISA or EISA bus transactions. When activated, the device is enabled for normal operation.

The code fragment that follows illustrates the activation of logical device two on a card. It assumes that the card has already been assigned a CSN, placed into the configure state, its resource data structure has been read, and its configuration registers have been programmed.

```
mov  dx,0279h    ;dx=address port
mov  al,07h      ;al=address of LDN reg
out  dx,al       ;select LDN reg
mov  al,02h      ;al=LDN 2
mov  dx,0A79h    ;dx=write data port
out  dx,al       ;select LDN 2
mov  al,30h      ;al=activate register address
mov  dx,0279h    ;dx=address port
out  dx,al       ;select activate register
mov  dx,0A79h    ;dx=write data port
mov  al,01h      ;al=activate bit set
out  dx,al       ;activate device
```

Figure 12-4: Activate Register

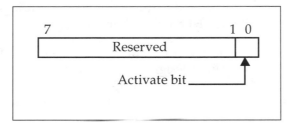

IO Range Check Register

There is one IO range check register associated with each logical device. This register permits the programmer to verify that the IO range assigned to one of a logical device's IO address decoders does not conflict with any IO addresses used by any other device. The range check register resides at configuration location 31h. The reserved bits in this register are read-only and must return zeros on a read, while the implemented bits are read/write. The register is illustrated in Figure 12-5 on page 158.

Assume that the currently-selected logical device has just been configured, has not yet been activated, and the IO range from 0300h through 030Fh has been assigned to one of its IO address decoders. The programmer then performs a test of the IO range as follows:

1. Write the value 02h to the range check register. This enables IO range checking and selects AAh as the pattern to be returned by the logical device for any read within the device's assigned IO range (0300h through 030Fh).

2. The programmer then proceeds to perform a series of IO reads from 0300h through 030Fh and testing for a pattern of AAh returned on each read. If the pattern is received properly for the entire range, proceed to step 3. If any pattern other than AAh is received, this indicates that another ISA device, probably a legacy ISA device, is set up to respond to the same address. The logical device is reconfigured for a different IO range and the range check is performed again.

3. Write the value 03h to the range check register. This enables range checking and selects 55h as the pattern to be returned by the logical device for any read within the device's assigned IO range (0300h through 030Fh).

4. The programmer then proceeds to perform a series of IO reads from 0300h through 030Fh and testing for a pattern of 55h returned on each read. If the pattern is received properly for the entire range, the selected IO range does not conflict with any other ISA device. If any pattern other than 55h is received, this indicates that another ISA device, probably a legacy ISA device, is set up to respond to the same address. The logical device is reconfigured for a different IO range and the range check is performed again.

Byte 5 of a device's logical device ID descriptor (refer to Table 11-8 on page 102) defines whether the device designer has implemented configuration locations 31h through 37h. Since the IO range check register resides at configuration location 31h, this indicates that the range check register is optional.

Figure 12-5: IO Range Check Register

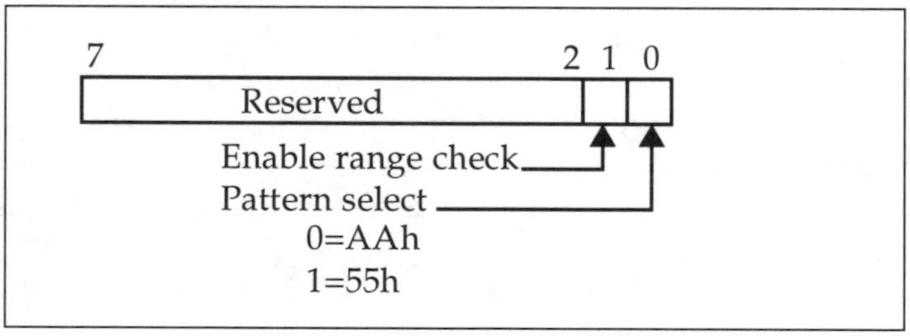

Reserved Device Control Registers

Configuration locations 32h through 37h in each logical device's configuration space are reserved by the specification and must not be used. Additional device-oriented control registers may be defined in these locations at a future date.

Chapter 12: The PnP Configuration Registers

Vendor-Defined Device Control Registers

Configuration locations 38h through 3Fh in each logical device's configuration space may be used by the device designer to implement device-specific control registers. The definition of these registers and the bits within them is outside the scope of the specification.

Device Configuration Registers

Introduction

In addition to its device control registers, each logical device on a card has its own device configuration registers. They are used to allocate IO space, memory space, an interrupt line, DMA channel, etc. to a device. The following sections define these registers.

The Memory Configuration Registers

Introduction. A logical device that includes one or more memory devices must include memory configuration registers. These registers permit the configuration software to assign memory ranges to the device. This section describes the manner in which the registers are implemented on a PnP card. In order to understand why these registers include bits defining whether the device is capable of functioning as an 8-, 16-, or 32-bit device, it is important to provide some background information. If you don't care about the background, you can skip to the section entitled "ISA 24-bit Memory Configuration Registers" on page 165.

Definition of an 8-Bit ISA Device. The original IBM PC and XT were based on the 8088 processor. The 8088 processor uses address bits A[19:0] to identify the precise location it wants to read or write. Furthermore, it only has one 8-bit data path, D[7:0], with which to read or write data. An 8-bit ISA device is only connected to data path D[7:0] and it uses the address (consisting of A[19:0]) to pinpoint the target location for the read or write. The memory responds to a read or a write whenever the byte-specific address is within its assigned range. The target byte is transferred over the only data path it is connected to, D[7:0].

Definition of a 16-Bit ISA Device. The IBM PC-AT was based on the 286 processor. This processor's address bus consists of A[23:0] and the BHE# (Bus High Enable) signal. Using the address bus, the processor can identify:

- a single, even-addressed location to read or write a single byte
- a single, odd-addressed location to read or write a single byte
- an even-addressed location and the next sequential, odd-addressed location to read or write two bytes simultaneously

The 286 has two data paths: D[15:8] is the upper data path; D[7:0] is the lower data path. It is a rule that the 286 always transfers data between itself and even-addressed locations over the lower data path; and between itself and odd-addressed locations over the upper data path. Logic external to the processor can determine the processor's intentions during a read or write transaction by observing its A0 and BHE# outputs:

- **A0 = 0 and BHE# deasserted**. A0 = 0 indicates that an even-addressed location is being addressed. The lower data path is therefore used for the byte transfer. BHE# deasserted indicates that the upper data path isn't used during this transaction.
- **A0 = 1 and BHE# asserted**. A0 = 1 indicates that an odd-addressed location is being addressed. The upper data path is therefore used for the byte transfer. BHE# asserted indicates that the upper data path is used during this transaction.
- **A0 = 0 and BHE# asserted**. A0 = 0 indicates that an even-addressed location is being addressed. The lower data path is therefore used for the byte transfer. BHE# asserted indicates that the upper data path is used during this transaction, implying that the processor is transferring a byte with an odd-addressed location over the upper data path. This combination indicates that the processor is performing a simultaneous two-byte transfer with an even and an odd-addressed location (the next sequential location) during this transaction (using both data paths).
- **A0 = 1 and BHE# deasserted**. This combination makes no sense and is not used.

A 16-bit ISA device is connected to both data paths and can interpret A0 and BHE#. It is capable of handling single-byte transfers with even- or odd-addressed locations and simultaneous transfers with the currently-addressed even location and the next sequential odd-addressed location.

ISA Steering Logic. The 286 processor assumes that all devices are capable of handling this addressing technique and data bus usage. It should be evident that 8-bit devices can't obey all of the rules.

For example, assume that the processor is attempting to read a byte from an odd-addressed location and that the target device is an 8-bit device. The processor drives the odd address onto A[23:0] and also asserts BHE#. A0 is set to 1, indicating that an odd location is being addressed. In addition, the assertion of BHE# indicates that the processor intends to read the byte over the upper data path. The 8-bit target device examines the address on A[23:0] and determines that the processor is addressing an odd-addressed location within its assigned range. 8-bit devices cannot see BHE# and couldn't do anything about it if they did see it asserted (because they are not connected to the upper data path).

The 8-bit target device outputs the requested byte onto the lower data path, but the processor expects to receive it over the upper data path. Unless something is done to fix it, the processor will read junk from the upper data path. This is the job of the ISA system's bus control logic. The bus control and the steering logic are pictured in Figure 12-6 on page 163. The bus control logic has two inputs that it uses to determine if the currently-addressed device is an 8- or a 16-bit device: M16# and IO16#. If the processor is performing a memory transaction, the bus control logic samples M16# at the end of the address phase of the transaction. M16# is only asserted if a 16-bit memory target decodes the address. It remains deasserted when an 8-bit device decodes the address.

On the one hand, the bus control logic examines the processor's A0 and BHE# outputs and determines that it is expecting to receive the byte over the upper data path. On the other hand, M16# is sampled deasserted, indicating that the device that decoded the address is an 8-bit device that will supply the requested byte over the lower data path. To steer the data to the correct path, the bus control logic enables a transceiver between the two data paths and commands it to copy the byte from the lower to the upper data path. The bus control logic asserts ready to the processor, indicating the presence of the requested data. The processor latches the data from the upper data path, completing the transaction.

The steering logic has to help out under the following circumstances:

- When the processor reads a byte from an odd-addressed location in an 8-bit device, the byte supplied by the target must be copied from the lower to the upper data path.
- When the processor writes a byte to an odd-addressed location in an 8-bit device, the byte supplied by the processor must be copied from the upper to the lower data path.
- When the processor performs a two-byte read from an 8-bit device, the steering logic must take the following actions:
  1. The 8-bit device initially only detects the access to its even-addressed location, and supplies the byte over the lower data path. This is the correct path, but the processor is expecting two bytes simultaneously, not one.

2. The steering logic latches the first byte and does not yet deliver it to the processor. It keeps the processor's ready line deasserted, forcing it to stretch out the transaction (by inserting wait states).

3. The processor does not change the address it's outputting, but the steering logic sets its A0 output to one, changing the address presented to the target device to the next, sequential, odd-addressed location.

4. The device doesn't look at the address again, however, unless the steering logic tricks it into thinking that another bus transaction has been initiated. This is accomplished by momentarily deasserting and then reasserting the read command line (either MRDC# or IORC#).

5. The target device examines the new, odd address and supplies the requested byte over the lower path (remember, it's an 8-bit device).

6. The steering logic copies the byte from the lower to the upper data path (because the processor expects to receive the contents of the odd-addressed location over the upper data path).

7. The steering logic then supplies the previously-latched byte to the processor over the lower path, while simultaneously supplying the byte from the odd-addressed location to it on the upper path. It then asserts the processor's ready signal, indicating the presence of the requested data on the bus.

8. The processor latches the two bytes, completing the two-byte read. The processor has been tricked into thinking that the target was a 16-bit target (albeit, a very, very slow one).

- When the processor performs a two-byte write to an 8-bit device, the steering logic must take the following actions:

1. The 8-bit device initially only detects the access to its even-addressed location. It accepts the byte presented to it on the lower data path. This is the correct path, but the processor is writing two bytes simultaneously, not one.

2. The steering logic keeps the processor's ready line deasserted, forcing it to stretch out the transaction. It copies the byte on the upper data path (destined for the odd-addressed location) to the lower path so it can get to the 8-bit device.

3. The processor does not change the address it's outputting, but the steering logic sets its A0 output to one, changing the address presented to the target device to the next, sequential, odd-addressed location.

4. The device doesn't look at the address again, however, unless the steering logic tricks it into thinking that another bus transaction has been initiated. This is accomplished by momentarily deasserting and then reasserting the write command line (either MWTC# or IOWC#).

5. The target device examines the new, odd address and accepts the byte presented to it on the lower path (remember, it's an 8-bit device).

6. The steering logic then asserts the processor's ready signal, indicating that it can end the write transaction.
7. The processor ends the transaction. It has been tricked into thinking that the target was a 16-bit target (albeit, a very, very slow one).

A detailed description of the ISA logic can be found in the MindShare book entitled *ISA System Architecture, Third Edition* (Addison-Wesley Publishing Company, 1995).

Figure 12-6: ISA Steering Logic

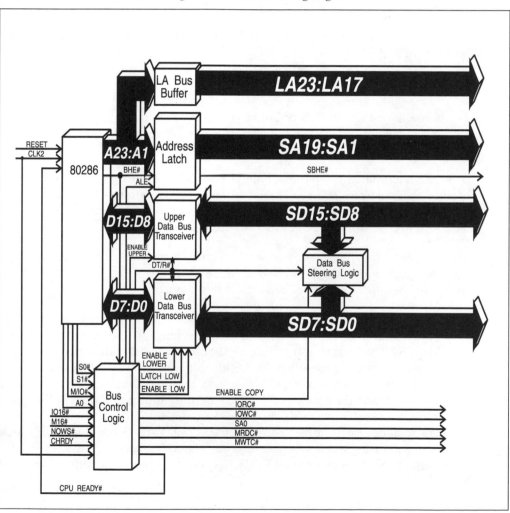

A Compatibility Problem. The operation of 8- and 16-bit devices has been described, as well as the steering logic's role in some transactions. This section describes a potential problem that can occur in an ISA machine.

Many 16-bit ISA memory devices decode address bits A[23:17] (these address address lines are actually named LA[23:17]) early in the transaction to determine if the address currently on the bus is within the range of addresses assigned to the device. Without examining address bits lower than A17, however, the smallest range a device could detect is 128K. Assume that a 16-bit ISA memory device has the following characteristics:

- It implements a 32KB memory buffer occupying the range from 0C0000h through 0C7FFFh.
- It decodes A[23:17] early looking for any address within the range 0C0000h through 0DFFFFh. Any access within this range causes it to assert M16#, indicating to the steering logic that a 16-bit memory device is the target of the transaction.
- Later in the transaction, it decodes A[16:15] to determine if the address is actually within its 32KB buffer. If within its range (0C0000h through 0C7FFFh), it takes part in the read or write transaction. If it isn't, the device does not respond to the transaction.

Also assume that the same machine is populated with an 8-bit ISA memory device that occupies the 8KB range from 0C8000h through 0C9FFF. In other words, it doesn't overlap the 16-bit memory device's 32KB buffer. It decodes A[23:15] to determine if the address is within its assigned 8KB range.

Now assume that the processor starts a read from memory address 0C8001 (actually, any odd address in the 8-bit device's range will serve for this example). This has the following effects on the two devices:

- The 16-bit memory device asserts M16# because the address is within the 128KB area it looks for early in the transaction. The steering logic detects M16# asserted, causing it to believe that the currently-addressed target can handle transfers over either (or both) data paths. Later in the transaction, the 16-bit memory examines A[16:15], determines that the address is actually not within the bounds of its 32KB memory buffer, and does not respond to the read.
- The 8-bit device examines address bits A[23:15] and determines that a location within its 8KB space is being addressed. Consequently, it drives the contents of memory location 0C8001h onto the lower data path.

Chapter 12: The PnP Configuration Registers

Because the steering logic sampled M16# asserted, it thinks that the target is a 16-bit memory that will supply the contents of the odd-addressed location on the upper data path. As a result, it doesn't copy the byte from the lower to the upper data path. The processor therefore latches junk from the upper data path.

A common fix on older ISA cards involved the inclusion of a switch or jumper on the 16-bit card that made it act as an 8-bit device. This causes it not to examine A[23:17] early in the transaction. Instead, it examines A[23:15] later in the transaction, sees that the target address is not within its assigned range, and therefore does not take part in the transaction. In addition, it does not assert M16#. This eliminates the compatibility problem, but results in diminished performance when communicating with the device (because it can only transfer one byte per transaction now). I'd rather have poor performance than a completely inoperable machine.

A better fix would be to design the 16-bit card to wait until later in the transaction before it did the decode and have it decode a sufficient amount of the address to accurately judge if it is truly the target. It can then assert M16#. This eliminates the problem and still permits it to function as a 16-bit device, yielding better performance.

This rather detailed description of the steering logic's function and the potential compatibility problem was included to highlight why the memory configuration registers include bits used to select whether the device operates as an 8-, 16-, or 32-bit device.

ISA vs. EISA Memory. The PnP specification defines configuration registers used to assign address ranges to ISA memory devices. In addition, it also defines registers used to assign address ranges to EISA memory cards. The sections that follow describe both the ISA and the EISA memory configuration registers.

ISA 24-bit Memory Configuration Registers. The ISA bus implements 24 address lines, A[23:0]. This provides an overall memory address range from 000000h through FFFFFFh—a total of 16MB of memory space. A memory device that resides on an ISA card must therefore decode the 24-bit address on the ISA bus to determine if it is the target of the current transaction. If the address decoder is designed to respond to a single, fixed memory address range, the configuration software cannot relocate the card's memory when its assigned range conflicts with that of another card. The designer should permit the address decoder to be programmed via the device's configuration registers.

Plug and Play System Architecture

Configuration locations 40h through 5Fh are populated with configuration registers used to program up to four separate memory address ranges to be recognized by the ISA memory associated with a device. Provision is made for more than one block of memory space because a logical device may incorporate more than one memory device. As an example, a device may incorporate a device ROM and a RAM memory buffer. This example would require two programmable address decoders to recognize the two separate ranges. Any access within one range should chip-select its ROM, while any access within the other range should chip-select its RAM.

Table 12-2 on page 169 provides a description of each of the ISA (also referred to as 24-bit) configuration registers. The ISA memory configuration registers consists of from zero to four register groups, each associated with a separate memory address decoder. Each register group is referred to as a memory descriptor in the specification and the descriptors are numbered from zero through three. Although the specification refers to these as descriptors, the author finds this term potentially confusing. The items in the resource data structure (described in the previous chapter) are also referred to as descriptors. For this reason, the author has chosen not to use the term "descriptor" during the remainder of this discussion of the configuration registers.

The configuration locations associated with a device's four ISA memory decoders occupy the following configuration locations:

- The configuration locations associated with ISA memory decoder zero are locations 40h through 44h.
- The configuration locations associated with ISA memory decoder one are locations 48h through 4Ch.
- The configuration locations associated with ISA memory decoder two are locations 50h through 54h.
- The configuration locations associated with ISA memory decoder three are locations 58h through 5Ch.

A logical device may implement anywhere from none of the decoders (if it has no ISA memory associated with it) up to all four of them (if it has multiple memory devices associated with it). If, for some reason, the configuration program has not programmed one of the decoders, this is indicated by clearing all five of that decoder's registers to zero, disabling the decoder.

Each of the up to four memory decoders consists of five locations (see Table 12-2 on page 169). The first two are used by the configuration software to assign the start memory address for the decoder. The third location specifies whether the decoder is an 8-bit or a 16-bit decoder and also specifies whether the fourth and fifth locations are used to assign the range's end address or its size.

Chapter 12: The PnP Configuration Registers

The first two locations are used to specify the base, or start, address of the memory range to be recognized. Using these two locations, the configuration program specifies the upper four hex digits of the six-digit base address. The address decoder always considers the lower two hex digits of the specified base address to be zeros. As an example, consider the case where the first location is set to 00h and the second to FAh. This means that the base address of the memory address range is 00FA00h. As a second example, setting the two locations to 20h and 00h respectively, indicates that the base memory address is 200000h.

The third location is referred to as the memory control register (see Figure 12-7 on page 168) and is used to define the decoder type (8- or 16-bit) and the usage of the fourth and fifth locations. Bit one of the memory control register can be implemented as either read/write or read-only. Making it read/write permits the configuration program to instruct a 16-bit ISA memory device's address decoder to act as an 8-bit ISA decoder. This would permit the configuration program to fix the type of problem that was described earlier in this chapter in the section entitled "A Compatibility Problem." If the ISA memory associated with the memory decoder does not permit selection of 16- or 8-bit operation, bit one can be hardwired to either a zero (if it's an 8-bit device) or a one (if it's a 16-bit device).

Bit zero of a decoder's memory control register is read-only and is used to define the usage of the fourth and fifth locations (these two locations comprise the limit/range register). If bit zero is hardwired to a one, the limit/range register is used by the configuration software to set the end (or limit) address (+1) of the range assigned to the decoder, and the start address assigned in the base address register can be any location (it doesn't need to be on an address divisible by the memory's size).

As an example, assume that bit zero is hardwired to one. This implies that the base address can be set at any location (i.e., it doesn't have to start at an address divisible by the memory's size). The configuration program writes the values 5Ch and 00h into configuration locations 40h and 41h, respectively. The assigned base address is therefore 5C0000h. It writes the values 5Ch and 30h into configuration locations 43h and 44h, respectively. This indicates that the end address of the decoder's assigned range is 5C3000h - 1, or 5C2FFFh. In other words, this address decoder has been programmed to recognize the 12KB range from 5C0000h through 5C2FFFh.

If bit zero of the memory control register is hardwired to zero, the limit/range register is used to assign a range length and the assigned base address must be set to an address divisible by the memory's size. As an example, assume that bit zero is hardwired to zero in the memory control register (implies that its start address must be located at an address divisible by its size) and that the configuration program writes the values FFh and 80h into configuration locations 43h and 44h, respectively. This indicates that the device has 32KB of memory (the easy way to figure this out is to note the binary-weighted value of the least-significant one bit in the 16-bit field in locations 43h and 44h; in this case, it's 32KB).

The memory on the device may be of a fixed size or it may vary. If the memory's size is fixed, only the base address would need to be set (the decoder inherently knows the size and therefore the range). The limit registers do not have to be implemented for a fixed-length device aligned on an address divisible by its size.

On the other hand, a particular memory device's size may be variable and/or it may support program-assignable address ranges. In this case, both the base and limit registers must be implemented. The memory's address decoder may be designed in one of two ways:

- It may be designed so that the base address does not have to be set on an address divisible by the memory's size. The designer would indicate this by hardwiring bit zero of the decoder's memory control register to a one.
- It may be designed so that the base address does have to be set on an address divisible by the memory's size. The designer would indicate this by hardwiring bit zero of the decoder's memory control register to a zero.

Figure 12-7: 24-bit (ISA) Memory Control Register

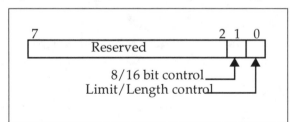

Chapter 12: The PnP Configuration Registers

Table 12-2: ISA 24-bit Memory Configuration Registers

Register	Location	Description
ISA Memory block 0 Base Address bits [23:16]	40h	This read/write register defines the upper 8-bits of the memory target's base address.
ISA Memory block 0 Base Address bits [15:8]	41h	This read/write register defines bits [15:8] of the memory target's base address.
Memory Control Register for ISA memory block 0	42h	• **Bits [7:2] are reserved**, read-only and must return zeros. • **Bit 1** is typically read/write. When set, the memory acts as 16-bit memory. When cleared, the memory acts as 8-bit memory. See description in the text. If the memory decoder does not permit selectable **8- or 16-bit** operation, this bit may be hardwired. • **Bit 0** is read-only and **indicates how the range/limit register is used**. If set, the range/limit register is used to set the memory's upper address (limit). If cleared, it is used as the range length. See text for additional explanation.
ISA memory block 0 range/ limit register bits [23:16]	43h	Defines bits [23:16] of either the upper memory limit (if bit 0 of memory control register set) or the range length (if bit 0 of memory control register cleared). See text for more information. Also see the next register.
ISA memory block 0 range/ limit register bits [15:8]	44h	Defines bits [15:8] of either the upper memory limit (if bit 0 of memory control register set) or the range length (if bit 0 of memory control register cleared). See text for more information.
Filler locations	45h-47h	Reserved. Do not use.

Table 12-2: ISA 24-bit Memory Configuration Registers (Continued)

Register	Location	Description
ISA memory block 1's register set	48h-4Ch	If implemented, these five registers are used to program the logical device's second ISA memory address decoder.
Filler locations	4Dh-4Fh	**Reserved**. Do Not use.
ISA memory block 2's register set	50h-54h	If implemented, these five registers are used to program the logical device's third ISA memory address decoder.
Filler locations	55h-57h	**Reserved**. Do not use.
ISA memory block 3's register set	58h-5Ch	If implemented, these five registers are used to program the logical device's fourth ISA memory address decoder.
Filler locations	5Dh-5F	**Reserved**. Do not use.

Intro to EISA Memory. EISA cards can implement PnP configuration registers and can be automatically configured in the same manner as PnP cards (in other words, isolated and then configured). These cards may implement 8-, 16- or 32-bit memory devices. An 8-bit device on an EISA card is implemented as either an 8-bit ISA or EISA device. A 16-bit memory device can be implemented as either an ISA or an EISA memory device. A 32-bit memory device must be implemented as an EISA memory device. If an EISA card only implements 8- and/or 16-bit ISA memory, the designer uses the 24-bit ISA memory configuration registers already described. If, on the other hand, the designer implements 8-, 16-, or 32-bit EISA memory on the card, the designer must use the 32-bit memory configuration registers described in the next section. The 32-bit memory decoder registers can be used to program 8-, 16-, or 32-bit memory decoders.

An EISA memory address decoder decodes A[31:2] plus the four byte enable signals, BE#[3:0]. A[31:2] identify the target doubleword (group of four locations) being addressed, while the four byte enable signals identify which of the four locations within the target doubleword are currently being addressed. BE0# corresponds to the lowest location in the doubleword, while BE3# corresponds to the highest location. The bus master generating the address communicates with the lowest location in the doubleword over data path 0 (D[7:0]), and with the highest location over data path 3 (D[31:24]).

Chapter 12: The PnP Configuration Registers

Note: It is a rule that a PnP card (either ISA or EISA) may implement either 24- or 32-bit memory decoders, but not both. They may not be mixed. To clarify, even if a card has multiple logical devices, each with memory, the memory decoders for all of them must be of the same type (ISA or EISA).

EISA Card Memory Configuration. Table 12-3 on page 171 provides a description of the programmable EISA memory configuration registers. With the following exceptions, they function in the same manner as the ISA memory configuration registers:

- While the ISA memory base address register is two bytes wide, the EISA register is four bytes wide.
- The memory control register uses a two bit field to define the address decoder as an 8-, 16-, or 32-bit decoder.
- The limit/range register is four rather than two bytes wide.

Table 12-3: Programmable EISA 32-bit Memory Configuration Registers

Register Name	Location	Description
EISA Memory block 0 Base Address bits [31:24]	76h	This read/write register defines bits [31:24] of the memory target's base address
EISA Memory block 0 Base Address bits [23:16]	77h	This read/write register defines bits [23:16] of the memory target's base address
EISA Memory block 0 Base Address bits [15:8]	78h	This read/write register defines bits [15:8] of the memory target's base address
EISA Memory block 0 Base Address bits [7:0]	79h	This read/write register defines bits [7:0] of the memory target's base address

Table 12-3: Programmable EISA 32-bit Memory Configuration Registers (Continued)

Register Name	Location	Description

EISA Control Register for memory block 0	7Ah	• **Bits [7:3] are reserved**, read-only and must return zeros.
		• **Bits [2:1]** are typically read/write and are defined as follows:
		    00b—8-bit memory
		    01b—16-bit memory
		    10b—Reserved
		    11b—32-bit memory
		If the memory decoder does not permit selectable **8- or 16-bit** operation, this bit may be hardwired.
		• **Bit 0** is read-only and **indicates how the range/limit register is used**. If set, the range/limit register is used to set the memory's upper address (limit). If cleared, it is used as the range length. See text for additional explanation.

EISA memory block 0 range/limit register bits [31:24]	7Bh	7Bh through 7Eh comprises the EISA memory block 0 range/limit register.
EISA memory block 0 range/limit register bits [23:16]	7Ch	7Bh through 7Eh comprises the EISA memory block 0 range/limit register.
EISA memory block 0 range/limit register bits [15:8]	7Dh	7Bh through 7Eh comprises the EISA memory block 0 range/limit register.
EISA memory block 0 range/limit register bits [7:0]	7Eh	7Bh through 7Eh comprises the EISA memory block 0 range/limit register.
Filler location	7Fh	Reserved. Do not use.
EISA memory block 1's register set	80h-88h	80h through 88h comprises the EISA memory block 1 configuration registers.
Filler locations	89h-8Fh	
EISA memory block 2's register set	90h-98h	90h through 98h comprises the EISA memory block 2 configuration registers.

Chapter 12: The PnP Configuration Registers

Table 12-3: Programmable EISA 32-bit Memory Configuration Registers (Continued)

Register Name	Location	Description
Filler locations	99h-9Fh	
EISA memory block 3's register set	A0h-A8h	A0h through A8h comprises the EISA memory block 3 configuration registers.

IO Configuration

The designer of a logical device may implement up to eight separate IO address decoders per device. They are referred to as IO decoders zero through seven. The designer must implement an IO decoder configuration register for each of the device's IO address decoders. Table 12-4 on page 174 defines the IO decoder registers, each of which is used to assign a base IO address for a separate IO address decoder. Unlike some memory devices, it is unnecessary to assign an end IO address for each decoder because IO devices have fixed-length blocks of IO ports. The only information the programmable IO address decoder requires is its base address.

ISA devices that only decode up to address bit nine do not need to implement bits [7:2] of the decoder's upper byte register. For a description of ISA 10-bit address decode, refer to the MindShare book entitled *EISA System Architecture* (Addison-Wesley Publishing Company, 1995), in the chapter on configuration.

As an example, assume that a PnP logical device implements two IO address decoders and that the configuration software has written the values 04h, 00h, 10h, and 00h, respectively into the device's configuration registers 60h through 63h. The base IO address assigned to address decoder zero is therefore 0400h, and the IO address assigned to decoder one is 1000h.

Table 12-4: IO Configuration Registers

Register Name	Location	Description
IO decoder 0 base address upper byte	60h	This read/write register is used to assign an IO base address to the logical device's IO decoder zero. If the device's resource data structure indicates that it only uses 10-bit ISA IO address decoding, bits [7:2] of the upper byte do not need to be supported.
IO decoder 0 base address lower byte	61h	
IO decoder 1 base address upper byte	62h	IO base address for device's IO decoder one. See description of IO decoder 0 in this table.
IO decoder 1 base address lower byte	63h	
IO decoder 2 base address upper byte	64h	IO base address for device's IO decoder two. See description of IO decoder 0 in this table.
IO decoder 2 base address lower byte	65h	
IO decoder 3 base address upper byte	66h	IO base address for device's IO decoder three. See description of IO decoder 0 in this table.
IO decoder 3 base address lower byte	67h	
IO decoder 4 base address upper byte	68h	IO base address for device's IO decoder four. See description of IO decoder 0 in this table.
IO decoder 4 base address lower byte	69h	
IO decoder 5 base address upper byte	6Ah	IO base address for device's IO decoder five. See description of IO decoder 0 in this table.
IO decoder 5 base address lower byte	6Bh	

Chapter 12: The PnP Configuration Registers

Table 12-4: IO Configuration Registers (Continued)

Register Name	Location	Description
IO decoder 6 base address upper byte	6Ch	IO base address for device's IO decoder six. See description of IO decoder 0 in this table.
IO decoder 6 base address lower byte	6Dh	
IO decoder 7 base address upper byte	6Eh	IO base address for device's IO decoder seven. See description of IO decoder 0 in this table.
IO decoder 7 base address lower byte	6Fh	

Interrupt Configuration

Each logical device on a card may be assigned up to two system interrupt request lines for its use. The selection is made via the interrupt configuration registers. The are two register pairs, referred to as interrupt configuration register 0 and interrupt configuration register 1. Table 12-5 on page 176 defines these registers. Bits [1:0] in the interrupt type registers are implemented as read/write when software has the ability to select these characteristics. When a device can only use an interrupt request line in one way (e.g., positive edge triggered), the designer hardwires these two bits to the appropriate values.

For a detailed explanation of interrupt operation in the ISA and EISA environments, refer to the MindShare books (Addison-Wesley Publishing Company, 1995) entitled *ISA System Architecture* and *EISA System Architecture* in the chapters on interrupts.

Table 12-5: Interrupt Configuration Registers

Name	Location	Description
IRQ select configuration register 0	70h	This read/write register is used to route the device's first interrupt to a system IRQ line. Bits [7:4] are reserved, while bits [3:0] are used to select a system IRQ line. A value of 01h selects IRQ1, 02h selects IRQ2, and 0Fh selects IRQ15. A value of 00h is used to indicate that a system IRQ line has not been assigned.
IRQ Type configuration register 0	71h	Bits [7:2] are reserved. Bits [1:0] are used to define the manner in which the device generates an interrupt request on its first interrupt line. Bit 1 Bit 0 Description 0 0 High-to-low transition 0 1 Active low, level sensitive 1 0 Low-to-high transition 1 1 Active high, level sensitive
IRQ select configuration register 1	72h	This read/write register is used to route the device's second interrupt to a system IRQ line. Bits [7:4] are reserved, while bits [3:0] are used to select a system IRQ line. A value of 01h selects IRQ1, 02h selects IRQ2, and 0Fh selects IRQ15. A value of 00h is used to indicate that a system IRQ line has not been assigned.
IRQ Type configuration register 1	73h	Bits [7:2] are reserved. Bits [1:0] are used to define the manner in which the device generates an interrupt request on its second interrupt line. Bit 1 Bit 0 Description 0 0 High-to-low transition 0 1 Active low, level sensitive 1 0 Low-to-high transition 1 1 Active high, level sensitive

Chapter 12: The PnP Configuration Registers

DMA Configuration

Each logical device on a card may be assigned up to two system DMA channels for its use. The selection is made via the two DMA configuration registers. There are two registers, referred to as DMA configuration registers zero and one. Table 12-6 on page 177 defines these registers. DMA channel four is not available for selection because it is used to cascade the slave DMA controller through the master DMA controller. For a detailed explanation of DMA in an ISA or EISA machine, refer to the MindShare books (Addison-Wesley Publishing Company, 1995) entitled *ISA System Architecture* and *EISA System Architecture* in the chapters on DMA and ISA bus masters.

Table 12-6: DMA Configuration Registers

Register	Location	Description
DMA configuration register 0	74h	Bits [7:3] are reserved. Bits [2:0] are used to select the first DMA channel used by the device. A value of 00h selects DMA channel zero, while a value of 07h selects DMA channel seven. A value of 04h indicates no DMA channel has been selected.
DMA configuration register 1	75h	Bits [7:3] are reserved. Bits [2:0] are used to select the second DMA channel used by the device. A value of 00h selects DMA channel zero, while a value of 07h selects DMA channel seven. A value of 04h indicates no DMA channel has been selected.

Reserved Device Configuration Registers

Configuration locations A9h through EFh and location FFh are reserved by the specification for the future definition of additional, device-oriented configuration registers and must not be used.

Vendor-Defined Configuration Registers

Configuration locations F0h through FEh are available for use as additional, vendor-defined, device-specific configuration registers. Definition of these registers and the bits within them is outside the scope of the PnP specification.

13 *Intro to PnP BIOS and OS*

The Previous Chapter

The previous chapter described the configuration register set associated with each PnP card and each logical device that resides on the card.

This Chapter

The purpose of this chapter is to provide a basic definition of some of the issues that must be dealt with by a PnP BIOS and a PnP OS. The term "BIOS" is defined, the configuration responsibilities of both the BIOS and the OS are introduced, static and dynamic configuration defined, and the PnP device ROM is introduced.

The Next Chapter

The next chapter provides a detailed description of the PnP POST/BIOS and device ROMs.

Definition of the Term "BIOS"

The term BIOS stands for Basic Input/Output System. It consists of a series of routines supplied by the system vendor. When a system is designed, the designers include a number of IO devices as part of the system's standard configuration. This would include devices such as the keyboard controller, display controller, a serial port, a parallel port, etc. Rather than require the operating system or the device driver programmer to know the exact IO register set usage for each of these devices, the system designers include a series of routines in the system ROM that is shipped with the system. These are referred to as the BIOS routines. When a programmer wishes to communicate with any of the standard devices, he or she issues a request to the ROM-based BIOS routine associated with that device. This routine converts the request into the corrected series of IO reads and/or writes to accomplish the request. The result is then returned to the calling program.

In addition to the BIOS routines, the system ROM also contains the power-on self-test, or POST, program. This program is the first one executed by the processor. It is used to test all of the embedded devices to determine if they appear to be working properly. In addition, the POST sets up all of the programmable embedded devices to operate in the manner desired by the system designers. The POST may also include a configuration utility that configures expansion cards (this functionality exists in EISA, PCI, and Micro Channel machines). In other words, the EISA, PCI, or Micro Channel configuration registers on each of the cards are programmed with the correct values to allocate non-conflicting resources to each of them.

At the conclusion of the POST and auto-configuration (if included), the system attempts to boot (i.e., load) the operating system software from the boot device. In a PC, this is typically floppy drive A. If there isn't a floppy in drive A, the boot program attempts to boot from the first hard drive. When the boot program finds the operating system (e.g., on drive A or C), it reads the operating system's startup code into memory and then executes it. The startup code is then responsible for reading the remainder of the operating system into memory and setting it up. To communicate with the standard devices, the operating system, device drivers and applications programs can call the BIOS routines in ROM. In some operating system environments, the OS and device drivers bypass the ROM-based BIOS routines and communicate directly with the IO devices.

The term "BIOS" is frequently (and incorrectly) used to refer to the POST, BIOS and the boot code in the system ROM. But, because it is now commonly used to refer to all of these entities together, the term BIOS is used in that manner throughout the remainder of the book.

Legacy ISA Devices Are a Problem

It is the responsibility of the system BIOS configuration program to allocate non-conflicting resources to the devices in the system. In order to achieve this goal, however, the BIOS must have explicit knowledge regarding the resources used by legacy ISA cards present in the system.

As mentioned earlier in the book, legacy ISA devices do not incorporate resource requirement lists, configuration registers, or any way to accurately determine the presence or absence of a card in the system. The revision 1.0A PnP BIOS specification contains the following text (in section 2.1.3):

> Unfortunately, it is very difficult, if not impossible, to accurately determine the resources used, unless these devices provide information about the system resources they will use. With this in mind, it is necessary for an external program to help isolate the resources that these devices are using. How this external program determines the resources consumed by these devices is beyond the scope of this document.

In other words, the PnP BIOS specification leaves it up to the system designer to provide a separate program that determines the resources consumed by legacy ISA cards. The method used by the separate program in making this determination is outside the scope of the PnP BIOS specification. Although the phrase "good luck" isn't used, it is heavily implied! In Windows 95, the combination of the Configuration Manager and the Device Installer fulfill this role.

Once the resource usage of legacy ISA devices has been determined, it is stored in some form of non-volatile memory (the type of memory and the format that the information is stored in are left up to the platform designer). The BIOS has explicit knowledge of where and in what form this information is stored and would access it to determine the resources available to be allocated to other devices (e.g., PCI, ISA PnP cards, PCMCIA cards, etc.).

BIOS and OS Share Configuration Responsibility

A typical PC system may incorporate the following types of devices:

- The processor.
- Main memory consisting of the DRAM installed on the system board.
- Embedded system board devices that may be configured by software.
- Devices embedded on the PCI bus on the system board.
- Devices on PCI add-in cards.
- Devices embedded on the EISA bus.
- Devices on EISA add-in cards.
- Devices on PnP ISA cards.
- Devices on PCMCIA cards.
- Embedded system board devices that reside at fixed IO locations.
- Devices on legacy ISA cards.

When the machine is first powered up, the OS has not yet been read into memory and executed. In addition, many of the devices installed in the system are not enabled and therefore cannot operate.

Ultimately, the combination of the firmware executed on power up (i.e., the POST/BIOS) and the OS initialization code are responsible for testing all devices, ensuring that non-conflicting resources are allocated to each of them, and activating all of them for normal operation. In addition, if any device(s) are installed or removed during run-time, the OS (and the BIOS) must have the ability to recognize the change in the machine's configuration.

- If a device has been removed, the OS must have the ability to deallocate the resources that were used by the device, thereby permitting them to be allocated to another device at a later time. It should also unload it driver from memory.
- If a device is added to the system, the OS must recognize its presence, read its resource requirements, allocate non-conflicting resources to it, and enable it for normal operation. It should also unload it driver from memory.

The BIOS may either handle the configuration of just the minimum number of devices necessary to boot the OS or may configure all of the devices in the system.

Case 1—Only Boot Devices Are Configured by the BIOS

The BIOS only configures and activates the devices to be used to boot the OS. When it has been read into memory and executed, a PnP OS is then responsible for configuring and activating all of the remaining devices. It is also responsible for any device removal or installation (deallocation/allocation of resources) that occurs from that point forward.

A non-PnP OS (e.g., MS-DOS) does not have the ability to detect and configure devices and therefore cannot utilize anything other than the devices activated by the BIOS. In order to permit full operation, the BIOS would have to configure and activate all devices. This topic is discussed in the next section.

Case 2—All Devices Are Configured by the BIOS

The BIOS configures and activates all of the devices in the system. When it has been read into memory, a PnP OS would then manage any device removal or installation event. A non-PnP OS (e.g., MS-DOS) can function correctly because all devices have already been activated by the BIOS.

The BIOS can handle the configuration of all devices in one of two ways: dynamic configuration or static configuration. The following two sections define these two methodologies.

Definition of Dynamic Configuration

Each time that the machine is powered up, the BIOS can automatically scan each bus in the system to determine the machine's device population and the resource requirements of each device. It can then allocate non-conflicting resources to each device and activate them. This is referred to as dynamic resource allocation.

Definition of Static Configuration

When the machine is initially set up, the BIOS scans all of the system buses to ascertain the machine's device population. The resource requirements of all devices are read. The BIOS determines a conflict-free allocation of resources and stores this information in non-volatile memory (e.g., in CMOS RAM). All of the devices are configured and activated.

When a PnP OS is loaded and executed, it assumes responsibility for handling any device removal or installation events. In both cases, it must update the system configuration information contained in non-volatile memory.

Each subsequent time that the machine is powered up, the BIOS uses the information contained in non-volatile(NV) memory to configure the machine. This is referred to as static configuration because the same, static resource image from non-volatile memory is used to configure the machine each time that it is powered on.

Of course, each time that the machine is powered on the BIOS would still have to scan the various system expansion buses to determine whether any new devices have been installed or any devices have been removed. In the event that one or more devices have been installed, the BIOS must then allocate non-conflicting resources to them and activate them for normal operation. Non-volatile memory must be updated by the BIOS to reflect the resources allocated to the new device(s). If any devices have been removed, the contents of non-volatile memory must be updated by the BIOS to deallocate their resources.

Definition of Static Device

A static device is one that is never installed or removed while power is applied to the machine. This would include all of the following:

Plug and Play System Architecture

- Devices embedded on the system board on any bus (e.g., PCI, VL, ISA, or EISA).
- Cards installed in ISA card slots.
- Cards installed in EISA card slots.
- Cards installed in Micro Channel card slots.
- Cards installed in VESA VL card slots.
- Cards installed in PCI card slots.

Definition of Dynamic Device

A dynamic device is one that can be installed or removed while power is applied to the machine. Some examples would be:

- Docking stations for laptop computers.
- PCMCIA cards (also referred to as PC cards).

The PnP system must recognize when a docking station or a PCMCIA card has been installed or removed. If a subsystem is installed, the subsystem is interrogated to determine the resources it needs. The configuration program assigns non-conflicting resources to the newly-installed device and activates it. If a device has been removed, the configuration software must note the fact that the resources formerly allocated to the device are available for future assignment to other devices.

Role of a Device ROM

General

The POST/BIOS code embedded within the system board ROM contains test and initialization code for the devices that are embedded on the system board. It does not contain test and initialization code for add-in devices that may reside on the PCI, EISA or ISA buses.

The developer of an add-in device frequently incorporates a ROM in the device, containing device-specific code designed to:

- provide a self-test for the device.
- initialize the device's registers to the desired state during system startup.
- provide a device-specific BIOS routine that understands how to interact with the device.
- provide a device-specific interrupt handler for the device.

Chapter 13: Intro to PnP BIOS and OS

In other words, the device ROM acts as an extension to the system board BIOS firmware. During the POST process, the system board POST/BIOS discovers device ROMs on each bus and executes their POST and initialization code. The method utilized to discover device ROMs is specific to the bus that the device resides on. The sections that follow provide a description of each method.

Legacy Device ROMs

The area of memory from 000C0000h through 000EFFFFh is reserved for assignment to legacy ISA device ROMs. It is a rule that a legacy device ROM must reside within this region and must start on an address divisible by 2K. The first four locations in the ROM must contain the following information:

- The first and second locations within the ROM must contain the hex characters 55h and AAh, respectively. This is the signature of a device ROM.
- The content of the third location indicates the size of the device ROM in increments of 512 bytes. As an example, the value 08h indicates a 4KB device ROM.
- The fourth location is the entry point (i.e., the start address) of the initialization code within the device ROM. After checksumming the ROM's contents to validate its contents, the system POST/BIOS executes a far call instruction to execute the initialization code within the ROM.

The last location in the ROM is the checksum byte.

The system board's POST/BIOS code scans the device ROM memory area (000C0000h through 000EFFFFh) attempting to locate a device ROM signature (55AAh) at each 2K address boundary. When a ROM is encountered, it is checksummed and a call is made to its initialization code entry point. Upon completion, the initialization code executes a return to the system board POST/BIOS's ROM scan program that called it. The scan program then proceeds to the next 2K address boundary to check for another device ROM. This process is repeated until the entire device ROM memory area has been scanned.

The ROM's initialization code sets up its device by performing the following actions:

- Executes a device-specific POST to test the device.
- Performs a series of IO writes to the device's control register set to set the device up for normal operation.
- If the device is interrupt-driven, the initialization program places the pointer to its ROM-based, device-specific interrupt service routine into the

entry in the memory-based interrupt table corresponding to the system interrupt request line used by the device.

- If the ROM contains a device-specific BIOS routine, it places the entry address of the routine into the correct entry in the interrupt table in memory.

The legacy device's ROM code has explicit knowledge of the device's register set base address and interrupt line usage. This information is either fixed at a predefined address and IRQ line or is selected by DIP switches on the card. The DIP switches can be read by the ROM code to determine the address and IRQ line.

It should be noted that the device ROM associated with a legacy ISA device may be upgraded to a PnP device ROM (assuming that the ROM is socketed). PnP device ROMs are discussed in more detail in the next chapter. Just upgrading the device ROM to a PnP device ROM does not give the legacy device the ability to be configured programmatically. However, it does permit the PnP system board POST/BIOS to automatically determine the device type and the resources utilized by the device.

PCI Device ROMs

The portion of the system board POST/BIOS that scans the PCI bus looking for devices (i.e., the ROM-based PCI bus enumerator) can detect the presence of a device ROM associated with a PCI device by probing its expansion ROM base address register. If the register is not implemented, the device does not have a device ROM. If it is implemented, the device implements a device ROM decoder. This does not necessarily mean that the device ROM is installed, however. The device may incorporate a ROM socket that may or may not be occupied.

The first four locations of a PCI device ROM are identical to that of a legacy ISA device ROM. The programmer reads the first two bytes of the ROM and checks for the device ROM signature, 55AAh. If detected, a device ROM is present. The ROM is checksummed, following which the system board POST/BIOS program executes a far call to the ROM's initialization code entry point.

This is where the process differentiates from that performed by a legacy device ROM's initialization code. The legacy initialization code "knows" the base address of its device's register set and the IRQ line that it utilizes. The PCI device, on the other hand, has a programmable IO base address for its register set and a software-selectable IRQ line. Before the body of its initialization code can be executed successfully, the base address and IRQ line assigned must be determined. This is accomplished by performing a series of calls to the PCI BIOS to access the device's IO base address register and to read its interrupt line register. Once this information has been acquired, the initialization program can perform its functions. In addition, it supplies this information to the body of the device driver in the device ROM so that it knows the base address of its device's IO control register set.

Another major difference in PCI ROMs is that they are **ALWAYS SHADOWED** (copied into) system memory. This means that the initialization portion of PCI device ROM code can perform memory writes into data structures within its own body (because it is really being executed out of system RAM). After the ROM's initialization code has completed execution, the POST write-protects the area of RAM that contains the ROM code.

A more detailed description of PCI device configuration and device ROMs can be found in the MindShare book entitled *PCI System Architecture (Addison-Wesley Publishing Company, 1995)*.

PnP Device ROM

As with the PCI device, ISA PnP devices utilize programmable configuration registers. In order for the ROM's initialization routine and the body of the device driver to determine the resources allocated to the device (e.g., base address of its IO control register set, etc.), it must be able to read its own configuration registers. To accomplish this, the PnP BIOS passes the initialization routine the card's assigned CSN and the IO address assigned to the configuration read address port. Utilizing this information, the initialization code can then read its device's configuration registers to determine its assigned base address, IRQ line, etc.

The next chapter contains a detailed description of the PnP device ROM.

EISA Device ROMs

EISA device ROMs are implemented in the same manner as those of legacy ISA cards. However, the ROM code can be rewritten to comply with the PnP device ROM model.

14 *The PnP POST and Device ROMs*

The Previous Chapter

The previous chapter provided a basic definition of some of the issues that must be dealt with by a PnP BIOS and a PnP OS. The term "BIOS" was defined, the configuration responsibilities of both the BIOS and the OS introduced, static and dynamic configuration defined, and the PnP device ROM introduced.

This Chapter

This chapter describes the PnP POST sequence and PnP device (option) ROMs.

The Next Chapter

The next chapter provides a detailed description of the services provided by the PnP BIOS.

The POST Sequence

General

When the machine is first powered up, the reset signal remains asserted until the power supply outputs have stabilized. This has two effects:

- it prevents any device from taking any action until the power has stabilized
- it initializes all device logic to a predefined state, thereby ensuring that all devices always start up in a predictable manner.

The assertion of reset at power up forces the processor to fetch its first instruction from the predefined power-on restart address when reset is deasserted.

This is the entry point of the POST (power on self-test) program in ROM memory. A typical PnP POST program has the following basic responsibilities:

1. Test all of the known devices for proper operation (to the extent that this is possible without user interaction and without the use of external test equipment). This includes testing main memory and initializing each memory location to a known state (to ensure proper parity is stored in each location).
2. After testing each of the embedded system board devices that are necessary for basic operation (e.g., the interrupt controller, DMA controller, programmable timers, etc.), software initializes these devices to the state they must be in for normal system operation. For a detailed description of these devices, refer to the MindShare book entitled *ISA System Architecture* (Addison-Wesley Publishing Company, 1995).
3. The software "knows" the resources (IO ranges, memory ranges, interrupt lines, etc.) consumed by embedded devices that are not configurable.
4. Software must scan all buses in the system (e.g., ISA, PCI and EISA) to identify all additional, configurable devices and determine their resource requirements.
5. Software then assigns resources to each configurable device, ensuring that the resources assigned to each do not conflict with those assigned to other configurable devices, nor with those consumed by legacy and embedded devices that use fixed resources (in other words, non-configurable devices).
6. If the software must boot a non-PnP OS, it must enable (i.e., activate) every device in the system so that they are available for use by the OS and application programs.
7. If the software must boot a PnP OS, it typically only activates the devices to be used during the process of reading the OS into memory. This may consist only of the mass storage device that the OS resides on, or, additionally, may include an input device (typically, the keyboard), and an output device (a display adapter).
8. Once the OS has been booted into memory, it is given control of the machine.

Detail of Typical POST Flow

The PnP BIOS specification is somewhat vague when describing the POST sequence. The specification does not define a strict sequence so as not to limit the BIOS writer's flexibility. Rather, it defines the major tasks that must be accomplished and the basic order in which they should be accomplished. The list that follows describes the sequence executed by a typical PnP POST. This example flow assumes that the POST configures and activates all devices in

Chapter 14: The PnP POST and Device ROMs

preparation for loading and executing a non-PnP OS. If loading a PnP OS, the POST might only configure and activate the devices to be used to boot the OS into memory.

1. Disable any configurable devices that come up in the enabled state. This might include PCI devices, EISA devices, etc. that have been designed to come up in the enabled state with predefined resources assigned to them. An example would be a VGA-compatible controller residing on the PCI bus that powers up responsive to the IO and memory ranges associated with a VGA-compatible device.

2. Using the process described earlier in the book, isolate each of the PnP E/ISA devices and assign a discrete CSN to each. Identify any of the PnP E/ISA devices that can be used as boot devices. Allocate non-conflicting resources to the PnP E/ISA devices. Do not activate any of the devices yet.

3. The POST builds a resource allocation map indicating the resources used by non-configurable devices (e.g., the IO address range used by the interrupt and DMA controllers). Assuming that the resources used by legacy ISA cards are stored in non-volatile memory, this information is included in the map as well.

4. A specific system may also maintain a list (in non-volatile memory) of the resources assigned to all of the installed devices configured during a previous session.

5. The POST selects and enables the input (typically the keyboard) and output (display) devices to be used during the OS boot process. An input and/or output device that comes up enabled that cannot be disabled is used as the input or output device. As an example, if present, an ISA-based VGA display adapter is used as the display output device. If the POST decides to use configurable devices, the selected devices should be enabled at this time. If any of these devices include PnP device ROMs, the POST should call the initialization code in the ROM at this time (to initialize the device). A detailed description of this process can be found in the latter part of this chapter.

6. Perform the scan for ISA device ROMs within the memory range from 000C0000h through 000EFFFFh. Each time that an ISA device ROM is discovered, call its initialization routine to initialize the ROM's associated ISA device. A detailed description of the ISA ROM scan process can be found in the MindShare book entitled *ISA System Architecture* (Addison-Wesley Publishing Company, 1995). If any PnP device ROMs are found during the scan, do not call their initialization routines at this time.

7. If a PnP device has been selected as the device to read the OS from (i.e., it is to be used as the IPL, or initial program load, device), perform a call to the device's PnP device ROM to initialize the device.

8. Allocate conflict-free resources to any devices in the system that have not yet been configured. As an example, scan the PCI bus and allocate resources to the devices found.
9. Activate all of these devices.
10. If any of these devices have option ROMs, call their initialization code to initialize the device. Do the same for the PnP ISA devices that have just been activated.
11. Call the program that attempts to read the OS into memory. This is referred to as the bootstrap loader program, and is called by executing an INT 19h instruction. For a detailed description of this process, refer to the section in this chapter entitled "Booting the OS."

At this point, the OS takes control of the machine, including resource management.

The PnP Device ROM

The PnP device ROM is also referred as an option ROM. The sections that follow provide a detailed description of its contents and usage.

The Purpose of a PnP Device ROM

The PnP BIOS specification provides an expanded definition of the format and function of the device ROM that is commonly found in legacy ISA devices. The primary purpose of the expanded definition is to aid the POST in discovering if a device can be used during the boot process. Although intended for PnP devices, non-PnP (i.e., legacy) devices may also include the PnP device ROM format. This has two advantages:

- Aids the POST in detecting if the device can be used during the OS boot process.
- Permits a PnP POST and/or OS to call a special routine within the PnP ROM that provides a list of the fixed resources used by the device. This aids the POST or BIOS in determining which non-conflicting resources are available for assignment to PnP devices.

It should be noted that the device ROM format defined by the specification relates only to x86-based platforms and may not be used by the POST in a system based on a different type of processor.

Chapter 14: The PnP POST and Device ROMs

Unless the reader wishes a detailed description of the PnP device ROM contents, skip the section that follows. For a description of the OS boot process, proceed to the section entitled "Booting the OS" on page 206.

The Format of a PnP Device ROM

Locations 00h through 19h of the ROM contain the same information that is found in the device ROM for a legacy ISA device. Table 14-1 on page 193 describes the elements found in this area. There are two deviations from the legacy ROM format:

- The area allocated (locations 03h through 06h) for the jump to the initialization routine has been expanded from three to four locations.
- Locations 1Ah and 1Bh are used to point to the PnP ROM header data structure (a description of the data structure follows the table).

Table 14-1: Option (Device) ROM Header

Locations	Length	Contents	Description
00h-01h	2	55h, AAh	Signature of a device ROM.
02h	1	*nn*	Where *nn* indicates the size of the device ROM in increments of 512 bytes. As an example, the value 04h indicates a ROM size of 2048 bytes.
03h-06h	4		Contains an instruction that causes the processor to jump to the entry point of the ROM's device initialization code.
07h-19h	13h		Used by many manufacturers to store copyright notice and/or other manufacturer-specific information.
1Ah-1Bh	2	nnnn	Address in the ROM of the PnP header data structure.

Plug and Play System Architecture

As stated earlier, the PnP ROM header data structure provides information to the PnP POST or OS regarding the ability of the device to act as one of the three boot devices. In addition, the designer of a non-PnP device may also supply a routine that reports the fixed resources used by the device. This aids the PnP POST and/or OS in ensuring that non-conflicting resources are allocated to PnP devices. Table 14-2 on page 194 provides a detailed description of the PnP ROM data structure's contents.

Table 14-2: PnP ROM Header Data Structure

Locations	Length (bytes)	Contents	Description
00h-03h	4	$PnP	These four ASCII characters are the **signature** of the PnP device ROM header data structure. The $ is stored in location 00h and the last character in location 03h.
04h	1	01h	This byte indicates the **revision** of the data structure format. The structure currently defined (defined by version 1.0a of the spec) is revision 01h.
05h	1	nn	Data structure **length** in increments of 16 bytes. As an example, a data structure length of 32 is indicated by a value of 02h.
06h-07h	2	nnnn	**Location of the next header data structure** in the ROM. If no other exists, this field contains 0000h. Additional data structures may be defined in the future and a ROM may contain more than one type of data structure.
08h	1	00h	Reserved.
09h	1	nn	This is the **checksum** of the entire data structure. Adding each byte of the data structure, including the checksum byte, must yield a result of 00h.
0Ah-0Dh	4	nnnnnnnn	32-bit PnP device ID (refer to Table 10-2 on page 73).

Table 14-2: PnP ROM Header Data Structure (Continued)

Locations	Length (bytes)	Contents	Description
0Eh-0Fh	2	nnnn	Start location of the device's **manufacturer ID**, represented by an ASCIIZ character string. This field contains 0000h if the manufacturer ID string is not present.
10h-11h	2	nnnn	Start location of the device's **product name**, represented by an ASCIIZ character string. This field contains 0000h if the product name string is not present.
12h-14h	3	nnnnnn	**Device type code**. The MSB of this three byte field is the general device type, while the second byte is the device sub-type. The LSB is the programming interface byte. The PnP BIOS specification refers the reader to appendix B of the spec for a description of this field, but the reference to appendix B is wrong. This information is missing from the specification. This is the same as the three byte class code field found in a PCI device's configuration header space. 'Appendix B—Class Code Assignments' on page 297 defines the currently-assigned class codes. For additional information, refer to the MindShare book entitled *PCI System Architecture, Third Edition* (Addison-Wesley Publishing Company, 1995), in the chapter on the configuration registers.
15h	1	nn	**Device indicator byte**. The bits within this byte provide information regarding the device's characteristics (refer to Table 14-3 on page 198).

Table 14-2: PnP ROM Header Data Structure (Continued)

Locations	Length (bytes)	Contents	Description
16h-17h	2	nnnn	**Boot connection vector.** Contains the start address (within the ROM) of the boot connection routine. If the POST determines to use this device as one of the three boot devices (IPL, input, or output), a far call is made to this routine with the parameters indicated in Table 14-4 on page 199. As a result, the called routine hooks the desired interrupt table entries. This value must be set to 0000h if the ROM does not implement a boot connection routine.
18h-19h	2	nnnn	**Disconnect vector.** Contains the start address (within the ROM) of the disconnect routine. If the system BIOS determines that the OS load failed, it calls this routine to perform a software clean up (e.g., restore interrupt table entries that were hooked by the device that failed).

Table 14-2: PnP ROM Header Data Structure (Continued)

Locations	Length (bytes)	Contents	Description
1Ah-1Bh	2	nnnn	**Bootstrap entry vector.** Contains the start address (within the ROM) of the device's bootstrap routine. This feature is primarily used to support RPL (remote program load). As an example, this may be the device ROM associated with a network adapter and a call to this routine causes an attempted OS boot over the network rather than from a local hard drive. The system calls this routine rather than the normal loader (via INT19h) under the following circumstances: • The device indicates (via its device indicator byte) that it is capable of acting as the IPL device. • The device indicates that it does not support the INT 13h block mode interface (in other words, INT 13h cannot be used to access the disk drive). • The device has a valid bootstrap entry vector. • The boot connection vector is not valid. The specification goes on to say that a complete description of RPL support is beyond the scope of the PnP BIOS specification and should be defined by a separate (undefined) specification.
1Ch-1Dh	2	0000h	Reserved.

Table 14-2: PnP ROM Header Data Structure (Continued)

Locations	Length (bytes)	Contents	Description
1Eh-1Fh	2	nnnn	**Static resource information vector.** Only used in a device ROM associated with a non-PnP device. A PnP device must set this value to 0000h. If valid, this field points to a routine that reports the device's static resource usage when called. When called, ES:DI must point to a memory buffer at least 1KB in size. Upon completion, this routine has loaded the buffer with a data structure describing the fixed, non-configurable resources used by to the device. The format of this data structure adheres to that described in the section entitled 'Structure of a System Device Node' on page 216. It deviates from the node definition in the following respects: • The device node number field must be set to zero. • It should only contain the **allocated resource configuration descriptor block**. The **possible resource configuration descriptor block** must consist only of the END TAG descriptor (because the resources used by the device are fixed and there are no other configuration possibilities).

Table 14-3: Device Indicator Byte Definition

Bit	Description
7	1 = indicates that the ROM supports the device driver initialization, or DDI, model. Additional information regarding DDI can be found on page 203.
6	1 = ROM may be shadowed in system RAM.
5	1 = ROM may be cached from.
4	1 = device code in this ROM is only needed if this device is to be used during the OS boot process.

Table 14-3: Device Indicator Byte Definition (Continued)

Bit	Description
3	Reserved (must be 0).
2	1 = device can be used to load the OS (in other words, it may be used as the IPL device).
1	1 = device can be used as the input device during the OS boot process.
0	1 = device can be used as the output device (i.e., the display device) during the OS boot process.

Table 14-4: Input Arguments for Boot Connection Routine

Register	Description of Parameter
AX	Although the specification specifies AX as one of the input registers, it only defines the contents of bits 7:0. The author assumes that this is the definition of the AL register contents and that AH must contain 00h. Bits 7:0 are defined as follows: Bit — Description 7:3 — Reserved (must be 0). 2 — 1 = Connect as IPL (hook INT13h, the disk BIOS function call entry point). 1 — 1 = Connect as primary output (hook INT 10h, the display BIOS function call entry point). 0 — 1 = Connect as primary input (hook INT 09h, the keyboard BIOS function call entry point).
ES:DI	Pointer to the PnP BIOS installation check structure. This structure supplies the ROM code with the system PnP BIOS entry points. This provides the ROM code with the ability to call the PnP BIOS. This subject is covered in the chapter entitled "The PnP BIOS Services."
BX	If this is an ISA PnP card, the BX register must contain the CSN assigned to this card. Using this and the IO address supplied in the DX register (see next entry in this table), the ROM code can access its card's configuration registers to determine the address ranges and interrupts that have been assigned to the device. If this is not an ISA PnP device, this value must be FFFFh.

Table 14-4: Input Arguments for Boot Connection Routine (Continued)

Register	Description of Parameter
DX	If this is an E/ISA PnP card, the DX register must contain the IO address of the E/ISA PnP read data port. See description (in this table) of BX contents. If this is not an E/ISA PnP device, this value must be FFFFh.

Discovering PnP Device ROMs

The POST discovers a PnP device ROM in the same manner as that used to detect legacy device ROMs—a signature of 55AAh is discovered in the first two locations on an address boundary divisible by 2K within the ROM scan memory range (000C0000h through 000EFFFFh).

When this signature is detected, a device ROM (either legacy or PnP) has been discovered. In order to determine if it is a PnP device ROM, use the pointer from ROM locations 1Ah and 1Bh to examine the PnP device ROM signature. If the signature stored in the first four locations of the data structure is $PnP, then a PnP device ROM has been discovered. If not, then the data structure is not present and this must be treated as a legacy device ROM. In other words, after checksumming the ROM, the POST performs a far call to the ROM's initialization entry point at location 3h in the ROM. It is not necessary to provide any input parameters, nor is it necessary to check for any return values in the processor's register set when the ROM initialization routine returns control to the POST.

Assuming that it is a PnP device ROM, the programmer then determines the data structure length and performs a checksum to validate the integrity of the header. If the checksum is correct, the ROM may be used. If not, an error should be reported to the end-user.

Calling the PnP ROM's Initialization Routine

The initialization routine within the ROM is executed by performing a far call to location 0003h in the ROM. The ROM contains a jump instruction starting at this location. When executed by the processor, it causes the processor to start fetching and executing the initialization code within the ROM.

Chapter 14: The PnP POST and Device ROMs

The functions that are typically performed by the PnP ROM's initialization routine include:

- Performance of a series of IO writes to the device's register set to set the device up for normal operation. In order to do this, the ROM code must know the base IO address assigned to the device's register set by the configuration software. Since this is a PnP device with a programmable IO address decoder, the ROM-based initialization routine must read its device's configuration registers in order to discover this address.
- If the device is interrupt driven and the designer has included a device-specific interrupt service routine in the ROM, the initialization code must write the start address of this interrupt service routine into the appropriate interrupt table entry. Since this is a PnP device with programmable interrupt line selection, the ROM-based initialization routine must read its device's configuration registers in order to discover which interrupt line has been assigned to its device.

For additional information regarding device initialization, refer to the section entitled 'The PnP Device ROM's Initialization Routine' on page 203.

To permit the ROM-based initialization routine to read from its device's configuration registers, the caller (i.e., the POST) must supply the input arguments indicated in Table 14-5 on page 202. It should be noted that this calling convention is only defined for x86-oriented PnP device ROMs. The PnP BIOS specification does not define the calling procedure to be used in other processor architectures (e.g., PowerPC).

The first argument (in the ES:DI register pair) tells the ROM code where the PnP BIOS installation check structure resides in memory. This structure (covered in the next chapter) supplies the entry point of the BIOS services so that the ROM code can call the BIOS to request the performance of configuration-related operations for it. It should be noted, however, that the ROM code cannot be assured that all of the BIOS services are currently available. Some of the BIOS services may only become available when the OS has been loaded into memory (i.e., the OS may provide a full-complement of PnP BIOS services while the system ROM may only supply a subset).

The second and the third input arguments supply the ROM code with the information required to access a PnP ISA card's configuration registers.

Table 14-5: Initialization Routine Input Arguments

Register	Parameter Description
ES:DI	Pointer to PnP BIOS installation check structure in memory (in segment:offset format).
BX	If a PnP E/ISA card, BX contains the CSN assigned to this card. If not an E/ISA PnP card, the value FFFFh must be placed in BX.
DX	If a PnP E/ISA card, DX contains the IO address assigned to the E/ISA PnP configuration read data port. If not an E/ISA PnP card, the value FFFFh must be placed in DX.

On Entry to PnP Device ROM's Initialization Routine

When the POST calls the initialization routine in a PnP device ROM, the routine must first determine if the system POST that called it is a PnP or a non-PnP POST. When it calls a PnP device ROM's initialization routine, a PnP POST supplies a pointer in ES:DI that points to the PnP installation check structure in memory. Using this pointer, the initialization routine reads the first four bytes from the data structure and determines if it consists of the ASCII character string "$PnP."

If the string is correct, this indicates that the POST is a PnP POST and has supplied the card's CSN and the address assigned to the ISA PnP read data port in the BX and DX registers, respectively. Using this information, the device can therefore access its own configuration registers to determine the resources that have been assigned to it. This information, in turn, can be used to initialize the device associated with the ROM.

If, on the other hand, the signature "$PnP" is not found, the caller is a non-PnP POST and the CSN and read data port address have not been supplied to the initialization routine. In this case, the BIOS specification says:

the PnP option ROM should initialize exactly as if it was a standard (non-PnP) ISA option ROM.

There are two situations: the device with a PnP option ROM may be a configurable or a non-configurable (legacy ISA) device. In the second case (legacy ISA device with a PnP option ROM), the ROM should use the legacy initialization method. In the first case, however, the configurable device has not been config-ured (i.e., resources have not been allocated to the device and it has not been activated). The initialization code cannot initialize the device if it doesn't know what resources it will be using. In the author's opinion, it would appear that the initialization routine should take no action other than to execute an interrupt return instruction (IRET) to return control back to the POST.

The specification states that some PnP BIOSs do not supply the check structure pointer in ES:DI when calling the option ROM's initialization routine. In this case, the option ROM's initialization code can determine if the system supports a PnP BIOS by scanning memory from F0000h through FFFFFh looking for the signature of the check structure on 16 byte boundaries. The specification also states that the option ROM's decision to perform a legacy or a PnP initialization must be solely based on the contents of ES:DI.

If the option ROM's initialization code detects the presence of a PnP BIOS, it may utilize the PnP BIOS to perform functions for it. However, because the OS has not yet been loaded into memory by the INT 19h boot loader program, it may not assume that the run-time BIOS services are available yet.

The PnP Device ROM's Initialization Routine

In some systems, the POST copies the device ROM code into system RAM, exe-cutes the ROM's initialization code, and then write protects the code image in system RAM. In other words, the ROM code is shadowed in system RAM mem-ory. This permits faster access due to RAM's faster access time and the fact that the data path between the system processor and system RAM is typically wider than that provided by ROM devices.

The PCI specification was the first to require shadowing of device ROMs (it is not required in ISA, EISA, Micro Channel, or PCMCIA). A detailed description of the PCI device ROM can be found in the MindShare publication entitled *PCI System Architecture, Third Edition* (Addison-Wesley Publishing Company, 1995). The sequence of actions taken by a PCI POST and the PCI device ROM code is outlined below:

1. The PCI device ROM is discovered in the same manner as any PC device ROM (by scanning on 2KB address boundaries from address C0000h through EFFFFh looking for the signature 55AAh).
2. When a ROM is found, the code image is checksummed and copied into system RAM.

3. The POST performs a far call to location 0003h of the ROM code. This is the entry point of the initialization portion of the ROM code.
4. The initialization code is executed. It performs actions such as initializing the device's IO register set, hooking an interrupt table entry to the interrupt service routine within the ROM's code image, and hooking an interrupt table entry to a device-specific BIOS routine within the ROM's code image. In addition, the initialization routine can update (because the ROM code has been copied into system RAM) any data structures within the ROM's code image (e.g., with the assigned IO base address and IRQ).
5. Upon completion, the initialization code may or may not adjust the length of the code image in RAM (e.g., to eliminate the initialization portion of the ROM code from RAM). This is accomplished by altering the image length field in the ROM header, re-computing the image checksum to reflect the new length, and storing the new checksum at the new end of the image. This can be done because the ROM header and code image are in RAM and can therefore be updated.
6. Upon completion, the initialization routine performs a far return to the POST.
7. The POST examines the length of the ROM image to determine if it has been adjusted by the initialization routine. If it has been shortened, the POST deallocates the RAM that is no longer consumed by the image, enabling it to be used again.
8. The POST then write-protects the ROM image in RAM so that it cannot be altered. The method used to do this is system design-specific.

The PnP BIOS specification refers to this method on the part of the POST and the device ROM as the DDIM (device driver initialization model).

Device ROMs designed for ISA, EISA, Micro Channel, and PCMCIA devices cannot be assured that the POST will shadow them. For this reason, the ROM code for these devices must be written so as not to perform memory updates within their code images. Optionally, these ROMs may include support for the DDIM as well. The ROM's initialization code can determine if the POST that called it has shadowed it by attempting to write to its data area. If it can successfully write into its data area, it has been shadowed and it may use the DDIM initialization sequence described earlier in this section.

The PnP BIOS specification states that PnP option ROMs *should* (the word *should* is 'fuzzy' and open to interpretation; the author thinks it should be changed to *must*) support DDIM. This permits the system POST to make better use of the device ROM area in memory (C0000h through EFFFFh). Memory isn't wasted on device ROM initialization code that is never executed again after the POST completes.

Return from PnP Device ROM's Initialization Routine

In its course of execution, the PnP initialization routine is permitted to hook any interrupts it requires and may update any data structures (e.g., the BIOS and extended BIOS data areas of memory). However, prior to completion and return to the POST, the routine must restore all of the items related to any boot devices to their original state.

On exit from the PnP ROM's initialization routine, information regarding the status of the associated boot device is returned in the processor's register set. Table 14-6 on page 205 defines the format of the information returned.

Table 14-6: Values Returned by Initialization Routine

Register Bit Field	Description of Returned Value
AH, bit 0	1 = IPL device supports INT13h (disk BIOS routine) block device format.
AL, bit 7	1 = output device supports INT 10h (display BIOS routine) character output.
AL, bit 6	1 = input device supports INT 09h (keyboard BIOS routine) character input.
AL, bits 5:4	00 = no IPL device attached 01 = unknown whether or not an IPL device is attached 10 = IPL device is attached (may be used for RPL) 11 = reserved
AL, bits 3:2	00 = no display device attached 01 = unknown whether or not a display device is attached 10 = display device is attached 11 = reserved
AL, bits 1:0	00 = no input device attached 01 = unknown whether or not an input device is attached 10 = input device is attached 11 = reserved

Booting the OS

Identification of the Boot Devices

The POST selects the devices to be used to boot the OS into memory in one of two ways:

- If any of the identified input, output or IPL devices come up in the enabled state, cannot be disabled, and used fixed resources, those devices are used by the POST to boot the OS.
- Assuming that the POST has no knowledge of any input, output, and/or IPL devices that come up enabled using fixed resources, and that it is able to identify (using the Device Indicator Byte in the PnP device ROM header) a configurable device that can be used to boot the OS, the POST configures and enables the PnP boot device(s) to be used to boot the OS.

Hooking Boot Device Interrupt Vector(s)

If a legacy ISA device is present, has a device ROM, and will be used to boot the OS, the POST calls the initialization routine within the legacy device ROM. This routine hooks the appropriate entry in the interrupt table to the device-specific interrupt service routine contained within its device ROM.

If a PnP device is chosen to be used to boot the OS into memory, and it has a PnP device ROM, the POST calls the boot connection routine within the ROM (see Table 14-2 on page 194). This routine hooks the appropriate interrupt table entry (or entries) to the device-specific interrupt service routine(s) within the ROM.

Reading Boot Sector Memory and Executing It

The POST reads the OS's boot sector into memory and executes it by performing one of the following actions:

- If the POST has selected a mass storage device within the machine as the boot device, it executes an INT 19h to call the bootstrap loader routine.
- If the POST has selected a device to perform the OS load from a remote site (e.g., RPL via the network), the POST executes the selected device's boot-

strap loader routine by calling the bootstrap entry vector found in the device ROM's header data structure (see Table 14-2 on page 194).

When executed, the bootstrap loader reads the OS boot program into memory and executes it. The OS boot program is responsible for reading the OS into memory. Once the OS has been read into memory, the OS boot jumps to the OS's entry point, thereby yielding control to the OS.

OS Startup

The OS initialization code is responsible for setting up all necessary data structures in memory (e.g., the page table, segment descriptor tables, etc.) and preparing to run applications programs.

OS Use of PnP BIOS

The OS may rely on PnP BIOS services contained within the system ROM or may contain its own set of routines to interface to the hardware platform (e.g., the HAL in Windows NT).

If the OS requires access to a PnP ROM BIOS, it must have some methodology to determine the existence of and the entry point to the PnP BIOS. This is accomplished in the following manner:

1. Scan the memory area from F0000h through FFFFFh looking for the ASCII signature "$PnP" starting at an address divisible by 16. If found, this signature resides at the start of a data structure referred to as the PnP BIOS support installation check data structure. The format of this structure is defined in Table 14-7 on page 208.
2. When the structure has been found, the OS performs a checksum to ensure it has not been corrupted.
3. In order to call the BIOS, the OS must know the entry point to the BIOS. For a real mode OS, this information is provided in locations 0Dh through 10h. The OS uses this as the target address of a far call to the BIOS. If the caller is a 16- or 32-bit protected mode OS, the entry point is provided by the information in locations 11h through 16h. The OS must create a read-only code segment descriptor in the segment descriptor table using the indicated base address. A far call is then performed with the segment portion of the call address specifying the segment table entry and the offset portion of the call address specifying the entry point of the BIOS within the code segment.

4. Prior to calling the BIOS, the OS must identify the data segment that contains the PnP BIOS's data area (thereby permitting the BIOS to access variables within its data area). If the OS is a real mode OS, this is accomplished by supplying the BIOS with the value specified in locations 1Bh and 1Ch. If the OS is a 16- or a 32-bit protected mode OS, this is accomplished by creating a segment table descriptor using the base address specified in locations 1Dh through 20h. The descriptor must define a data segment length of 64KB and make it a read/write segment. After creating the descriptor in the segment descriptor table, the OS must supply the BIOS with this segment selector. Upon entry to the BIOS, the DS register is set with the value supplied by the OS.

For a more detailed description of the PnP BIOS calling conventions, refer to the next chapter.

Table 14-7: PnP BIOS Support Installation Check Data Structure

Field	Offset	Length (bytes)	Value
Signature	00h	4	ASCII string "$PnP", where location 00h contains "$" and location 3h contains the last character.
Structure Version	04h	1	2-digit BCD revision of PnP BIOS that the BIOS complies with. The high-order nibble is the major rev number, while the low-order nibble is the stepping within the rev level.
Structure Length	05h	1	21h. Length of the data structure starting with location 00h.

Table 14-7: PnP BIOS Support Installation Check Data Structure (Continued)

Field	Offset	Length (bytes)	Value
BIOS Control Field	06h	2	This 16-bit field provides information regarding the PnP BIOS's capabilities. Bits Description 15:2 Reserved (must be zero) 1:0 00= no event notification 01=notification via polling 10=notification via interrupt 00=Reserved For more information on event notification, refer to the section entitled "Services Related to Handling of Run-Time Events" on page 240.
Structure Checksum	08h	1	Adding all bytes in the structure (including the checksum byte) must result in 00h.
Event Notification Flag Address	09h	4	If the BIOS control field indicates that events are signalled via polling, then this value represents the memory address to be polled to determine if an event has occurred. The BIOS indicates that an event has occurred by setting bit zero of this memory location.
Real mode 16-bit offset (IP value) to BIOS entry point	0Dh	2	PnP BIOS entry point in CS:IP format. The CS value represents the start address of the area of memory that contains the BIOS, while the IP value (instruction pointer) identifies the exact location of the entry point within the code segment). Locations 0Fh and 10h specify the start address of the code segment. Locations 0Dh and 0Eh specify the entry point within the code segment. A real mode OS uses this entry point to call the PnP BIOS. Also see description of locations 1Bh and 1Ch.
Real mode 16-bit BIOS code segment (CS value) start address	0Fh	2	

Table 14-7: PnP BIOS Support Installation Check Data Structure (Continued)

Field	Offset	Length (bytes)	Value
16-bit protected mode offset of BIOS entry point	11h	2	PnP BIOS entry point in base:offset format. The base value represents the 32-bit start address of the area of memory (code segment) that contains the BIOS, while the offset value identifies the exact location of the entry point within the code segment. Locations 13h through 16h specify the start address of the code segment. Locations 11h and 12h specify the entry point within the code segment (CS length is 64KB, so only a 16-bit offset is required). A protected mode OS uses this entry point to call the PnP BIOS. Also see description of locations 1Dh through 20h.
16-bit protected mode BIOS segment base address	13h	4	
OEM device ID	17h	4	The 32-bit EISA ID for the system board. This field is not required and must be set to zero if the system board doesn't have an EISA ID.
Real-mode 16-bit BIOS segment start address	1Bh	2	Indicates the start address of the system memory segment that contains the PnP BIOS data area. When the processor is operating in real mode, the caller must supply this value to the PnP BIOS. This enables the BIOS to access variables within its data area.

Chapter 14: The PnP POST and Device ROMs

Table 14-7: PnP BIOS Support Installation Check Data Structure (Continued)

Field	Offset	Length (bytes)	Value
16-bit protected mode DS segment selector	1Dh	4	Indicates the 32-bit start address of the system PnP BIOS data area. When the processor is operating in protected mode, the caller must create a data segment descriptor using this base address and supply it to the PnP BIOS. This enables the BIOS to access variables within its data area. The descriptor must specify a segment length of 64KB and provide read/write access to the BIOS data segment.

Boot Error Recovery

The Old Way (Boot Error Unrecoverable)

When INT 19h is executed, the boot loader program in a non-PnP PC typically performs the following steps:

1. The boot program attempts to read the first physical sector (512 bytes) from drive A: into memory.
2. If unsuccessful because there isn't a diskette in the drive, go to step 8.
3. When a diskette is present, the first physical sector is read into memory and checked for the boot sector signature, 55AAh, in the first two bytes. Go to next step.
4. If the signature is correct, the code in the boot sector is executed. This is the program that starts reading the OS into memory. Go to step 6.
5. If the signature is incorrect, an error message is displayed to the end user and the OS load process aborts. Stop!
6. Assuming that the boot sector program executes without error, the OS is read into memory and control is passed to it. If there's an error during the OS load, go to next step.
7. If there is an error during the OS load process, the actions taken are OS-specific. Typically, an error is display and the boot process aborts. Stop!
8. There wasn't a diskette present in drive A, so the boot program attempts to read the first physical sector (512 bytes) from the first hard drive. Go to next step.

9. If the attempt to read the first sector from the hard drive fails, an error message is displayed and the load process is aborted. Stop! If the boot sector is read into memory successfully, go to next step.
10. The sector is checked for the boot sector signature, 55AAh, in the first two bytes. Go to next step.
11. If the signature is correct, the code in the boot sector is executed. This is the program that starts reading the OS into memory. Go to step 13 if good signature or next step if not.
12. If the signature is incorrect, an error message is displayed to the end user and the OS load process aborts. Stop!
13. The code in the boot sector is executed. Go to step 6.

In other words, if the boot fails, the machine stops!

The New Way (Boot Error Recovery)

In the event that the OS boot fails when attempting to boot from a device with a PnP device ROM, a PnP machine doesn't give up! It attempts to boot from another device with a PnP device ROM.

When a PnP device ROM's initialization code is called by the POST, it should not hook any interrupts, nor should it alter the system BIOS data area in any way. When the PnP BIOS selects a device with a PnP device ROM to act as the IPL device, it either calls:

- the ROM's boot connection routine (BOOT_CONNECTION_VECTOR) and instructs it to hook INT13h and INT 19h. The POST then executes INT19h to execute the device's boot program.
- the ROM's BOOTSTRAP_ENTRY_POINT if the ROM incorporates its own bootstrap program (e.g., for remote program load, RPL, over a network).

When called, the ROM's bootstrap loader program attempts to load the OS from its associated device. If the selected boot device incurs an error while attempting to load the OS, it should restore the resources it modified (e.g., the INT13h and INT19h entries in the interrupt table, and any data in the system BIOS data area).

The specification states that the ROM code should then return to the PnP BIOS using INT19h or INT18h (the alternate boot loader instruction). The author is of the opinion (maybe mistakenly) that this is open to interpretation and will hopefully be clarified in the next revision of the PnP BIOS specification. Consider the following possible interpretations:

1. If an INT19h (or INT 18h) is executed without any further action, this will just re-execute the device's boot program, yielding the same failure again.
2. A far return can be executed to return control to the PnP BIOS.
3. The contents of entry 19h (or INT 18h) in the interrupt table could be altered to point to the BIOS entry point and INT 19h (or INT 18h) could then be executed. Although this would call the BIOS, what function call would be supplied to the BIOS?

It is the author's opinion that number two is the correct action. BIOS execution resumes at the instruction that follows the INT 19h in the BIOS. The BIOS can then select another device that also has a PnP device ROM to attempt to boot from and then re-attempt the boot.

15 *The PnP BIOS Services*

The Previous Chapter

The previous chapter described the PnP POST sequence and PnP device (option) ROMs.

This Chapter

This chapter provides a detailed description of the PnP BIOS Services.

Purpose of the PnP BIOS

The PnP BIOS not only is responsible for ensuring a conflict-free OS boot process, but may also provide configuration services to the OS during run-time. These services may include:

- providing the OS with information regarding non-configurable, embedded system board devices.
- providing the OS with the ability to interrogate and update the list of resources consumed by PnP, configurable devices.
- alerting the OS when a change in system configuration occurs during run-time (e.g., a docking station is attached while the system is running, a PCM-CIA card is installed or removed, etc.).
- a mechanism permitting the OS to utilize the PnP BIOS to manage the power consumption of devices that support advanced power management.

Embedded System Board Devices

General

The BIOS services permit the OS to access the node list to ascertain the resources allocated to the embedded devices. If a device's node indicates that it is configurable, the BIOS provides a service that permits the OS to select the resources to be used by the device. The system device configuration list consists of a series of data structures, also referred to as nodes, that identify the resources used by devices embedded in the system that provide basic system board services. This would include devices such as:

- interrupt controller
- DMA controller
- keyboard controller
- floppy disk controller
- system board timers
- an integrated (i.e., embedded) video controller
- etc.

These embedded devices may or may not be configurable. If a device is configurable, the device's data structure (i.e., node) defines the possible resource assignments for the device. The system device configuration list does not provide information about expansion bus (i.e., add-in) devices, nor does it provide information about peripherals connected to system board devices (e.g., the keyboard, or the display).

The section that follows defines the structure of a device node. Later sections in this chapter define the PnP BIOS services that interact with a device node.

Structure of a System Device Node

The PnP BIOS must implement one system device node for each device embedded on the system board. Each device node is a data structure that describes the resources consumed by the device. Optionally, an embedded device may be configurable (as opposed to using fixed resources). In this case, the possible combinations of resources that may be assigned to the device may be described in one of the following ways:

- in the device node data structure.
- in a configuration file (e.g., an EISA configuration file) supplied by the device vendor.
- in an image of the device's configuration file that is supplied in the system ROM.

In the event that the assignable resource list for the device is provided in both its node and a configuration file, the information in the configuration file will be used (it is assumed that the file contains more recent information than the ROM).

Table 15-1 on page 217 defines the format of a system device node data structure.

Table 15-1: System Device Node Structure (one per device)

Field	Size (bytes)	Description
Device node size (in bytes)	2	Size, in bytes, of this data structure.
Device node number (or handle)	1	Each node is assigned a unique handle by the PnP BIOS designer. This handle is used as an input parameter when the OS calls the BIOS and identifies which node is to be accessed by the OS.
Device product ID	4	The EISA device ID for the device. An example of an EISA ID can be found in Table 11-21 on page 131.

Table 15-1: System Device Node Structure (one per device) (Continued)

Field	Size (bytes)	Description
Device type code	3	The PnP BIOS specification refers the reader to the *Device Identifier Table & Device Type Code Table* for a description of this value, but the author could not find these tables in the referenced document. However, this three byte value is the same as the PCI class code field. If the OS cannot find a loadable device driver that matches the EISA device ID (see previous field), the OS can look for a generic device driver that has a match on the device type code. A complete listing of the class codes can be found in "Appendix B—Class Code Assignments" on page 297. For more information regarding the class code assignments, refer to the MindShare publication entitled *PCI System Architecture* (Addison-Wesley Publishing Company, 1995).
Device node attributes	2	This bit field provides information regarding the configurability of the device, as well as other device characteristics. Refer to Table 15-2 on page 220 for a detailed definition of this field.
Allocated resource configuration descriptor field	n	This is a sub-structure within the node and describes the **resources currently allocated to the device**. The format of this descriptor block is the same as that defined in the chapter entitled "Card Resource Requirements" in the section entitled "Format of a Logical Device's Resource List" on page 92.

Table 15-1: System Device Node Structure (one per device) (Continued)

Field	Size (bytes)	Description
Possible resource configuration descriptor field	n	This is an optional field. It is a sub-structure within the node and describes all of the **possible resources that may be allocated to the device.** If the node does not define the possible resources that may be assigned to the device, the only item contained in this field is the END TAG descriptor and the field checksum. In this case, the possible resource selections for the device may optionally be supplied in a configuration file delivered with the system board. In the event that this information is not supplied in either the node or a configuration file, the BIOS (and the OS) considers the device to be non-configurable. It uses the resources described in the allocated resource configuration descriptor field (see previous entry in this table).
Compatible device IDs	n	This is a list of the EISA IDs for compatible devices. This information can be used to identify and load a device driver that is compatible with the device. In the event that there are no compatible device IDs, this field only contains the END TAG descriptor and the field's checksum. For a detailed description of the compatible device ID, refer to "Compatible Device ID" on page 104.

Table 15-2: Device Node Attribute Field

Bit(s)	Description
15:9	Reserved (must be zero).
8:7	00 device configuration can be changed, but the new configuration does not take effect until the next time the system is booted (static configuration). 01 device configuration can be changed during run-time and the new configuration takes effect immediately (dynamic configuration). 10 reserved for future use. 11 device can only be configured during run-time (dynamic configuration only).
6	0=device is not a removable system device 1=device is a removable system device
5	0=device is not a docking station device 1=device is a docking station device
4	0=device is not capable of functioning as the primary IPL device 1=device is capable of functioning as the primary IPL device
3	0=device is not capable of functioning as the primary input device 1=device is capable of functioning as the primary input device
2	0=device is not capable of functioning as the primary output device 1=device is capable of functioning as the primary output device
1	0=device is configurable 1=device is not configurable
0	0=device can be disabled 1=device cannot be disabled

Calling the PnP BIOS

Prior to calling the PnP BIOS, the OS must establish the existence of and the entry point to the PnP BIOS. This procedure is described in the section entitled "OS Use of PnP BIOS" on page 207.

The OS calling the PnP BIOS is either a real mode OS (in other words, MS-DOS) or a protected mode OS. If it is a protected mode OS, it may be either a 16- or a

32-bit OS. The PnP BIOS specification defines a real mode and a 16-bit protected mode interface. A 32-bit protected mode OS must use the 16-bit protected mode entry point.

The Code Segment Descriptor

If the OS is a protected mode OS, the OS must construct a code segment descriptor in the segment descriptor table prior to calling the PnP BIOS. The descriptor must be set up as follows:

- uses the code segment base address specified in the PnP BIOS support installation check data structure.
- segment limit must be 64KB.
- code segment must permit read access.
- IO permission bit map for the current task must permit access to any IO ports the BIOS may need to access in order to perform the requested function.
- current privilege level, or CPL, must be less than or equal to the IO privilege level. This permits the BIOS to use instructions such as CLI and STI without causing an interrupt.

Data Segment Definition

The caller (i.e., the OS) must define the data segment to be used by the PnP BIOS. If the OS is a real mode OS, it supplies the BIOS with the value specified in the PnP BIOS support installation check data structure.

If the OS is a protected mode OS, it must create a data segment descriptor in the segment descriptor table. In creating the descriptor entry, it uses the 32-bit data segment base address specified in the PnP BIOS support installation check data structure as the segment base address. If it is a 16-bit protected mode OS, it uses the lower 24 bits of the base address as the segment base address. A 32-bit protected mode OS uses the entire 32-bit base address. The segment length is set to 64KB and the descriptor's access rights are set to permit read/write access to the data segment. The selector for this descriptor is supplied to the BIOS by the OS. Upon entry to the BIOS, the BIOS loads DS with the OS-supplied data segment value or selector.

Stack Segment Definition

The parameters associated with each PnP BIOS function call are supplied by the OS in the currently-defined stack segment. The stack segment must be defined as at least 1KB in size (thereby permitting the PnP BIOS sufficient stack space for its own use). Prior to performing the PnP BIOS call, the OS pushes the required parameters (the parameters required for each BIOS function request are defined later in this chapter) onto the stack. Because the PnP BIOS is implemented using 16- rather than 32-bit code, a 32-bit OS must only push 16-bit parameters onto the stack. The BIOS expects them in this form. If it is a flat model 32-bit OS, it must also convert any arguments that represent 32-bit memory pointers into segment:offset form and push them onto the stack as two 16-bit values. Figure 15-1 on page 224 illustrates the expected content of the stack on entry to the BIOS.

Assuming that a 32-bit OS follows these rules when placing arguments on the stack to be used by the BIOS, the BIOS always receives the input arguments in the correct form (as a series of 16-bit values) whether it is called by a 16- or a 32-bit OS.

Upon entry to the BIOS, the BIOS code must access the arguments that have been placed on the stack. To do this, it must know the base address of the argument list in stack memory. This is supplied by the current contents of the stack pointer register. There are two possible cases:

1. If the caller is a 16-bit OS, the 16-bit SP register points to the base address of the argument list.
2. If the caller is a 32-bit OS, the 32-bit ESP register points to the base address of the argument list.

The BIOS must determine if the caller is a 16- or a 32-bit OS and then copy the appropriate stack pointer register to the 32-bit base pointer register, EBP. EBP is then used along with an offset value to access the arguments on the stack. If the caller is a 16-bit OS, the BIOS copies SP to EBP (the upper 16-bits of EBP are cleared to zero) and then uses EBP to access the arguments on the stack. If the caller is a 32-bit OS, the BIOS copies ESP to EBP and uses EBP to access the arguments.

As an example:

```
mov  ax,[ebp+4] ;move function number from stack to AX
```

The PnP BIOS can determine which register to copy to EBP by interrogating the B bit (big bit; the specification refers to this as the 'big' segment indicator, but Intel documentation refers to as the 'G', or granularity, bit) in the 7th digit of the stack segment descriptor (refer to Figure 12-8 on page 223). The byte can be examined using the LAR instruction (load access rights). If the B bit = 0, all stack instructions (e.g., push and pop and call) use the 16-bit SP register and the processor assumes a stack upper limit of FFFFh (64KB). If the B bit = 1, the stack instructions use the 32-bit ESP register and a stack upper limit of FFFFFFFFh (4GB) is assumed.

Figure 12-8: 32-bit Segment Descriptor Entry

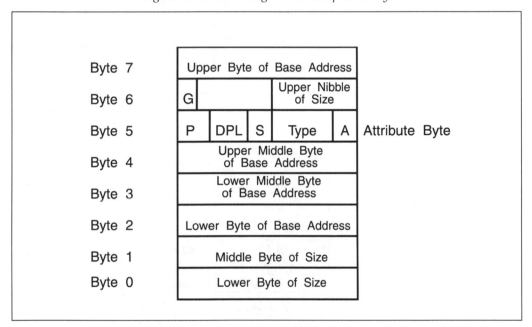

Plug and Play System Architecture

The following code fragment would be placed at the start of the BIOS entry code:

```
push    eax             ;save current eax contents on stack
mov     ax,ss           ;stack segment selector to ax for test
lar     eax,ax          ;load 2nd dw of descriptor into eax
test    eax,400000h     ;test 'G' bit for 32-bit segment
pop     eax             ;restore eax to original value
push    ebp             ;save current ebp value
jz      16BitStack      ;jmp if 'G' bit=0 (16-bit stack segment)
mov     ebp,esp         ;32-bit stack segment, so copy esp to ebp
                        ;execute body of BIOS


16BitStack:             ;jmp here if 16-bit stack segment
movzx   ebp,sp          ;sp->ebp and clear upper 16 bits of ebp
jmp     body of BIOS
```

Figure 15-1: Stack Contents on Entry to BIOS

MSB Arg 4	Location n
LSB Arg 4	Location n-1
MSB Arg 3	Location n-2
LSB Arg 3	Location n-3
MSB Arg 2	Location n-4
LSB Arg 2	Location n-5
MSB Arg 1	Location n-6
LSB Arg 1	Location n-7
MSB CS	Location n-8
LSB CS	Location n-9
MSB IP	Location n-10
LSB IP	Location n-11

Basic Calling Convention

The basic skeleton of 'C' language PnP BIOS function call is:

PnPBios (Function, arg1, arg2, arg3, etc.);

This procedure call causes the processor to push the function number and all specified parameters (arguments) onto the stack and perform a far call to the PnP BIOS entry point (supplied from the PnP installation check structure in memory). Upon entry to the PnP BIOS, the function and its associated parameters (arguments) are read from the stack and the request is processed. On return from the call, the SP register is adjusted to the start of the stack and the integer returned in the AX register is tested for a successful BIOS call (AX = 0000h if the request is successfully processed). A return with bit 7 of AX set indicates an error code, while a non-zero return with bit 7 cleared is a warning code (see Table 15-3 on page 225).

The following is an example of an assembly language call to the PnP BIOS:

```
push argument 4
push argument 3
push argument 2
push argument 1
push function number
call FAR PTR entryPoint
add  sp, n                 ;reset stack pointer
cmp  ax,SUCCESS
jne  error
.
```

Table 15-3: Error and Warning Return Codes

Return Code (in AX)	Value	Description
Success Code		
SUCCESS	00h	Function completed successfully
Warning Codes		

Table 15-3: Error and Warning Return Codes (Continued)

Return Code (in AX)	Value	Description
Reserved	01h - 7Eh	Reserved. The specification actually only states that 01h is reserved, but the author thinks this is an oversight. Also refer to Table 15-9 on page 245.
NOT_SET_STATICALLY	7Fh	The request asked the BIOS to reconfigure the device right now (i.e., dynamic reconfiguration), and the device's configuration options in non-volatile memory were to be changed as well (static reconfiguration). The device would be configured using the new configuration options each time the machine is rebooted. This warning indicates that the BIOS was able to reconfigure the device right now, but was unsuccessful in changing its configuration options in non-volatile memory.
Error Codes		
Reserved	80h	Reserved. The specification doesn't say that this error code is reserved, but each code must be defined in some fashion. The author would treat it as reserved.
UNKNOWN_FUNCTION	81h	Unknown or invalid function number passed.
FUNCTION_NOT_SUPPORTED	82h	The target function is not supported on this system.
INVALID_HANDLE	83h	Target device node number is invalid or out of range.

Table 15-3: Error and Warning Return Codes (Continued)

Return Code (in AX)	Value	Description
BAD_PARAMETER	84h	The function detected invalid resource descriptors or resource descriptors were specified out of order.
SET_FAILED	85h	The attempt to assign new device node data failed.
EVENTS_NOT_PENDING	86h	There are no events pending.
SYSTEM_NOT_DOCKED	87h	The system is not currently docked.
NO_ISA_PNP_CARDS	88h	No E/ISA PnP cards are currently installed in the system.
UNABLE_TO_DETERMINE_DOCK_CAPABILITIES	89h	The system could not determine the capabilities of the docking station.
CONFIG_CHANGE_FAILED_NO_BATTERY	8Ah	The system (a battery-operated laptop system) failed the undocking sequence because it does not have a battery. It can operate while docked by using the docking station's power supply.
CONFIG_CHANGE_FAILED_RESOURCE_CONFLICT	8Bh	The system failed to dock successfully because it detected a resource conflict with one or more of the primary boot devices (input, output, and/or IPL).
BUFFER_TOO_SMALL	8Ch	The memory buffer passed to the PnP BIOS by the caller (the OS) was not large enough to hold the data to be returned by the PnP BIOS.

Table 15-3: Error and Warning Return Codes (Continued)

Return Code (in AX)	Value	Description
USE_ESCD_SUPPORT	8Dh	This return code is used by functions 09h and 0Ah to instruct the caller that reporting resources explicitly assigned to the devices in the system to the PnP BIOS must be handled through the functions defined by the ESCD specification (functions 41h, 42h, and 43h).
MESSAGE_NOT_SUPPORTED	8Eh	Indicates that the message passed to the PnP BIOS via function 04h, Send Message, is not supported on this system.
HARDWARE_ERROR	8Fh	Indicates that the PnP BIOS has detected a hardware failure.
Reserved Error Codes		
Reserved	90h - FFh	Reserved. The specification doesn't say they are reserved, but they have to be defined in some fashion. The author would treat them as reserved.

Introduction to the PnP BIOS Services

Table 15-4 on page 229 lists all of the PnP BIOS functions and indicates whether each of them must be implemented by the PnP BIOS designer. A detailed description of each function follows the table.

Table 15-4: PnP BIOS Functions

Function Number	Function	Description
00h	Get Number of System Device Nodes	Required. This function returns the number of system board device nodes (data structures) and the size, in bytes, of the largest device node. The OS uses this information to calculate the size of the memory buffer required to receive all of the device nodes (number of nodes x size of the largest node). Each device node defines the resources used by a device embedded on the system board.
01h	Get System Device Node	Required. This function returns the node (data structure) of the specified device node in the specified memory buffer. It also indicates the number of the next device node (or FFh if this is the last node).
02h	Set System Device Node	Required. This function is used to provide a new configuration for the specified device node (assuming the device associated with the node is configurable).
03h	Get Event	Required if BIOS supports notification of dynamic events. This function returns a message indicating what type of system event occurred (e.g., docking station connected), or an indication that no event occurred.
04h	Send Message	Required if BIOS supports notification of dynamic events. This function can be used by the OS after the Get Event function has indicated that an event has been detected. The OS uses this function to instruct the BIOS as to how to handle the previously-reported event.
05h	Get Docking Station Info	Required if BIOS supports notification of dynamic events. This function permits the OS to get information regarding the type of docking station and its capabilities.
06h	Reserved	
07h	Reserved	

Table 15-4: PnP BIOS Functions (Continued)

Function Number	Function	Description
08h	Reserved	
09h	Set Statically Allocated Resource Info	Required if the system has an ISA bus on which legacy ISA cards may installed. The OS uses this function to tell the BIOS the resources that are consumed by all of the legacy ISA cards installed in the system.
0Ah	Get Statically Allocated Resource Info	Required if the system has an ISA bus on which legacy ISA cards may installed. The OS uses this function to obtain the list of resources consumed by the entire community of legacy ISA cards installed in the system.
0Bh	Get APM ID Table	Required if the system supports the Advanced Power Management (APM) specification (rev 1.1 or greater). This function returns a table that maps the APM device IDs to PnP device IDs.
40h	Get PnP ISA Configuration Table	Required if the system has an E/ISA bus with add-in connectors. This function returns a data structure that provides the total number of CSNs assigned and the IO address of the E/ISA PnP configuration read data port. Using this information, the OS can access each E/ISA PnP card's configuration registers to ascertain its current configuration and/or to alter its configuration.
41h	Get ESCD Info	Required if the BIOS supports the ESCD specification. This function returns information regarding the non-volatile memory (e.g., its size and location) used to store the ESCD data structure.
42h	Read ESCD Data	Required if the BIOS supports the ESCD specification. This function is used to read the contents of the ESCD from non-volatile memory.
43h	Write ESCD Data	Required if the BIOS supports the ESCD specification. This function is used to update the ESCD in non-volatile memory.

Static vs. Dynamic Device Configuration

The PnP BIOS specification makes frequent reference to static and dynamic configuration of a device. A request issued to the BIOS to change the configuration of a device immediately by altering the contents of one or more of its configuration registers is referred to as dynamic configuration (in other words, reconfigure the device right now!).

Alternatively, the OS can request that the BIOS alter the configuration information in non-volatile memory that is associated with a device. The altered configuration will not take effect until the next time that the machine is rebooted. This is referred to as static configuration.

If a device's dynamic configuration is changed, but not its static configuration, the device's configuration is altered for the duration of the current session but will revert to the original configuration the next time that the machine is rebooted.

Services Related to Embedded Devices

Functions 00h, 01h, and 02h are used to read and update the configuration information for devices embedded on the system board. The sections that follow provide a detailed explanation of each of these functions.

Function 00h—Get Number of System Device Nodes

Function 00h Description. This is a required function. Function 00h supplies the OS with the total number of embedded system board device nodes. It also returns the size of the largest of the device nodes (in bytes). This value may be multiplied by the total number of device nodes to determine the size of the memory buffer necessary to hold all of the device nodes (the contents of each device node may be fetched into the buffer using function 01h).

After a warm or a hot docking, the BIOS must update the system board node list to include any newly discovered system devices found in the docking station. When the system is undocked, the docking station devices must be removed from the node list. The PnP OS must cause the PnP BIOS to re-enumerate all embedded system board devices and docking station system devices each time that a DOCK_CHANGED or a SYSTEM_DEVICE_CHANGED message is received from the BIOS. The system devices must also be re-enumerated whenever the system emerges from sleep (suspend) mode (to ensure that no devices were removed or installed during the sleep period).

The BIOS must ensure that the node numbers of the system devices (those located in the system, not those in the docking station) do not change when the system is docked or undocked. The specification provides the following example:

> An undocked system may report device nodes 0-11. When the system detects the hot-insertion of a modem (in the base system, not in a docking station) it then reports device nodes 0-12. When the system is later docked, it can report more devices (e.g., 0-12 for the system devices and 20-22 for the additional system devices detected in the docking station). If the modem is removed, the BIOS reports device nodes 0-11 and 20-22.

Backward-Compatibility Note. In the first version of the PnP BIOS specification, the NumNodes argument (see Table 15-5 on page 232) was originally specified as a WORD (two bytes) and then later changed to a CHAR (one byte). In order to ensure backward-compatibility, all OSs and other programs that may call function 00h must expect a word and then clear the upper byte upon return.

Function 00h Input Arguments. Table 15-5 on page 232 defines the input arguments that must be supplied to the PnP BIOS when calling function 00h.

Table 15-5: Function 00h Input Arguments

Name	Size (bytes)	Description
Function	2	Function number value 0000h, represented as a 16-bit signed integer.
NumNodes	4	32-bit pointer to the 8-bit memory location where the function returns the number of nodes that the PnP BIOS has access to. The number returned is represented as an unsigned 8-bit value. Each node is a data structure that describes the resources used by an embedded system board device. The pointer is supplied in segment:offset form.

Table 15-5: Function 00h Input Arguments (Continued)

Name	Size (bytes)	Description
NodeSize	4	32-bit pointer to the two memory locations where the function returns the size, in bytes, of the largest device node. The value returned is represented as a 16-bit unsigned integer. The pointer is supplied in segment:offset form.
BiosSelector	2	• If the caller is a protected mode OS, the OS must create a data segment descriptor in the descriptor table using the base address obtained from the PnP installation check structure. The data segment must have a length of 64KB and permit read/write access. The value supplied in the BiosSelector argument is the 16-bit selector that identifies the location of the descriptor within the descriptor table. • If the caller is a real mode OS, the value supplied is the 16-bit real mode DS value obtained from the installation check structure. Upon entry, the BIOS loads the supplied value into the DS register so that it can access its data area in memory.

Synopsis of Function 00h Procedure. The following is a synopsis of the function 00h procedure:

```
int FAR (*entryPoint)(Function, NumNodes, NodeSize, BiosSelector);
int Function;                      /* PnP function 0000h */
unsigned char FAR *NumNodes;       /* Number of nodes that exist */
unsigned int FAR *NodeSize;        /* Size, in bytes, of largest node */
unsigned int BiosSelector;         /* PnP BIOS DS value */
```

Example Function 00h Assembly Language Procedure Call. The following is an example assembly language function 00h PnP BIOS call.

```
push  BiosSelector         ;DS value>stack
push  segment of NodeSize  ;NodeSize segment address>stack
push  offset of NodeSize   ;NodeSize offset address>stack
push  segment of NumNodes  ;NumNodes segment address>stack
push  offset of NumNodes   ;NumNodes offset address>stack
push  GET_NUM_NODES        ;Function 0000h>stack
call  FAR PTR entryPoint   ;call BIOS
add   sp,12                ;reset stack pointer
cmp   ax,SUCCESS           ;test return code
jne   error                ;jmp to error if non-zero,else proceed
```

Function 00h Return Values. On return, all registers other than AX are preserved. The content of the AX register indicates success or failure of the function request. A value of 0000h indicates success. A non-zero value with bit 7 set to one indicates an error code, while a non-zero value with bit 7 cleared to zero indicates a warning code. These codes are defined in Table 15-3 on page 225.

Function 01h—Get System Device Node

Function 01h Description. This is a required function. Function 01h copies the specified device node's (Node) data structure into the devNodeBuffer in memory. The node data is formatted as indicated in Table 15-1 on page 217. A Node number of 00h indicates the first node, 01h the second, etc. Also refer to the description of the Control argument in Table 15-5 on page 232.

Function 01h Input Arguments. Table 15-5 on page 232 defines the input arguments that must be supplied to the PnP BIOS when calling function 01h.

Table 15-6: Function 01h Input Arguments

Name	Size (bytes)	Description
Function	2	Function number value 0001h, represented as a 16-bit signed integer.
Node	4	32-bit pointer to the 8-bit memory location where caller (i.e., the OS) supplies the device node to be fetched. The number supplied in Node is represented as an unsigned 8-bit value. The pointer is supplied in segment:offset form.
devNodeBuffer	4	32-bit pointer to the memory buffer (data structure) where the function must return the requested device node. The pointer is supplied in segment:offset form.

Table 15-6: Function 01h Input Arguments (Continued)

Name	Size (bytes)	Description
Control	2	The lower two bits (1:0) of this 16-bit value tell the BIOS to return either the current configuration of the device (dynamic configuration information), or the way it will be configured the next time the machine is rebooted (the device's static configuration information). The Control argument is defined as follows: Bit(s)　Description 15:2　　Reserved. 　1　　　0=do not return the info regarding how the device will be configured on the next boot. 　　　　　1=return the info regarding how the device will be configured on the next boot. 　0　　　0=do not return the device's current configuration. 　　　　　1=return the device's current configuration. If both bits are set to one by the OS, the BIOS must return the BAD_PARAMETER error code.
BiosSelector	2	• If the caller is a protected mode OS, the OS must create a data segment descriptor in the descriptor table using the base address obtained from the PnP installation check structure. The data segment must have a length of 64KB and permit read/write access. The value supplied in the BiosSelector argument is the 16-bit selector that identifies the location of the descriptor within the descriptor table. • If the caller is a real mode OS, the value supplied is the 16-bit real mode DS value obtained from the installation check structure. Upon entry, the BIOS loads the supplied value into the DS register so that it can access its data area in memory.

Synopsis of Function 01h Procedure. The following is a synopsis of the function 01h procedure:

```
int FAR (*entryPoint)(Function,Node,devNodeBuffer,Control,BiosSelector);
int Function;                    /* PnP function 0001h */
unsigned char FAR *Node;         /* Number of node to retrieve */
struct DEV_NODE FAR *devNodeBuffer; /* Buffer to deposit node data in */
unsigned int Control;            /* Control Flag */
unsigned int BiosSelector;       /* PnP BIOS DS value */
```

Example Function 01h Assembly Language Procedure Call. The following is an example assembly language function 01h PnP BIOS call.

```
push  BiosSelector              ;DS value>stack
push  Control Flag              ;Control Flag>stack
push  segment of devNodeBuffer  ;devNodeBuffer segment>stack
push  offset of devNodeBuffer   ;devNodeBuffer offset>stack
push  segment of Node           ;Node segment>stack
push  offset of Node            ;Node offset>stack
push  GET_DEVICE_NODE           ;Function 0001h>stack
call  FAR PTR entryPoint        ;call BIOS
add   sp,14                     ;reset stack pointer
cmp   ax,SUCCESS                ;test return code
jne   error                     ;jmp to error if non-zero,
                                ;else proceed
```

Function 01h Return Values. On return, the Node argument is updated with the number of the next node, or with FFh if this is the last node. The devNodeBuffer in memory contains the node data for the requested device. The node data is formatted as indicated in Table 15-1 on page 217. All registers other than AX are preserved. The content of the AX register indicates success or failure of the function request. A value of 0000h indicates success. A non-zero value with bit 7 set to one indicates an error code, while a non-zero value with bit 7 cleared to zero indicates a warning code. These codes are defined in Table 15-3 on page 225.

Function 02h—Set System Device Node

Function 02h Description. This is a required function. Function 02h updates the configuration of the device (either immediately or the next time the machine is rebooted, as defined by the Control argument in Table 15-5 on page 232) associated with the specified device node's (Node) data structure using the information supplied in the devNodeBuffer in memory. The format of the data supplied in the devNodeBuffer is defined in Table 15-1 on page 217. A Node number of 00h indicates the first node, 01h the second, etc. The correct procedure would be:

1. Use function 01h, GET_DEVICE_NODE, to fetch a copy of the current device configuration into a memory buffer.
2. Within the supplied copy of the node data, alter the items to be changed in the **allocated resource configuration block** to alter the desired aspects of the device's configuration.
3. Use function 02h, specifying the updated memory buffer as the source buffer, to update the device's configuration (statically or dynamically).

The OS must supply a buffer containing all of the resource assignments for the target device, including those that are not being changed. This is necessary because the content and order of the elements within the buffer define the order of the device's configuration registers for the BIOS. For this reason, leaving out resource descriptors or supplying them in the incorrect order will cause the BIOS to configure the device' configuration registers incorrectly. This function does not validate the new resource settings or the checksum passed by the OS, and may not return an error code if there are errors in these areas.

To disable the device, set all of the resource descriptors in the **allocated resource configuration block** of the buffer to zero. If a device has only a single configuration option and it can be enabled and disabled via software, that configuration option must be included in the **possible resource configuration options** for that device.

Function 02h Input Arguments. Table 15-5 on page 232 defines the input arguments that must be supplied to the PnP BIOS when calling function 02h.

Table 15-7: Function 02h Input Arguments

Name	Size (bytes)	Description
Function	2	Function number value 0002h, represented as a 16-bit signed integer.
Node	2	Caller (i.e., the OS) supplies the device node to be updated. The number supplied in Node is represented as an unsigned 8-bit value. The upper 8-bits aren't used by the BIOS.

Table 15-7: Function 02h Input Arguments (Continued)

Name	Size (bytes)	Description
devNodeBuffer	4	32-bit pointer to the memory buffer that contains the data structure to be used in updating the target node. The pointer is supplied in segment:offset form.
Control	2	The lower two bits (1:0) of this 16-bit value tell the BIOS to either change the configuration of the device immediately (dynamic configuration), or to store the new configuration for use in reconfiguring the device at the next reboot (static configuration). The Control argument is defined as follows:

Bit(s)   Description

15:2	Reserved.
1	0=do not instruct the BIOS to reconfigure the device on the next boot. 1=instruct the BIOS to reconfigure the device on the next boot.
0	0=do not reconfigure the device immediately. 1=reconfigure the device immediately.

If both bits are cleared to zero by the OS, the BIOS must return the BAD_PARAMETER error code. If both bits are set to one, the BIOS reconfigures the device immediately and should also attempt to update non-volatile memory so the device configuration is also changed at the next boot. If the immediate device configuration completes successfully, but the configuration memory cannot be updated, the BIOS must return the NOT_SET_STATICALLY warning code.

Chapter 15: The PnP BIOS Services

Table 15-7: Function 02h Input Arguments (Continued)

Name	Size (bytes)	Description
BiosSelector	2	• If the caller is a protected mode OS, the OS must create a data segment descriptor in the descriptor table using the base address obtained from the PnP installation check structure. The data segment must have a length of 64KB and permit read/write access. The value supplied in the BiosSelector argument is the 16-bit selector that identifies the location of the descriptor within the descriptor table. • If the caller is a real mode OS, the value supplied is the 16-bit real mode DS value obtained from the installation check structure. Upon entry, the BIOS loads the supplied value into the DS register so that it can access its data area in memory.

Synopsis of Function 02h Procedure. The following is a synopsis of the function 02h procedure:

```
int FAR (*entryPoint)(Function,Node,devNodeBuffer,Control,BiosSelector);
int Function;                      /* PnP function 0002h */
unsigned char Node;                /* Number of node to update */
struct DEV_NODE FAR *devNodeBuffer; /* Buffer containing update data */
unsigned int Control;              /* Control Flag */
unsigned int BiosSelector;         /* PnP BIOS DS value */
```

Example Function 02h Assembly Language Procedure Call. The following is an example assembly language function 02h PnP BIOS call.

```
    push  BiosSelector              ;DS value>stack
    push  Control Flag              ;Control Flag>stack
    push  segment of devNodeBuffer  ;devNodeBuffer segment>stack
    push  offset of devNodeBuffer   ;devNodeBuffer offset>stack
    push  Node                      ;Node number>stack
    push  SET_DEVICE_NODE           ;Function 0002h>stack
    call  FAR PTR entryPoint        ;call BIOS
    add   sp,12                     ;reset stack pointer
    cmp   ax,SUCCESS                ;test return code
    jne   error                     ;jmp to error if non-zero,
                                    ;else proceed
```

Plug and Play System Architecture

Function 02h Return Values. All registers other than AX are preserved. The content of the AX register indicates success or failure of the function request. A value of 0000h indicates success. A non-zero value with bit 7 set to one indicates an error code, while a non-zero value with bit 7 cleared to zero indicates a warning code. These codes are defined in Table 15-3 on page 225.

Services Related to Handling of Run-Time Events

Background

The PnP BIOS <u>may optionally provide</u> support for run-time changes in the system configuration. A classic example is a notebook system that supports the 'hot' installation of the system into a docking station. In this case, the PnP BIOS must have the capability to signal an event to the OS both when the system is first docked as well as when it is removed from the docking station. It must also provide the ability for the OS to fetch information about the docking station from the BIOS. The system may also support the hot installation and removal of system devices such as the floppy drive unit, or may support other, manufacturer-specific events. As part of event management, the PnP BIOS must also support the ability of the OS to pass messages that permit it to communicate with the BIOS in response to an event.

The functions associated with event management are:

- Function 03h—Get Event
- Function 04h—Send Message
- Function 05h—Get Docking Station Information

It should be noted that these functions (and the PnP BIOS in general) are only associated with events associated with the system board logic—not with expansion devices such as PCMCIA cards. The installation and removal events generated by PCMCIA cards are handled (as they have always been) by the PCMCIA Card Services program (in Windows 95, the PCMCIA bus enumerator).

The sections that follow provide detailed information regarding each of these functions.

Methods Used for Event Notification

If event notification is implemented by the PnP BIOS, the occurrence of an event is signalled to the OS by one of two methods:

- generation of an interrupt
- setting a status bit in memory that is periodically polled by the OS

The OS determines whether or not the BIOS supports event notification and, if it does, the notification method by looking at the Control field in the BIOS support installation check data structure (see Table 14-7 on page 208).

Notification Via Polling

If the BIOS uses status bit polling to notify the OS of a change in configuration (e.g., a docking or undocking event), the OS must periodically read the memory location that contains the event notification flag bit. The event notification flag address field in the BIOS support installation check data structure (see Table 14-7 on page 208) contains the address of the memory location that contains the notification flag. Bit zero of this location is set by the BIOS when an event has been detected, otherwise the bit is cleared to zero. If the OS detects bit zero set to one, this indicates that an event has occurred. When an event is detected, the OS must clear bit zero and then use the BIOS function calls documented in the sections that follow to determine the type of event and to handle it.

Notification Via Interrupt

If the BIOS control field in the PnP BIOS support installation check data structure (see Table 14-7 on page 208) indicates that the system generates an interrupt to signal an event, the OS must install an interrupt handler to service events. To do this, the OS must know which system IRQ line the system uses to signal an event. Once the IRQ line has been determined, the OS places the pointer to its event interrupt service routine into the interrupt table entry associated with the indicated IRQ line.

It must be noted, however, that the indicated IRQ line may be shared with one or more other devices in the system. For this reason, before inserting the pointer to the event interrupt service routine into the indicated interrupt table entry, the OS first reads the current contents from the entry and saves it. If another device had already hooked that entry to its device-specific routine, this is the pointer to its routine. In addition, whenever its interrupt service routine is entered, the event interrupt service routine must check the system event interrupt generation logic's interrupt pending bit to determine if the interrupt was generated by the event logic or by another device that had previously hooked the same interrupt. In order to do this, the event service routine must know the IO port to read that contains the event logic's interrupt pending bit.

The IRQ entry to hook and the IO port address that contains the event logic's interrupt pending bit is determined by scanning the system board device configuration list (using the Get Node function) looking for the device node that contains the device ID "PNP0C03" (the EISA ID "PNP" has been reserved for Microsoft; in addition, Microsoft has assigned 32-bit EISA IDs to many of the devices commonly found in a PC; "PNP0C03" is the ID for the event notification interrupt; the device ID list can be found in the appendix on page 279). This node contains the selected IRQ number and the IO port address. It is a requirement that bit zero in the indicated IO port is the event logic's interrupt pending bit. This bit is set to one when the event logic has generated an event interrupt request. If bit zero is set to one, the event interrupt service routine is responsible for clearing the bit to zero and servicing the interrupt. If the bit is cleared to zero, the event logic has not generated an interrupt. Rather, another device that shares the same line has generated an interrupt. The event interrupt service routine must perform a far jump to the entry point of the next device's interrupt service routine (using the address it read from the interrupt table entry before it hooked it).

Alternately, the system vendor can supply their own event logic device identifier and a system-specific event interrupt service routine.

Loading the Event Device Driver

The steps typically performed by the OS are provided in the list that follows:

1. Read the BIOS Control field from the BIOS support installation check data structure and test it to determine if the system implements event notification using interrupts.
2. Assuming interrupts are used for event notification, the OS uses the device ID "PNP0C03" to locate the loadable device driver that handles events. This device driver contains the interrupt service routine that handles events.
3. The device driver is loaded into memory and the OS performs a far call to the driver's initialization code.

4. The driver initialization code uses the Get Node BIOS function to scan the system board device node list looking for the event logic's device ID "PNP0C03."
5. When the node is found, the driver reads the node data structure to determine the IRQ to hook and the IO port that contains the interrupt pending bit.
6. The driver hooks the interrupt table entry associated with the indicated IRQ to the interrupt service routine that is contained within the driver body and also saves the IO port address for use by the service routine.
7. The driver performs a far return to return control to the OS.

Device Driver Event Handing

The steps associated with handling an event are listed below:

1. When an event occurs during run-time, the processor suspends execution of the currently running program and jumps to the event interrupt service routine within the device driver.
2. At the front end of the routine, the IO port is read and the interrupt pending bit checked. If it is cleared to zero, a far jump is performed to the interrupt service routine for another device that uses the same IRQ line. If it is set to one, the body of the event service routine is executed.
3. In the body of the event service routine, the programmer clears the interrupt pending bit in the IO port.
4. The programmer uses the Get Event BIOS function to determine the type of event that has occurred.
5. If the event is the installation of a docking station, the Get Docking Station Information BIOS function is used to obtain information about the docking station.
6. The service routine may use the Send Message BIOS function to instruct the BIOS as to how to handle the event.
7. When the event has been handled, the service routine executes an IRET (interrupt return) instruction, returning control to the interrupted program.

Intro to the Event-Oriented Services

The sections that follow provide a detailed description of the following BIOS services:

- Function 03h—Get Event
- Function 04h—Send Message
- Function 05h—Get Docking Station Information

Function 03h—Get Event

Function 03h Description. <u>This function is required if the BIOS supports event notification</u>. Function 03h is called by the OS or the event device driver in response to the BIOS indicating that an event has occurred (via either polling or an interrupt). It is used to obtain a message indicating the type of event that has been detected by the BIOS.

Function 03h Input Arguments. Table 15-5 on page 232 defines the input arguments that must be supplied to the PnP BIOS when calling function 03h.

Table 15-8: Function 03h Input Arguments

Name	Size (bytes)	Description
Function	2	Function number value 0003h, represented as a 16-bit signed integer.
Message	4	32-bit pointer to the two-byte memory buffer the BIOS stores the message in, indicating the type of event that occurred. The pointer is supplied in segment:offset form.
BiosSelector	2	• If the caller is a protected mode OS, the OS must create a data segment descriptor in the descriptor table using the base address obtained from the PnP installation check structure. The data segment must have a length of 64KB and permit read/write access. The value supplied in the BiosSelector argument is the 16-bit selector that identifies the location of the descriptor within the descriptor table. • If the caller is a real mode OS, the value supplied is the 16-bit real mode DS value obtained from the installation check structure. Upon entry, the BIOS loads the supplied value into the DS register so that it can access its data area in memory.

Chapter 15: The PnP BIOS Services

Synopsis of Function 03h Procedure. The following is a synopsis of the function 03h procedure:

```
int FAR (*entryPoint)(Function,Message,BiosSelector);
int Function;                    /* PnP function 0003 */
unsigned int FAR *Message;       /* Pointer to message buffer */
unsigned int BiosSelector;       /* PnP BIOS DS value */
```

Example Function 03h Assembly Language Procedure Call. The following is an example assembly language function 03h PnP BIOS call.

```
push  BiosSelector           ;DS value>stack
push  segment of Message     ;Message buffer segment>stack
push  offset of Message      ;Message buffer offset>stack
push  GET_EVENT              ;Function 0003h>stack
call  FAR PTR entryPoint     ;call BIOS
add   sp,8                   ;reset stack pointer
cmp   ax,SUCCESS             ;test return code
jne   error                  ;jmp to error if non-zero,
                             ;else proceed
```

Function 03h Return Values. The Message buffer contains the two-byte message indicating the type of event that occurred. The possible message codes are listed in Table 15-9 on page 245. All registers other than AX are preserved. The content of the AX register indicates success or failure of the function request. A value of 0000h indicates success. A non-zero value with bit 7 set to one indicates an error code, while a non-zero value with bit 7 cleared to zero indicates a warning code. These codes are defined in Table 15-3 on page 225.

Table 15-9: Event Message Codes Returned by Function 03h

Message	Value	Description
ABOUT_TO_CHANGE_CONFIG	0001h	This message is sent to the OS by the BIOS to indicate that the docking station is about to be installed or removed. Using the Send Message BIOS function, the OS responds with a message indicating OK to proceed or ABORT the action.

Table 15-9: Event Message Codes Returned by Function 03h (Continued)

Message	Value	Description
DOCK_CHANGED	0002h	This message is sent to the OS by the BIOS when the docking station has been successfully removed or installed.
SYSTEM_DEVICE_CHANGED	0003h	This message is sent to the OS by the BIOS when a removable system board device (other than a docking station) has been removed or installed in the system.
CONFIG_CHANGE_FAILED	0004h	This message is sent to the OS by the BIOS when an error is incurred while a docking station or a removable system board device is being attached or removed. The OS should examine the error code returned in the AL register for more information regarding the type of error.
Reserved	0005h-7FFFh	Reserved.
OEM_DEFINED_EVENTS	8000h-FFFEh	This message is sent to the OS by the BIOS when a system board-specific event has occurred. These message codes are defined by the system vendor and are outside the scope of the spec. The PnP BIOS spec states that all of the message codes in this range have bit 7 set to a one, but it should say bit 15.

Table 15-9: Event Message Codes Returned by Function 03h (Continued)

Message	Value	Description
UNKNOWN_SYSTEM_EVENT	FFFFh	This message is sent to the OS by the BIOS when an event has occurred, but the BIOS is unable to determine the type of event.

Function 04h—Send Message

Function 04h Description. This function is required if the BIOS supports event notification. Function 04h is used by the OS or the device driver to respond to the BIOS after an event is signalled. It can also be used to initiate an event (e.g., undocking, or power down) under software control. The three categories of messages that may be sent to the BIOS are:

- **Response messages**—These messages (OK and ABORT) are sent to the BIOS in response to the BIOS signalling an event. The OS or the device driver uses the Get Event function to determine the event type, and the Send Message function to send a response message to the BIOS. The response message sent to the BIOS tells it to permit the previously signalled event (e.g., undocking) to continue (the OK message), or to abort the operation (the ABORT message). Table 15-11 on page 249 defines the response message codes.
- **Control messages**—The OS or the device driver can use these messages to cause the BIOS to initiate an event (e.g., power down or undocking). Table 15-12 on page 249 defines the control message codes.
- **OEM-defined messages**—These messages are defined by the system manufacturer. The effect on the BIOS is system design-dependent. Table 15-13 on page 251 defines the OEM-defined message codes.

Function 04h Input Arguments. Table 15-5 on page 232 defines the input arguments that must be supplied to the PnP BIOS when calling function 04h.

Table 15-10: Function 04h Input Arguments

Name	Size (bytes)	Description
Function	2	Function number value 0004h, represented as a 16-bit signed integer.
Message	2	16-bit unsigned integer representing the message to be sent to the BIOS by the OS or the event device driver in response to an event. The message sent to the BIOS is one of the following types: • A **response message** is sent to the BIOS to instruct it to permit the event to proceed (e.g., the undocking operation) or to abort the event. Table 15-11 on page 249 lists the response message codes. • A **control message** permits the OS or the event device driver to initiate an event. Table 15-12 on page 249 lists the control message codes. • **OEM-defined messages** are system specific and the effect that it has on the BIOS (and the system) is system specific. Table 15-13 on page 251 lists the OEM message codes.
BiosSelector	2	• If the caller is a protected mode OS, the OS must create a data segment descriptor in the descriptor table using the base address obtained from the PnP installation check structure. The data segment must have a length of 64KB and permit read/write access. The value supplied in the BiosSelector argument is the 16-bit selector that identifies the location of the descriptor within the descriptor table. • If the caller is a real mode OS, the value supplied is the 16-bit real mode DS value obtained from the installation check structure. Upon entry, the BIOS loads the supplied value into the DS register so that it can access its data area in memory.

Table 15-11: Response Message Codes

Message	Value	Description
OK	0000h	Instructs the BIOS to continue with the sequence (e.g., continue with the undocking operation) that initiated the event previously reported to the OS or the device driver. This message is only valid when the Get Event function has returned one of the ABOUT_TO_ event messages.
ABORT	0001h	Instructs the BIOS to abort the sequence (e.g., undocking the system) that initiated the event previously reported to the OS or the device driver. This message is only valid when the Get Event function has returned one of the ABOUT_TO_ event messages. It is assumed that the OS will alert the user as to the reason for the abort.
Reserved	0002h-003Fh	Reserved.

Table 15-12: Control Message Codes

Message	Value	Description
UNDOCK_DEFAULT_ACTION	0040h	The OS or the device driver uses this control message to instruct the BIOS to execute the series of actions necessary to eject the system from the docking station under software control.

Table 15-12: Control Message Codes (Continued)

Message	Value	Description
POWER_OFF	0041h	The OS or the device driver uses this control message to instruct the BIOS to execute the series of actions necessary to power down the system. It is assumed that the OS has already taken any software actions necessary before the system is powered down (e.g., flushing any file updates in the L1 or L2 caches to memory, and all modified pages to disk).
PNP_OS_ACTIVE	0042h	During its initialization sequence, a PnP OS must register with the BIOS using this message. When this message is received, the PnP BIOS will wait forever after signalling an event for the PnP OS to perform the Get Event function. The PnP BIOS may default (at power up time) to either the PnP OS active or inactive state). Although a PnP BIOS is not required to support this message, support is recommended in systems that generate events. If this message is not supported, the Send Message function must return the MESSAGE_NOT_ SUPPORTED warning code in the AX register.
PNP_OS_INACTIVE	0043h	See message code 42h above.
Reserved	0044h-7FFFh	Reserved

Table 15-13: OEM Message Codes

Message	Value	Description
OEM defined messages	8000h-FFFFh	OEM defined messages.

Synopsis of Function 04h Procedure. The following is a synopsis of the function 04h procedure:

```
int FAR (*entryPoint)(Function,Message,BiosSelector);
int Function;                       /* PnP function 0004h */
unsigned int FAR Message;           /* message value */
unsigned int BiosSelector;          /* PnP BIOS DS value */
```

Example Function 04h Assembly Language Procedure Call. The following is an example assembly language function 04h PnP BIOS call.

```
push   BiosSelector         ;DS value>stack
push   Message              ;Message>stack
push   SEND_MESSAGE         ;Function 0004h>stack
call   FAR PTR entryPoint   ;call BIOS
add    sp,6                 ;reset stack pointer
cmp    ax,SUCCESS           ;test return code
jne    error                ;jmp to error if non-zero,
                            ;else proceed
```

Function 04h Return Values. All registers other than AX are preserved. The content of the AX register indicates success or failure of the function request. A value of 0000h indicates success. A non-zero value with bit 7 set to one indicates an error code, while a non-zero value with bit 7 cleared to zero indicates a warning code. These codes are defined in Table 15-3 on page 225.

Function 05h—Get Docking Station Information

Function 05h Description. This function is required if the BIOS supports event notification. BIOS function 05h is performed in response to a docking event to obtain information about the docking station. This includes the station's product ID, its serial number, and whether it supports cold (system must be powered off), warm (system must be in suspend mode), or hot docking (system may be fully powered up).

If the BIOS is unable to obtain cold/warm/hot information, the UNABLE_TO_DETERMINE_DOCK_CAPABILITIES warning code must be returned in the AX register. The data structure will contain the product ID and the serial number, however. If the system does not support docking, the BIOS will return the FUNCTION_NOT_SUPPORTED warning code in AX. If the system supports docking but is currently not docked, this function will return the SYSTEM_NOT_DOCKED warning code in AX.

Function 05h Input Arguments. Table 15-5 on page 232 defines the input arguments that must be supplied to the PnP BIOS when calling function 05h.

Table 15-14: Function 05h Input Arguments

Name	Size (bytes)	Description
Function	2	Function number value 0005h, represented as a 16-bit signed integer.
DockingStationInfo	4	The docking station information (see Table 15-15 on page 253) is returned in the memory buffer identified by the 32-bit pointer contained in DockingStationInfo. The pointer is represented in segment:offset format.
BiosSelector	2	• If the caller is a protected mode OS, the OS must create a data segment descriptor in the descriptor table using the base address obtained from the PnP installation check structure. The data segment must have a length of 64KB and permit read/write access. The value supplied in the BiosSelector argument is the 16-bit selector that identifies the location of the descriptor within the descriptor table. • If the caller is a real mode OS, the value supplied is the 16-bit real mode DS value obtained from the installation check structure. Upon entry, the BIOS loads the supplied value into the DS register so that it can access its data area in memory.

Synopsis of Function 05h Procedure. The following is a synopsis of the function 05h procedure:

```
int FAR (*entryPoint)(Function,DockingStationInfo,BiosSelector);
int Function;                        /* PnP function 0005 */
unsigned char FAR *DockingStationInfo;/* pointer to info buffer */
unsigned int BiosSelector;           /* PnP BIOS DS value */
```

Example Function 05h Assembly Language Procedure Call. The following is an example assembly language function 05h PnP BIOS call.

```
push  BiosSelector                ;DS value>stack
push  segment DockingStationInfo  ;segment of buffer>stack
push  offset DockingStationInfo   ;offset of buffer>stack
push  GET_DOCK_INFO               ;Function 0005h>stack
call  FAR PTR entryPoint          ;call BIOS
add   sp,8                        ;reset stack pointer
cmp   ax,SUCCESS                  ;test return code
jne   error                       ;jmp to error if non-zero,
                                  ;else proceed
```

Function 05h Return Values. Upon return, the DockingStationInfo memory buffer contains the docking station information in the format defined in Table 15-15 on page 253. All registers other than AX are preserved. The content of the AX register indicates success or failure of the function request. A value of 0000h indicates success. A non-zero value with bit 7 set to one indicates an error code, while a non-zero value with bit 7 cleared to zero indicates a warning code. These codes are defined in Table 15-3 on page 225.

Table 15-15: Docking Station Information Data Structure

Field	Offset	Length (bytes)	Description
Docking station location ID	00h	4	The EISA device ID for the docking station. This value is set to FFFFFFFFh if the station does not have an ID.

Table 15-15: Docking Station Information Data Structure (Continued)

Field	Offset	Length (bytes)	Description
Serial Number	04h	4	This value is not required, but is useful to verify that the system is installed in a docking station that it is authorized to access. A value of 00000000h should be returned if the station does not have a serial number.

Capabilities	08h	2	This 16-bit field is defined as follows:
			<u>Bit(s)</u> Description
			15:3 Reserved.
			2:1 00=system must be powered off to dock /undock (cold docking).
			     01=warm docking supported (system must be in suspend mode).
			     10=Hot docking supported (system does not have to be in suspend mode).
			0 0=station does not provide support for controlling the dock/undock process. This is referred to as "surprise" style.
			     1=station provides support for controlling the dock /undock process. This is referred to as "VCR" style.

Service Supporting PnP ISA Cards

Function 40h—Get PnP E/ISA Configuration Table

Function 40h Description. This function is required, but returns the FUNCTION_NOT_SUPPORTED warning code in the AX register if the system does not have an ISA bus. When called (assuming the system has an ISA bus), it returns the total number of CSNs assigned to PnP E/ISA cards and the IO address of the PnP configuration read data port. Using this information, the OS can directly access the required resource list and the configuration registers on each PnP card. This permits the OS to ascertain the current configuration of each card and, if necessary to select an alternative configuration for the card.

If there aren't any PnP E/ISA cards in the system, the total number of CSNs assigned is cleared to zero and the configuration read data port address is invalid and must not be used. If the system is a laptop with docking capability, this function must have more flexibility. For a detailed description of the values returned after a cold, warm, or hot docking event, refer to the section entitled "Function 40h Return Values." on page 257.

Function 40h Input Arguments. Table 15-5 on page 232 defines the input arguments that must be supplied to the PnP BIOS when calling function 40h.

Table 15-16: Function 40h Input Arguments

Name	Size (bytes)	Description
Function	2	Function number value 0040h, represented as a 16-bit signed integer.
Configuration	4	Points to the six-byte memory buffer that the function uses to return the total number of CSNs assigned to PnP E/ISA cards and the PnP configuration read data port IO address. The format of this data structure is defined in Table 15-17 on page 256. This buffer pointer is represented in segment:offset format.

Table 15-16: Function 40h Input Arguments (Continued)

Name	Size (bytes)	Description
BiosSelector	2	• If the caller is a protected mode OS, the OS must create a data segment descriptor in the descriptor table using the base address obtained from the PnP installation check structure. The data segment must have a length of 64KB and permit read/write access. The value supplied in the BiosSelector argument is the 16-bit selector that identifies the location of the descriptor within the descriptor table. • If the caller is a real mode OS, the value supplied is the 16-bit real mode DS value obtained from the installation check structure. Upon entry, the BIOS loads the supplied value into the DS register so that it can access its data area in memory.

Table 15-17: PnP E/ISA Configuration Data Structure Format

Field	Offset	Length (bytes)	Description
Structure Revision	00h	1	The data structure format defined in this table is revision 01h.
Total number of CSNs assigned	01h	1	00h if no PnP E/ISA cards were detected in the system. Otherwise, this field indicates the total number of CSNs assigned to PnP E/ISA cards.
IO address of PnP configuration read data port	02h	2	Meaningless and must not be used by OS if the CSN field contains 00h. Otherwise, this field returns the 16-bit IO address of the read data port.
Reserved	04	2	Reserved. Cleared to 0000h.

Chapter 15: The PnP BIOS Services

Synopsis of Function 40h Procedure. The following is a synopsis of the function 40h procedure:

```
int FAR (*entryPoint)(Function,Configuration,BiosSelector);
int Function;                     /* PnP function 0040h */
unsigned char FAR *Configuration; /* buffer pointer */
unsigned int BiosSelector;        /* PnP BIOS DS value */
```

Example Function 40h Assembly Language Procedure Call. The following is an example assembly language function 40h PnP BIOS call.

```
push  BiosSelector            ;DS value>stack
push  segment Configuration   ;buffer segment>stack
push  offset Configuration    ;buffer offset>stack
push  GET_ISA_CONFIG_STRUC    ;Function 0040h>stack
call  FAR PTR entryPoint      ;call BIOS
add   sp,8                    ;reset stack pointer
cmp   ax,SUCCESS              ;test return code
jne   error                   ;jmp to error if non-zero,
                              ;else proceed
```

Function 40h Return Values. All registers other than AX are preserved. The content of the AX register indicates success or failure of the function request. A value of 0000h indicates success. A non-zero value with bit 7 set to one indicates an error code, while a non-zero value with bit 7 cleared to zero indicates a warning code. These codes are defined in Table 15-3 on page 225.

A system without an ISA bus returns the FUNCTION_NOT_SUPPORTED warning code in AX. If the system has an E/ISA bus but no PnP E/ISA cards were identified by the BIOS, it returns SUCCESS in AX, a CSN value of 00h, and a meaningless read data port IO address. On a laptop system with docking capability, there are a number of possible scenarios:

- When the ISA bus is present (i.e., the system is docked), the information returned in the data structure is valid after a cold boot (a system power up).
- After a cold boot has occurred with the system undocked (i.e., there is no ISA bus), function 40h returns all fields cleared to zero.
- After a warm docking (the laptop is docked while in the suspend state), if the BIOS scans the E/ISA bus for PnP E/ISA cards before returning control to the OS after the docking has completed, the data structure contains valid data.
- After a hot docking (the laptop is docked while it is fully powered up), if the BIOS does not scan the E/ISA bus for PnP E/ISA cards before returning control to the OS after the docking has completed, the BIOS returns zeros in all fields.
- After the system is removed from the docking station (i.e., no ISA bus is present), the BIOS returns zeros in all fields.

Services Related to ISA Cards

Functions 09h and 0Ah support legacy ISA cards. BIOS support for these functions is optional because:

- The system may not have any legacy ISA devices (a system may not have E/ISA bus connectors into which legacy ISA cards may be installed).
- The BIOS may use functions 41h, 42h, and 43h, rather than 09h and 0Ah, to access non-volatile memory in order to keep track of the resources used by devices (including legacy ISA devices).

The OS can use function 09h to supply the BIOS with a summary list of the resources used by the entire community of legacy ISA cards in the system. Function 0Ah is used by the OS to fetch the list from the BIOS.

Any time that a new legacy card is installed in the system, an OS-specific configuration utility program must be run. The user is prompted to enter the IO space, memory space, interrupt line, and DMA channels used by the new card. In Windows 95, this is performed by the Device Installer under the direction of the CM. The configuration utility calls BIOS function 0Ah to get the list of resources currently used by legacy cards. It adds the new card's resources to the summary list and calls BIOS function 09h to send the updated list back to the BIOS (to be written to NV memory). The summary resource list is stored in non-volatile memory by the BIOS in a system implementation-specific, compacted form.

A positive aspect of this method is that the summary resource list consumes a very small amount of non-volatile memory. On the other hand, a negative aspect of functions 09h and 0Ah is that the resources consumed by legacy ISA cards are stored in non-volatile memory in summary form rather than maintaining a list of the resources consumed by each individual card.

As an alternative method, the BIOS may implement functions 41h, 42h, and 43h. These functions support the ESCD (extended system configuration data) method of storing the resource usage information in non-volatile memory. The resource usage is tracked for each individual device. The amount of non-volatile memory consumed is greater (typically 2-4KB), but the system has greatly enhanced ability to resolve resource usage problems. A separate specification, the ESCD spec, details the exact format of the information stored in non-volatile memory. Detailed coverage of the ESCD specification is outside the scope of this book.

Using the ESCD functions, the OS maintains a complete list of the resources used by all legacy ISA cards, as well as those currently-assigned to PnP E/ISA cards, PCI devices, PCMCIA devices, etc. This information is used to configure all of the configurable devices every time the machine is restarted and to ensure that the configuration of the boot devices does not conflict with any of the non-configurable devices.

In addition, the OS can change the configuration of any configurable device immediately (while the machine is running), or may alter the configuration information for the configurable device in non-volatile memory, causing the device to be configured differently the next time the machine is restarted (or the device's configuration can be altered immediately and may simultaneously be changed in non-volatile memory to be used each time that the machine is restarted).

Determining if Functions 09h and 0Ah are Implemented

If the OS calls BIOS function 09h or 0Ah and the USE_ESCD_SUPPORT warning message is returned in the AX register, this indicates that the BIOS implements the ESCD functions, rather than 09h and 0Ah.

Function 09h—Set Statically Allocated Resource Information

Function 09h Description. This function is optional. It is not required if the system does not implement an E/ISA expansion bus and does not have any legacy ISA devices. It must be called by the OS each time that a legacy ISA device is installed in or removed from the system and must supply the BIOS with an updated list of the resources consumed by all legacy ISA devices. The BIOS then stores the list in non-volatile memory, usually in a system-specific, compressed form.

In the act of compressing the information, some of the resource detail may be lost. As an example, assume that the BIOS tracks the IO port usage of legacy ISA devices using 24 bytes of non-volatile memory. This is a total of 192 bits. Assume that each bit represents a doubleword (four bytes) of IO space. This permits the mapping of 768 locations of IO space. All legacy ISA cards occupy the IO region from 0100h through 03FFh, a total of 768 locations. If any subset of a group of four locations within this area are reported used, the corresponding bit is set to one. If none of the four locations are used, the corresponding bit is cleared to zero.

On entry, the OS must supply a memory buffer (the ResourceBlock buffer) that contains a summary list of all resources consumed by the legacy ISA devices in the system. The information supplied to the BIOS in the buffer indicates the resources consumed by the legacy devices and is presented as a series of resource descriptors terminated by an END TAG descriptor. The descriptors have the same format as that used for PnP ISA devices. For a complete description of the descriptor format, refer to the section "Format of a Logical Device's Resource List" on page 92.

Function 09h Input Arguments. Table 15-5 on page 232 defines the input arguments that must be supplied to the PnP BIOS when calling function 09h.

Table 15-18: Function 09h Input Arguments

Name	Size (bytes)	Description
Function	2	Function number value 0009h, represented as a 16-bit signed integer.
ResourceBlock	4	The list of resources used by all legacy ISA cards is supplied to the BIOS in the ResourceBlock memory buffer. For a complete description of the descriptor format, refer to the section "Format of a Logical Device's Resource List" on page 92. This buffer pointer is represented in segment:offset format.

Chapter 15: The PnP BIOS Services

Table 15-18: Function 09h Input Arguments (Continued)

Name	Size (bytes)	Description
BiosSelector	2	• If the caller is a protected mode OS, the OS must create a data segment descriptor in the descriptor table using the base address obtained from the PnP installation check structure. The data segment must have a length of 64KB and permit read/write access. The value supplied in the BiosSelector argument is the 16-bit selector that identifies the location of the descriptor within the descriptor table. • If the caller is a real mode OS, the value supplied is the 16-bit real mode DS value obtained from the installation check structure. Upon entry, the BIOS loads the supplied value into the DS register so that it can access its data area in memory.

Synopsis of Function 09h Procedure. The following is a synopsis of the function 09h procedure:

```
int FAR (*entryPoint)(Function,ResourceBlock,BiosSelector);
int Function;                        /* PnP function 0009h */
unsigned char FAR *ResourceBlock;    /* Resource buffer pointer */
unsigned int BiosSelector;           /* PnP BIOS DS value */
```

Example Function 09h Assembly Language Procedure Call. The following is an example assembly language function 09h PnP BIOS call.

```
push  BiosSelector                              ;DS value>stack
push  segment ResourceBlock                     ;buffer segment>stack
push  offset ResourceBlock                      ;buffer offset>stack
push  SET_STATICALLY_ALLOCATED_RESOURCES ;Function 0009h>stack
call  FAR PTR entryPoint                         ;call BIOS
add   sp,8                                       ;reset stack pointer
cmp   ax,SUCCESS                                 ;test return code
jne   error                                      ;jmp to error if non-zero,
                                                 ;else proceed
```

Function 09h Return Values. All registers other than AX are preserved. The content of the AX register indicates success or failure of the function request. A value of 0000h indicates success. A non-zero value with bit 7 set to one indicates an error code, while a non-zero value with bit 7 cleared to zero indicates a warning code. These codes are defined in Table 15-3 on page 225.

If the function returns the USE_ESCD_FUNCTION warning code in the AX register, the OS must use the ESCD functions to access the configuration information stored in non-volatile memory.

Function 0Ah—Get Statically Allocated Resource Information

Function 0Ah Description. <u>This function is optional</u>. It is not required if the system does not implement an ISA expansion bus and does not have any legacy ISA devices.

On entry, the OS must supply a memory buffer (the ResourceBlock buffer) that will receive the summary list (from the BIOS) of all resources consumed by the legacy ISA devices in the system. The ResourceBlock buffer must be at least 2KB in size to ensure that there is adequate space for the information returned by the BIOS. The information supplied by the BIOS indicates the resources consumed by the legacy devices and is presented as a series of resource descriptors terminated by an END TAG descriptor. As noted in the description of function 09h, the information returned may not be a completely faithful report (because it has been compressed and some granularity is therefore lost) of the resources used by the community of legacy devices. In the example given in the function 09h description, if any of a group of four IO addresses is used by the legacy cards, the BIOS would report that all four were used.

The descriptors have the same format as that used for PnP E/ISA devices. For a complete description of the descriptor format, refer to the section "Format of a Logical Device's Resource List" on page 92.

Function 0Ah Input Arguments. Table 15-5 on page 232 defines the input arguments that must be supplied to the PnP BIOS when calling function 0Ah.

Table 15-19: Function 0Ah Input Arguments

Name	Size (bytes)	Description
Function	2	Function number value 000Ah, represented as a 16-bit signed integer.

Table 15-19: Function 0Ah Input Arguments (Continued)

Name	Size (bytes)	Description
ResourceBlock	4	The list of resources used by all legacy ISA cards is supplied by the BIOS in the ResourceBlock memory buffer. For a complete description of the descriptor format, refer to the section "Format of a Logical Device's Resource List" on page 92. This buffer pointer is represented in segment:offset format.
BiosSelector	2	• If the caller is a protected mode OS, the OS must create a data segment descriptor in the descriptor table using the base address obtained from the PnP installation check structure. The data segment must have a length of 64KB and permit read/write access. The value supplied in the BiosSelector argument is the 16-bit selector that identifies the location of the descriptor within the descriptor table. • If the caller is a real mode OS, the value supplied is the 16-bit real mode DS value obtained from the installation check structure. Upon entry, the BIOS loads the supplied value into the DS register so that it can access its data area in memory.

Synopsis of Function 0Ah Procedure. The following is a synopsis of the function 0Ah procedure:

```
int FAR (*entryPoint)(Function,ResourceBlock,BiosSelector);
int Function;                      /* PnP function 000Ah */
unsigned char FAR *ResourceBlock;  /* Resource buffer pointer */
unsigned int BiosSelector;         /* PnP BIOS DS value */
```

Example Function 0Ah Assembly Language Procedure Call. The following is an example assembly language function 0Ah PnP BIOS call.

```
push  BiosSelector                            ;DS value>stack
push  segment ResourceBlock                   ;buffer segment>stack
push  offset ResourceBlock                    ;buffer offset>stack
push  GET_STATICALLY_ALLOCATED_RESOURCES ;Function 000Ah>stack
call  FAR PTR entryPoint                       ;call BIOS
add   sp,8                                      ;reset stack pointer
cmp   ax,SUCCESS                                ;test return code
jne   error                                     ;jmp to error if non-zero
```

Function 0Ah Return Values. All registers other than AX are preserved. The content of the AX register indicates success or failure of the function request. A value of 0000h indicates success. A non-zero value with bit 7 set to one indicates an error code, while a non-zero value with bit 7 cleared to zero indicates a warning code. These codes are defined in Table 15-3 on page 225.

If the function returns the USE_ESCD_FUNCTION warning code in the AX register, the OS must use the ESCD functions (rather than functions 09h and 0Ah) to access the configuration information stored in non-volatile memory.

Service Related to Automatic Power Management (APM)

Function 0Bh—Get APM ID Table

Function 0Bh Description. This function is required to permit power management of PnP devices that support power management via the APM BIOS. Function 0Bh supports an APM BIOS compliant with version 1.1 or later of the APM specification. This BIOS function provides the OS with a list that identifies the PnP devices with power management capabilities controlled via the APM BIOS. The returned list consists of a series of ID pairs: the PnP device ID, and its corresponding APM ID. A device driver or the OS calls function 0Bh and receives the list. The list is then scanned for a match on the PnP device ID. If the ID isn't found, the device either does not implement power management capability or its power management capabilities are not controlled via the APM BIOS. Assuming a match is found, the APM ID associated with the PnP device ID is used when calling the APM BIOS to identify the target device for the power management request.

Function 0Bh Input Arguments. Table 15-5 on page 232 defines the input arguments that must be supplied to the PnP BIOS when calling function 0Bh.

Table 15-20: Function 0Bh Input Arguments

Name	Size (bytes)	Description
Function	2	Function number value 000Bh, represented as a 16-bit signed integer.

Table 15-20: Function 0Bh Input Arguments (Continued)

Name	Size (bytes)	Description
BufSize	4	This 32-bit pointer points to the start address of the two byte value in memory in which the caller specifies the ApmIdTable buffer size to the BIOS. If the specified buffer size is too small to hold the entire device ID/APM ID table, function 0Bh returns the required buffer size in BufSize. The caller can therefore ascertain the required buffer size by passing the BIOS a buffer size of 0000h in BufSize. The BIOS then returns the required buffer size in BufSize. The pointer is in segment:offset form.
ApmIdTable	4	This 32-bit pointer points to the start address of the memory buffer in which the BIOS should return the table. The pointer is in segment:offset form. The format of the returned data is defined in Table 15-21 on page 266.
BiosSelector	2	• If the caller is a protected mode OS, the OS must create a data segment descriptor in the descriptor table using the base address obtained from the PnP installation check structure. The data segment must have a length of 64KB and permit read/write access. The value supplied in the BiosSelector argument is the 16-bit selector that identifies the location of the descriptor within the descriptor table. • If the caller is a real mode OS, the value supplied is the 16-bit real mode DS value obtained from the installation check structure. Upon entry, the BIOS loads the supplied value into the DS register so that it can access its data area in memory.

Synopsis of Function 0Bh Procedure. The following is a synopsis of the function 0Bh procedure:

```
int FAR (*entryPoint)(Function,BufSize, ApmIdTable, BiosSelector);
int Function;                    /* PnP function 000Bh */
unsigned integer FAR *BufSize;   /* buffer size */
unsigned char FAR *ApmIdTable;   /* buffer pointer */
unsigned int BiosSelector;       /* PnP BIOS DS value */
```

Example Function 0Bh Assembly Language Procedure Call. The following is an example assembly language function 0Bh PnP BIOS call.

```
push  BiosSelector          ;DS value>stack
push  segment ApmIdTable     ;segment>stack
push  offset ApmIdTable      ;offset>stack
push  segment BufSize        ;segment>stack
push  offset BufSize         ;offset>stack
push  GET_APM_TABLE          ;Function 000Bh>stack
call  FAR PTR entryPoint     ;call BIOS
add   sp,12                  ;reset stack pointer
cmp   ax,SUCCESS             ;test return code
jne   error                 ;jmp to error if non-zero,
                            ;else proceed
```

Function 0Bh Return Values. All registers other than AX are preserved. The content of the AX register indicates success or failure of the function request. A value of 0000h indicates success. A non-zero value with bit 7 set to one indicates an error code, while a non-zero value with bit 7 cleared to zero indicates a warning code. These codes are defined in Table 15-3 on page 225.

The requested table is returned in the specified memory buffer. The format of the returned data is defined in Table 15-21 on page 266. If the buffer size specified by the caller is too small, on return, BufSize contains the required buffer size and the BUFFER_TOO_SMALL warning code is returned in AX.

Table 15-21: Format of the APM ID Table

Field	Length (bytes)	Description
PnP device ID	4	EISA device ID of 1st device.
APM deviceID	2	Corresponding APM device ID for 1st device.
PnP device ID	4	EISA-style PnP device ID of 2nd device.

Table 15-21: Format of the APM ID Table (Continued)

Field	Length (bytes)	Description
APM deviceID	2	Corresponding APM device ID for 2nd device.
PnP device ID	4	EISA-style PnP device ID of 3rd device.
APM deviceID	2	Corresponding APM device ID for 3rd device.
...	...	...
PnP device ID	4	EISA-style PnP device ID of nth device.
APM deviceID	2	Corresponding APM device ID of nth device.

ESCD Services

What Is ESCD?

ECSD stands for extended system configuration data and it defines:

- a method for storing detailed configuration information in non-volatile (NV) memory
- three PnP BIOS functions that are used to access this information.

The ESCD specification was developed by Compaq, Intel and Phoenix Technologies.

Providing the BIOS and the OS with detailed information regarding the resources allocated to each individual device in the system permits the startup program to automatically configure all configurable devices the same way each time that the machine is restarted. This ensures that the configuration of other devices does not conflict with that of the boot devices, and that the system can successfully boot the OS into memory.

The ESCD specification provides a detailed format of the configuration data structures stored in NV memory. Each data structure defines the resources used by a device or a card in the system. This includes legacy and PnP E/ISA cards and PCI devices. The reconfiguration of embedded system board devices is accomplished using functions 00h, 01h, and 02h, rather than the ESCD BIOS functions.

What About EISA Cards?

The BIOS functions defined by the EISA specification permit the current resource selections for an EISA card to be stored in NV memory, but do not support storage of a list of the alternative resources that the card may be configured to use. In order to reconfigure an EISA card, the EISA configuration utility program must be executed and it must have access to the EISA configuration file associated with the card.

A combination of the information stored in NV memory by the EISA BIOS functions and the ESCD BIOS functions may be used to store:

- the current configuration of the EISA card
- the choices of alternative resources that the card can be configured for
- the IO port addresses of the card's EISA configuration registers
- the bits (in the configuration registers) that must be changed and the values they must be changed to in order to select one or more of the alternative resources to be used by the card.

This permits the automatic reconfiguration of EISA cards to be performed much as it is for PCI and PnP ISA devices.

Is ESCD BIOS Support Required?

Support for the ESCD BIOS functions is optional. The OS can determine if the ESCD functions are implemented by calling function 09h or 0Ah. If either of these functions returns the USE_ESCD_FUNCTIONS warning code, this indicates that the ESCD functions are implemented and must be used in lieu of functions 09h and 0Ah to store configuration information for legacy ISA cards, PnP ISA cards, PCI devices, and possibly EISA devices.

ESCD Data Format

A complete description of the ESCD data structures is outside the scope of this book. This information can be found in the ESCD specification (available for download on the Compuserve PlugPlay forum). The format very closely resembles that defined by the EISA BIOS specification (available from BCPR Services in Spring, Texas, phone 713-251-4770).

What Are the ESCD Services?

The three ESCD functions are GET_ESCD_SIZE (function 41h), READ_ESCD (function 42h), and WRITE_ESCD (function 43h). A complete description of these three functions follows.

Additional Error Return Codes

When a system BIOS implements the ESCD BIOS functions, additional error codes (in addition to those listed in Table 15-3 on page 225) may be returned when these functions are called. These error codes are listed in Table 15-22 on page 269. It should be noted that some of the ESCD error codes may conflict with those returned for non-ESCD functions. The meaning of an error code must therefore be qualified within the context of the function that returned the error.

Table 15-22: ESCD Error Return Codes

Return Code	Value	Description
ESCD_IO_ERROR_READING	55h	The BIOS could not read or write the ESCD from NV memory.
ESCD_INVALID	56h	The ESCD data in NV memory is invalid (battery dead or checksum error).
ESCD_BUFFER_TOO_SMALL	59h	The memory buffer supplied by the caller is too small to hold the ESCD data.

Table 15-22: ESCD Error Return Codes (Continued)

Return Code	Value	Description
ESCD_NVRAM_TOO_SMALL	5Ah	The area of NV memory allocated for the storage of the ESCD data is too small to hold the ESCD data supplied to the BIOS.

Function 41h—Get ESCD Size

Function 41h Description. This function is optional and is only implemented if the system BIOS supports storage of a complete image (rather than just a compressed summary of the resources used by the entire community of legacy ISA devices) of the resources used by all devices (both non-configurable and configurable) in the system. If the OS receives a USE_ESCD_SUPPORT warning message when it calls function 09h or 0Ah, this indicates that the system implements the ESCD functions and they must be used to record and access the resources used by all devices in the system.

Function 41h provides information to be used when calling functions 42h and 43h to access configuration information stored in non-volatile memory (NV). The caller supplies the function with the pointers to three storage areas in memory and the BIOS returns the total amount of NV memory allocated to hold ESCD data, the size of the ESCD buffer which must be used by function 43h when writing updated ESCD data into NV memory, and, if the NV memory is memory-mapped, the base memory address of the NV memory.

Function 41h Input Arguments. Table 15-5 on page 232 defines the input arguments that must be supplied to the PnP BIOS when calling function 41h.

Table 15-23: Function 41h Input Arguments

Name	Size (bytes)	Description
Function	2	Function number value 0041h, represented as a 16-bit signed integer.

Table 15-23: Function 41h Input Arguments (Continued)

Name	Size (bytes)	Description
MinESCDWriteSize	4	This 32-bit memory pointer points to a 16-bit unsigned integer that is returned by the BIOS. This integer indicates the minimum size of the ESCD buffer that must be used when performing a function 43h call to write the ESCD data buffer into non-volatile memory. The pointer is presented in segment:offset form. For more information, refer to the section entitled "Function 43h—Write ESCD" on page 275.
ESCD Size	4	This 32-bit memory pointer points to a 16-bit unsigned integer that is returned by the BIOS. This integer indicates the total amount of space allocated for storage of ESCD data within non-volatile memory (the amount of NV memory and how much is available for storage of ESCD data is system BIOS-dependent). When calling function 42h to read the ESCD data from non-volatile memory into a memory buffer, this value is used to select the size of the buffer. This is necessary because the caller doesn't know how much ESCD data will be returned so the maximum must be assumed. The pointer is presented in segment:offset form. For more information, see the section entitled "Function 42h—Read ESCD" on page 273.
NVStorageBase	4	This 32-bit memory pointer points to a 32-bit value that represents the start address of the non-volatile memory (if the system's non-volatile memory is memory-mapped). If the non-volatile memory is not memory-mapped, this value must be zero. For more information, refer to the sections entitled "Function 42h—Read ESCD" on page 273 and "Function 43h—Write ESCD" on page 275.

Table 15-23: Function 41h Input Arguments (Continued)

Name	Size (bytes)	Description
BiosSelector	2	• If the caller is a protected mode OS, the OS must create a data segment descriptor in the descriptor table using the base address obtained from the PnP installation check structure. The data segment must have a length of 64KB and permit read/write access. The value supplied in the BiosSelector argument is the 16-bit selector that identifies the location of the descriptor within the descriptor table. • If the caller is a real mode OS, the value supplied is the 16-bit real mode DS value obtained from the installation check structure. Upon entry, the BIOS loads the supplied value into the DS register so that it can access its data area in memory.

Synopsis of Function 41h Procedure. The following is a synopsis of the function 41h procedure:

```
int FAR (*entryPoint)(Function,MinESCDWriteSize,ESCD Size, NVStorageBase,
        BiosSelector);
int Function;                       /* PnP function 0041h */
unsigned integer FAR *MinESCDWriteSize;/* minimum write buffer size */
unsigned int FAR *ESCDSize;         /* total size of ESCD memory */
unsigned long FAR *NVStorageBase;   /* if NV memory-mapped,base address */
unsigned int BiosSelector;          /* PnP BIOS DS value */
```

Example Function 41h Assembly Language Procedure Call. The following is an example assembly language function 41h PnP BIOS call:

```
push  BiosSelector              ;DS value>stack
push  segment NVStorageBase     ;segment>stack
push  offset NVStorageBase      ;offset>stack
push  segment ESCDSize          ;segment>stack
push  offset ESCDSize           ;offset>stack
push  segment MinESCDWriteSize  ;segment>stack
push  offset MinESCDWriteSize   ;offset>stack
push  GET_ESCD_SIZE             ;Function 0041h>stack
call  FAR PTR entryPoint        ;call BIOS
add   sp,16                     ;reset stack pointer
cmp   ax,SUCCESS                ;test return code
jne   error                     ;jmp to error if non-zero
```

Function 41h Return Values. All registers other than AX are preserved. The content of the AX register indicates success or failure of the function request. A value of 0000h indicates success. A non-zero value with bit 7 set to one indicates an error code, while a non-zero value with bit 7 cleared to zero indicates a warning code. These codes are defined in Table 15-3 on page 225.

Function 42h—Read ESCD

Function 42h Description. This function is optional and is used to read the complete ESCD structure from NV memory into a memory buffer. It can then be examined to ascertain the resources currently assigned to each device, and can be updated (using function 43h) to:

- define the resources assigned to a new device that has been added to the system.
- delete the record of resources that were assigned to a device that has been removed from the system.
- alter the resources assigned to a device already configured so that the new configuration is used the next time that the system is restarted.

At a minimum, a PnP EISA system is required to support the standard PnP BIOS functions and must include access to NV memory using the EISA BIOS functions. Ideally though, an EISA system should implement (in addition to the EISA BIOS functions) PnP BIOS functions 09h, 0A, 42h, and 43h, thus providing the OS (and any programs that access NV memory) with a single, consistent interface to NV memory and the configuration information.

Function 42h Input Arguments. Table 15-5 on page 232 defines the input arguments that must be supplied to the PnP BIOS when calling function 42h.

Table 15-24: Function 42h Input Arguments

Name	Size (bytes)	Description
Function	2	Function number value 0042h, represented as a 16-bit signed integer.
ESCDBuffer	4	This 32-bit pointer points to the memory buffer to receive the ESCD structure supplied by the BIOS. The pointer is in segment:offset form.

Table 15-24: Function 42h Input Arguments (Continued)

Name	Size (bytes)	Description
ESCDSelector	2	This value is required if function 41h has indicated that the NV memory is located in memory space. In this case, a protected mode OS must (prior to calling function 42h) create a segment descriptor using the base address of the memory-mapped NV memory and a segment length of 64KB. The segment must be designated read/writable. The ESCDSelector value is then set to the entry number of the segment descriptor in the segment descriptor table. If the OS is a real mode OS, the ESCDSelector value must be set to the segment base address of the NV memory area (supplied by function 41h). If the NV memory is mapped into memory space, this argument is necessary to permit the function to access the memory data area that the NV memory resides in. If function 41h indicated that the NV memory is not located in memory space, this argument must be set to zero.
BiosSelector	2	• If the caller is a protected mode OS, the OS must create a data segment descriptor in the descriptor table using the base address obtained from the PnP installation check structure. The data segment must have a length of 64KB and permit read/write access. The value supplied in the BiosSelector argument is the 16-bit selector that identifies the location of the descriptor within the descriptor table. • If the caller is a real mode OS, the value supplied is the 16-bit real mode DS value obtained from the installation check structure. Upon entry, the BIOS loads the supplied value into the DS register so that it can access its data area in memory.

Synopsis of Function 42h Procedure. The following is a synopsis of the function 42h procedure:

```
int FAR (*entryPoint)(Function,ESCDBuffer,ESCDSelector,BiosSelector);
int Function;                    /* PnP function 0042h */
char FAR *ESCDBuffer;            /* buffer pointer */
unsigned int ESCDSelector;       /* used if NV in memory space */
unsigned int BiosSelector;       /* PnP BIOS DS value */
```

Example Function 42h Assembly Language Procedure Call. The following is an example assembly language function 42h PnP BIOS call.

```
push  BiosSelector             ;DS value>stack
push  segment ESCDSelector     ;buffer segment>stack
push  offset ESCDSelector      ;buffer offset>stack
push  segment ESCDBuffer       ;segment>stack
push  offset ESCDBuffer        ;offset>stack
push  READ_ESCD                ;Function 0042h>stack
call  FAR PTR entryPoint       ;call BIOS
add   sp,12                    ;reset stack pointer
cmp   ax,SUCCESS               ;test return code
jne   error                    ;jmp to error if non-zero,
                               ;else proceed
```

Function 42h Return Values. All registers other than AX are preserved. The content of the AX register indicates success or failure of the function request. A value of 0000h indicates success. A non-zero value with bit 7 set to one indicates an error code, while a non-zero value with bit 7 cleared to zero indicates a warning code. These codes are defined in Table 15-3 on page 225.

On return, the ESCDBuffer in memory contains the ESCD structure.

Function 43h—Write ESCD

Function 43h Description. This function is optional and is used to write the complete ESCD structure to NV memory from a memory buffer. It is used to update the ESCD structure when:

- a new device has been added to the system.
- deleting the record of resources assigned to a device that has been removed from the system.
- first storing configuration information for the initial machine configuration.
- altering the resources assigned to a device already configured so that the new configuration is used the next time the system is restarted.

When calling this function, the OS provides the start address of the memory buffer to be written to NV memory. The size of the memory buffer containing the ESCD data structure is the MinESCDWriteSize value returned by function 41h. Upon entry to function 43h, the BIOS determines the size of the ESCD data structure from the ESCD header in the buffer (for a detailed description of the ESCD data structure format, refer to the ESCD specification). The ESCDSelector input argument must be supplied if function 41h indicates that the NV memory is mapped into memory space. If function 41h indicates that it isn't memory-mapped, the selector value must be set to zero.

Reconfiguration of the embedded system board devices must be handled using functions 0, 1, and 2.

Function 43h Input Arguments. Table 15-5 on page 232 defines the input arguments that must be supplied to the PnP BIOS when calling function 43h.

Table 15-25: Function 43h Input Arguments

Name	Size (bytes)	Description
Function	2	Function number value 0043h, represented as a 16-bit signed integer.
ESCDBuffer	4	This 32-bit pointer points to the memory buffer that contains the ESCD structure supplied to the BIOS to be written to NV memory. The pointer is in segment:offset form.

Table 15-25: Function 43h Input Arguments (Continued)

Name	Size (bytes)	Description
ESCDSelector	2	This value is required if function 41h has indicated that the NV memory is located in memory space. In this case, a protected mode OS must (prior to calling function 42h) create a segment descriptor using the base address of the memory-mapped NV memory and a segment length of 64KB. The segment must be designated read/writable. The ESCDSelector value is then set to the entry number of the segment descriptor in the segment descriptor table. If the OS is a real mode OS, the ESCDSelector value must be set to the segment base address of the NV memory area (supplied by function 41h). If the NV memory is mapped into memory space, this argument is necessary to permit the function to access the memory data area that the NV memory resides in. If function 41h indicated that the NV memory is not located in memory space, this argument must be set to zero.
BiosSelector	2	• If the caller is a protected mode OS, the OS must create a data segment descriptor in the descriptor table using the base address obtained from the PnP installation check structure. The data segment must have a length of 64KB and permit read/write access. The value supplied in the BiosSelector argument is the 16-bit selector that identifies the location of the descriptor within the descriptor table. • If the caller is a real mode OS, the value supplied is the 16-bit real mode DS value obtained from the installation check structure. Upon entry, the BIOS loads the supplied value into the DS register so that it can access its data area in memory.

Synopsis of Function 43h Procedure. The following is a synopsis of the function 43h procedure:

```
int FAR (*entryPoint)(Function,ESCDBuffer,ESCDSelector,BiosSelector);
int Function;                    /* PnP function 0043h */
char FAR *ESCDBuffer;            /* buffer pointer */
unsigned int ESCDSelector;       /* NV memory segment selector */
unsigned int BiosSelector;       /* PnP BIOS DS value */
```

Example Function 43h Assembly Language Procedure Call. The following is an example assembly language function 43h PnP BIOS call.

```
push  BiosSelector          ;DS value>stack
push  ESCDSelector          ;NV memory selector
push  segment ESCDBuffer    ;buffer segment>stack
push  offset ESCDBuffer     ;buffer offset>stack
push  WRITE_ESCD            ;Function 0043h>stack
call  FAR PTR entryPoint    ;call BIOS
add   sp,10                 ;reset stack pointer
cmp   ax,SUCCESS            ;test return code
jne   error                 ;jmp to error if non-zero,
                            ;else proceed
```

Function 43h Return Values. All registers other than AX are preserved. The content of the AX register indicates success or failure of the function request. A value of 0000h indicates success. A non-zero value with bit 7 set to one indicates an error code, while a non-zero value with bit 7 cleared to zero indicates a warning code. These codes are defined in Table 15-3 on page 225.

Appendix A— Device ID Assignments

Introduction

The PnP device ID permits the OS to associate a device with its associated device driver. Microsoft has assigned PnP device IDs to many of the devices most commonly found integrated onto the system board. This includes devices within the following categories:

- Interrupt controllers
- Timers
- DMA controllers
- Keyboards
- Parallel ports
- Serial ports
- Disk controllers
- Display controllers
- Expansion buses
- Real-time clock and other miscellaneous system board devices
- PCMCIA controller chip sets
- Mouse
- Modems
- Network controllers
- SCSI and proprietary CD-ROM controllers
- Sound, video capture, and multimedia controllers

Microsoft Windows 95 requires that each system board device have a unique device ID. This EISA-style, PnP ID is assigned by Microsoft. The EISA manufacturer ID of "PNP" has been assigned to Microsoft and Microsoft has created a list of IDs built upon this manufacturer ID. Windows 95 uses a device's ID to identify a device driver information file (a file with a .INF extension). The contents of this file identifies the loadable device driver associated with the device. During the OS load process, Windows 95 uses this information to locate the device driver associated with the device and loads the driver into memory.

Plug and Play System Architecture

To permit Windows 95 to locate and load the driver associated with a device, manufacturers of all add-in devices are required to assign a unique device ID to the device and to supply an .INF file and a loadable device driver file.

The tables that follow provide a list of the device IDs assigned to common system board devices by Microsoft. The current list may be downloaded from the Compuserve PlugPlay forum. Eventually, these IDs will be incorporated into the PnP ISA specification.

Table A-1: EISA Device IDs for Interrupt Controllers

Device ID	Device
PNP0000	AT interrupt controller
PNP0001	EISA interrupt controller
PNP0002	MCA interrupt controller
PNP0003	Intel APIC
PNP0004	Cyrix SLiC MP interrupt controller

Table A-2: EISA Device IDs for System Timers

Device ID	Device
PNP0100	AT timers
PNP0101	EISA timers
PNP0102	MCA timers

Appendix A— Device ID Assignments

Table A-3: EISA Device IDs for DMA Controllers

Device ID	Device
PNP0200	AT DMA controller
PNP0201	EISA DMA controller
PNP0202	MCA DMA controller

Table A-4: EISA Device IDs for Keyboards

Device ID	Device
PNP0300	IBM PC/XT keyboard controller (83-key)
PNP0301	IBM PC/AT keyboard controller (86-key)
PNP0302	IBM PC/XT keyboard controller (84-key)
PNP0303	IBM enhanced (101/102-key, PS/2 mouse support)
PNP0304	Olivetti keyboard (83-key)
PNP0305	Olivetti keyboard (102-key)
PNP0306	Olivetti keyboard (86-key)
PNP0307	Microsoft Windows keyboard
PNP0308	General input device emulation interface (GIDEI) legacy
PNP0309	Olivetti keyboard (A101/102-key)
PNP030A	AT&T 302 keyboard

Table A-5: EISA Device IDs for Parallel Ports

Device ID	Device
PNP0400	Standard LPT printer port
PNP0401	ECP printer ports

Table A-6: EISA Device IDs for Serial Ports

Device ID	Device
PNP0500	Standard PC COM port
PNP0501	16550A-compatible COM port

Table A-7: EISA Device IDs for Disk Controllers

Device ID	Device
PNP0600	Generic ESDI/IDE/ATA hard disk controller
PNP0601	Plus Hardcard II
PNP0602	Plus Hardcard IIXL/EZ
PNP0603	HP Omnibook IDE controller
PNP0604	PC standard floppy disk controller
PNP0605	HP Omnibook floppy disk controller

Appendix A— Device ID Assignments

Table A-8: EISA Device IDs forDisplay Controllers

Device ID	Device
PNP0900	VGA compatible
PNP0901	Video Seven VRAM/VRAM II/1024i
PNP0902	8514/A compatible
PNP0903	Trident VGA
PNP0904	Cirrus Logic laptop VGA
PNP0905	Cirrus Logic VGA
PNP0906	Tseng ET4000
PNP0907	Western Digital VGA
PNP0908	Western Digital laptop VGA
PNP0909	S3 911/924
PNP090A	ATI Ultra Pro/Plus (Mach 32)
PNP090B	ATI Ultra (Mach 8)
PNP090C	XGA compatible
PNP090D	ATI VGA Wonder
PNP090E	Weitek P9000 graphics adapter
PNP090F	Oak Technology VGA
PNP0910	Compaq QVision
PNP0911	XGA/2
PNP0912	Tseng W32/W32i/W32p
PNP0913	S3 801/928/964
PNP0914	Cirrus Logic 5429/5434 (memory-mapped)

Table A-8: EISA Device IDs forDisplay Controllers (Continued)

Device ID	Device
PNP0915	Compaq advanced VGA (AVGA)
PNP0916	ATI Ultra Pro Turbo (Mach64)
PNP0917	Reserved by Microsoft
PNP0930	C&T Super VGA
PNP0931	C&T Accelerator
PNP0940	NCR 77c22e Super VGA
PNP0941	NCR 77c32blt
PNP09FF	Plug and Play monitors (VESA DDC)

Table A-9: EISA Device IDs for Expansion Buses

Device ID	Device
PNP0A00	ISA bus
PNP0A01	EISA bus
PNP0A02	MCA bus
PNP0A03	PCI bus
PNP0A04	VESA VL bus

Table A-10: EISA Device IDs for RTC and Miscellaneous System Board Devices

Device ID	Device
PNP0800	AT speaker
PNP0B00	AT RTC
PNP0C00	PnP BIOS (only created by the system device node enumerator)
PNP0C01	System board
PNP0C02	ID for reserving resources required by PnP system board registers (not specific to a particular device)
PNP0C03	PnP BIOS event notification interrupt
PNP0C04	Math coprocessor
PNP0C05	APM BIOS (all versions)
PNP0C06	Reserved for identification of early PnP BIOS implementation
PNP0C07	Reserved for identification of early PnP BIOS implementation

Table A-11: EISA Device IDs for PCMCIA Controller Chipsets

Device ID	Device
PNP0E00	Intel 82365-compatible PCMCIA controller
PNP0E01	Cirrus Logic CL-PD6720 PCMCIA controller
PNP0E02	VLSI VL82C146 PCMCIA controller

Table A-12: EISA Device IDs for Mice

Device ID	Device
PNP0F	Microsoft bus mouse

Table A-12: EISA Device IDs for Mice (Continued)

Device ID	Device
PNP0F	Microsoft serial mouse
PNP0F	Microsoft Inport mouse
PNP0F	Microsoft PS/2 mouse
PNP0F	MouseSystems mouse
PNP0F	MouseSystems 3-button mouse (COM2)
PNP0F	Genius mouse (COM1)
PNP0F	Genius mouse (COM2)
PNP0F	Logitech serial mouse
PNP0F	Microsoft Ballpoint serial mouse
PNP0F	Microsoft PnP mouse
PNP0F	Microsoft PnP ballpoint mouse
PNP0F	Microsoft-compatible serial mouse
PNP0F	Microsoft-compatible Inport mouse
PNP0F	Microsoft-compatible PS/2 mouse
PNP0F	Microsoft-compatible serial ballpoint mouse
PNP0F	TI QuickPort mouse
PNP0F	Microsoft-compatible bus mouse
PNP0F	Logitech PS/2 mouse
PNP0F	PS/2 port for PS/2 mice
PNP0F	Microsoft Kids mouse
PNP0F	Logitech bus mouse
PNP0F	Logitech SWIFT device
PNP0F	Logitech-compatible serial mouse

Table A-12: EISA Device IDs for Mice (Continued)

Device ID	Device
PNP0F	Logitech-compatible bus mouse
PNP0F	Logitech-compatible PS/2 mouse
PNP0F	Logitech-compatible SWIFT device
PNP0F	HP Omnibook mouse
PNP0F	Compaq LTE Trackball PS/2 mouse
PNP0F	Compaq LTE trackball serial mouse
PNP0F	Microsoft Kids trackball mouse
PNP0F	Reserved by Microsoft input device group
PNP0F	Reserved by Microsoft input device group
PNP0F	Reserved by Microsoft input device group
PNP0F	Reserved by Microsoft input device group
PNP0F	Reserved by Microsoft systems

Table A-13: EISA Device IDs for Network Controllers

Device ID	Device
PNP8001	Novell/Anthem NE3200
PNP8004	Compaq NE3200
PNP8006	Intel EtherExpress/32
PNP8008	HP EtherTwist EISA LAN Adapter/32 (HP27248A)
PNP8065	Ungermann-Bass NIUps or NIUps/EOTP
PNP8072	DEC (DE211) EtherWorks MC/TP
PNP8073	DEC (DE212) EtherWorks MC/TP_BNC

Table A-13: EISA Device IDs for Network Controllers (Continued)

Device ID	Device
PNP8078	DCA 10Mb MCA
PNP8074	HP MC LAN Adapter/16 TP (PC27246)
PNP80C9	IBM Token ring
PNP80CA	IBM Token ring II
PNP80CB	IBM token ring II/short
PNP80CC	IBM Token ring 4/16Mbs
PNP80D3	Novell/Anthem NE1000
PNP80D4	Novell/Anthem NE2000
PNP80D5	NE1000 compatible
PNP80D6	NE2000 compatible
PNP80D7	Novell/Anthem NE1500T
PNP80D8	Novell/Anthem NE2100
PNP80DD	SMC ARCNETPC
PNP80DE	SMC ARCNET PC100,PC200
PNP80DF	SMC ARCNET PC110,PC210,PC250
PNP80E0	SMC ARCNET PC130/E
PNP80E1	SMC ARCNET PC120,PC220,PC260
PNP80E2	SMC ARCNET PC270/E
PNP80E5	SMC ARCNET PC600W,PC650W
PNP80E7	DEC DEPCA
PNP80E8	DEC (DE100) EtherWorks LC
PNP80E9	DEC (DE200) EtherWorks Turbo
PNP80EA	DEC (DE101) EtherWorks LC/TP

Table A-13: EISA Device IDs for Network Controllers (Continued)

Device ID	Device
PNP80EB	DEC (DE201) EtherWorks Turbo/TP
PNP80EC	DEC (DE202) EtherWorks Turbo/TP_BNC
PNP80ED	DEC (DE102) EtherWorks LC/TP_BNC
PNP80EE	DEC EE101 (built-in)
PNP80EF	DECpc 433 WS (built-in)
PNP80F1	3Com EtherLink Plus
PNP80F3	3Com EtherLink II or IITP (8 or 16-bit)
PNP80F4	3Com TokenLink
PNP80F6	3Com EtherLink 16
PNP80F7	3Com EtherLink III
PNP80FB	Thomas Conrad TC6045
PNP80FC	Thomas Conrad TC6042
PNP80FD	Thomas Conrad TC6142
PNP80FE	Thomas Conrad TC6145
PNP80FF	Thomas Conrad TC6242
PNP8100	Thomas Conrad TC6245
PNP8015	DCA 10Mb
PNP8106	DCA 10Mb Fiber Optic
PNP8107	DCA 10Mb twisted pair
PNP8113	Racal NI6510
PNP811C	Ungermann-Bass NIUpc
PNP8120	Ungermann-Bass NIUpc/EOTP
PNP8123	SMC StarCard PLUS (WD/8003S)

Table A-13: EISA Device IDs for Network Controllers (Continued)

Device ID	Device
PNP8124	SMC StarCard PLUS with on-board hub (WD/8003SH)
PNP8125	SMC EtherCard PLUS (WD/8003E)
PNP8126	SMC EtherCard PLUS with boot ROM socket (WD/8003EBT)
PNP8127	SMC EtherCard PLUS with boot ROM socket (WD/8003EB)
PNP8128	SMC EtherCard PLUS TP (WD/8003WT)
PNP812A	SMC EtherCard PLUS 16 with boot ROM socket (WD/8013EBT)
PNP812D	Intel EtherExpress 16 or 16TP
PNP812F	Intel TokenExpress 16/4
PNP8130	Intel TokenExpress MCA 16/4
PNP8132	Intel EtherExpress 16 (MCA)
PNP8137	Artisoft AE-1
PNP8138	Artisoft AE-2 or AE-3
PNP8141	Amplicard AC210/XT)
PNP8142	Amplicard AC210/AT
PNP814B	Everex SpeedLink/PC16 (EV2027)
PNP8155	HP PC LAN Adapter/8 TP (HP27245)
PNP8156	HP PC LAN Adapter/16 TP (HP27247A)
PNP8157	HP PC LAN Adapter/8 TL (HP27250)
PNP8158	HP PC LAN Adapter/16 TP Plus (HP27247B)
PNP8159	HP PC LAN Adapter/16 TL Plus (HP27252)
PNP815F	National Semiconductor Ethernode *16AT
PNP8160	National Semiconductor AT/LANTIC Ethernode 16-AT3
PNP816A	NCR Token ring 4 Mbs ISA

Table A-13: EISA Device IDs for Network Controllers (Continued)

Device ID	Device
PNP816D	NCR Token ring 16/4 Mbs ISA
PNP8191	Olicom 16/4 Token ring adapter
PNP81C3	SMC EtherCard PLUS Elite (WD/8003EP)
PNP81C4	SMC EtherCard PLUS 10T (WD/8003W)
PNP81C5	SMC EtherCard PLUS Elite 16 (WD/8013EP)
PNP81C6	SMC EtherCard PLUS Elite 16T (WD/8013W)
PNP81C7	SMC EtherCard PLUS Elite 16 Combo (WD/8013EW or 8013EWC)
PNP81C8	SMC EtherElite Ultra 16
PNP81E4	Pure Data PDI9025-32 (token ring)
PNP81E6	Pure Data PDI508+ (ArcNet)
PNP81E7	Pure Data PDI516+ (ArcNet)
PNP81EB	Proteon Token ring (P1390)
PNP81EC	Proteon Token ring (P1392)
PNP81ED	Proteon ISA token ring (P1340)
PNP81EE	Proteon ISA token ring (P1342)
PNP81EF	Proteon ISA token ring (P1346)
PNP81F0	Proteon ISA token ring (P1347)
PNP81FF	Cabletron E2000 Series DNI
PNP8200	Cabletron E2100 Series DNI
PNP8209	Zenith Z-Node
PNP820A	Zenith NE2000 compatible
PNP8213	Xircom Pocket Ethernet II
PNP8214	Xircom Pocket Ethernet I

Table A-13: EISA Device IDs for Network Controllers (Continued)

Device ID	Device
PNP821D	RadiSys EXM-10
PNP8227	SMC 3000 Series
PNP8231	AMD AM2100/AM1500T
PNP8263	Tulip NCC-16
PNP8277	Exos 105
PNP828A	Intel '595-based Ethernet
PNP828B	TI 2000-style token ring
PNP828C	AMD PCNet family cards
PNP828D	AMD PCNet32 (VL version)
PNP82BD	IBM PCMCIA-NIC
PNP8321	DEC Ethernet (all types)
PNP8323	SMC EtherCard (all types except 8013/A)
PNP8324	ARCNET compatible
PNP8326	Thomas Conrad (all ArcNet types)
PNP8327	IBM token ring (all types)
PNP8385	Remote network access driver
PNP8387	Remote network access point-to-point protocol driver

Table A-14: EISA Device IDs for SCSI and Proprietary CD Adapters

Device ID	Device
PNPA000	Adaptec 154x compatible SCSI controller
PNPA001	Adaptec 174x compatible SCSI controller

Appendix A— Device ID Assignments

Table A-14: EISA Device IDs for SCSI and Proprietary CD Adapters (Continued)

Device ID	Device
PNPA002	Future Domain 16-700 compatible controller
PNPA003	Panasonic proprietary CD-ROM adapter (SBPro/SB16)
PNPA01B	Trantor 128 SCSI controller
PNPA01D	Trantor T160 SCSI controller
PNPA01E	Trantor T338 Parallel SCSI controller
PNPA01F	Trantor T348 Parallel SCSI controller
PNPA020	Trantor Media Vision SCSI controller
PNPA022	Always IN-2000 SCSI controller
PNPA02B	Sony proprietary CD-ROM controller
PNPA02D	Trantor T13b 8-bit SCSI controller
PNPA02F	Trantor T358 parallel SCSI controller
PNPA030	Mitsumi LU-005 single speed CD-ROM controller and drive
PNPA031	Mitsumi FX-001 single speed CD-ROM controller and drive
PNPA032	Mitsumi FX-001 double speed CD-ROM controller and drive

Table A-15: EISA Device IDs for Sound, Video Capture, and Multimedia

Device ID	Device
PNPB000	Sound Blaster 1.5 compatible sound device
PNPB001	Sound Blaster 2.0 compatible sound device
PNPB002	Sound Blaster pro compatible sound device
PNPB003	Sound Blaster 16 compatible sound device
PNPB004	Thunderboard compatible sound device
PNPB005	Adlib compatible FM synthesizer device
PNPB006	MPU401 compatible
PNPB007	Microsoft Windows Sound System compatible sound device
PNPB008	Compaq business audio
PNPB009	PnP Microsoft Windows Sound System device
PNPB00A	MediaVision Pro Audio Spectrum (Trantor SCSI enabled, Thunder chip disabled)
PNPB00B	MediaVision Pro Audio 3D
PNPB00C	MusicQuest MQX-32M
PNPB00D	MediaVision Pro Audio Spectrum Basic (No Trantor SCSI, Thunder chip enabled)
PNPB00E	MediaVision Pro Audio Spectrum (Trantor SCSI enabled, Thunder chip enabled)
PNPB00F	MediaVision Jazz-16 chipset (OEM versions)
PNPB010	Auravision VxP500 chipset, Orchid Videola
PNPB018	MediaVision Pro Audio Spectrum 8-bit
PNPB019	MediaVision Pro Audio Spectrum Basic (No Trantor SCSI, Thunder chip disabled)

Appendix A— Device ID Assignments

Table A-15: EISA Device IDs for Sound, Video Capture, and Multimedia (Continued)

Device ID	Device
PNPB020	Yamaha OPL3 compatible FM synthesizer device
PNPB02F	Joystick/gameport

Table A-16: EISA Device IDs for Modems

Device ID	Device
PNPC000	Compaq 14400 Modem (TBD)
PNPC001	Compaq 2400/9600 modem (TBD)

Appendix B—Class Code Assignments

Introduction

The system BIOS must implement a data structure, referred to as a device node, for each device embedded on the system board. A complete description of the node format can be found in the section entitled. One of the items in the device node is the device type code. In PCI, this referred to as the class code.

If the OS cannot find a loadable device driver that matches the device ID, the OS can look for a generic device driver that has a match on the device type code.

Table B-1: Class Code (Device Type Code) Assignments

Sub Class	Programming I/F	Description
Class Code 00h—Reserved (Sub Class and Prog. I/F bytes are 00h)		
Class Code 01h—Mass Storage Controllers		
00h	00h	SCSI controller
01h	nnh	IDE Controller. See Table B-2, "IDE Programming Interface Definition," on page 301 for definition of the programming interface byte.
02h	00h	Floppy disk controller
03h	00h	IPI controller
04h	00h	RAID controller
80h	00h	Other mass storage controller

Table B-1: Class Code (Device Type Code) Assignments (Continued)

Sub Class	Programming I/F	Description
		Class Code 02h—Network Controllers
00h	00h	Ethernet controller
01h	00h	Token ring controller
02h	00h	FDDI controller
03	00h	ATM controller
80h	00h	Other network controller
		Class Code 03h—Display Controllers
00h	00h	VGA-compatible controller, responding to memory addresses 000A0000h through 000BFFFFh, and IO ports 03B0h through 3BBh and all aliases of these addresses.
	01h	8514-compatible controller, responding to IO ports 02E8 and its aliases, and IO ports 02EAh and 02EFh.
01h	00h	XGA controller
80h	00h	Other display controller
		Class Code 04h—Multimedia Devices
00h	00h	Video device
01h	00h	Audio device
80h	00h	Other multimedia device
		Class Code 05h—Memory Controllers
00h	00h	RAM memory controller
01h	00h	Flash memory controller
80h	00h	Other memory controller
		Class Code 06h—Bridges

Table B-1: Class Code (Device Type Code) Assignments (Continued)

Sub Class	Programming I/F	Description
00h	00h	Host/PCI bridge
01h	00h	PCI/ISA bridge
02h	00h	PCI/EISA bridge
03h	00h	PCI/MCA bridge
04h	00h	PCI/PCI bridge
05h	00h	PCI/PCMCIA bridge
06h	00h	NuBus bridge
07h	00h	Cardbus bridge
80h	00h	Other bridge type
Class Code 07h—Simple Communications Controllers		
00h	00h	Generic XT compatible serial controller
	01h	16450 compatible serial controller
	02h	16550 compatible serial controller
01h	00h	Parallel port (output only)
	01h	Bi-directional parallel port
	02h	ECP 1.x parallel port
80h	00h	Other communications controller
Class Code 08h—Base System Peripherals		
00h	00h	Generic 8259 programmable interrupt controller (PIC)
	01h	ISA compatible PIC
	02h	EISA compatible PIC

Table B-1: Class Code (Device Type Code) Assignments (Continued)

Sub Class	Programming I/F	Description
01h	00h	Generic 8237A compatible DMA controller
	01h	ISA compatible DMA controller
	02h	EISA compatible DMA controller
02h	00h	Generic 8254 compatible timer
	01h	ISA compatible timer
	02h	EISA compatible timer
03h	00h	Generic RTC controller
	01h	ISA RTC controller
80h	00h	Other system device
Class Code 09h—Input Devices		
00h	00h	Keyboard controller
01h	00h	Digitizer (pen)
02h	00h	Mouse controller
80h	00h	Other input device
Class Code 0Ah—Docking Stations		
00h	00h	Generic docking station
80h	00h	Other type of docking station
Class Code 0Bh—Processors		
00h	00h	386
01h	00h	486
02h	00h	Pentium
10h	00h	Alpha

Appendix B—Class Code Assignments

Table B-1: Class Code (Device Type Code) Assignments (Continued)

Sub Class	Programming I/F	Description
40h	00h	Co-processor
Class Code 0Ch—Serial Bus Controllers		
00h	00h	Firewire (IEEE 1394)
01h	00h	ACCESS.bus
02h	00h	SSA

Table B-2: IDE Programming Interface Definition

Bit(s)	Description
0	Operating mode (primary)
1	Programmable indicator (primary)
2	Operating mode (secondary)
3	Programmable indicator (secondary)
6:4	Reserved. Must be zero
7	Master IDE device

Appendix C—Glossary

activate register. Each PnP logical device implements an activate register that is used to activate the device after it has been configured.

adapter description file. Each Micro Channel device (adapter) is accompanied by an adapter description file (ADF) that describes the resources required by the card. The file also defines the card's configuration registers and the bit settings in each that select various resource settings.

adapter enable/setup register. A Micro Channel card must be placed into setup mode in order to access its configuration registers. The configuration program uses this register to select the target Micro Channel card to place into setup mode. Once the card has been configured, this register is written with the appropriate value to take the card out of setup mode.

address port. Refers to the PnP configuration address port, used to select one of a logical device's stack of configuration registers to act as the target of subsequent configuration reads and writes.

ADF file. See "adapter description file."

alias. Refers to an IO address that "aliases" to one more other ranges. In other words, some IO cards perform an inadequate IO address decode and recognize addresses that are not really meant for them. Legacy ISA IO cards are a classic example—they only decode up to address bit nine, ignoring A[15:10].

Allocated resource descriptor. Refers to the allocated resource descriptor block in a system device node data structure. This set of descriptors defines the resources currently selected for the device's use.

alternate boot loader. Refers to the INT 18h instruction. In the original IBM PC, INT 18h was used to invoke ROM BASIC. Some machines, however, use this instruction to invoke an alternate OS boot loader program. The primary boot loader is invoked using INT 19h.

APIC IO Module. Refers to the Intel Advanced Programmable Interrupt Controller IO module. This module receives interrupt requests from various IO subsystems and distributes them to the next available processor (in a machine with an array of host processors). Each Intel Pentium P54C processor incorporates an APIC module that interacts with the external IO module.

APIC. See "APIC IO Module."

base address register (BAR). PCI configuration registers used to detect the address space requirements of the device and then assign a range of memory or IO space to the device's decoder(s). Each PCI device can implement up to six BARs.

BIOS installation check structure. A data structure residing on a 16-byte boundary within the memory range from F0000h through FFFFFh. The OS (and any other software that requires access to the PnP BIOS) searches for this structure. When found, it identifies the revision of the PnP BIOS services and its entry point.

BIOS. Basic Input Output Services. The set of platform-specific routines that are included in ROM to be used in communicating with the system hardware.

boot connection vector. In a PnP device ROM, the pointer to a ROM-based routine that may be called by the PnP BIOS to cause it to hook its device (or devices) to the boot interrupt vectors (INT 09h, INT 10h, and INT13h).

boot process. The process of reading the OS into memory and passing control to it.

bootstrap entry vector. A PnP device ROM may include a boot program that may be called by the PnP BIOS to boot the OS from the device.

bootstrap loader. The program that reads the first physical block from a mass storage device, verifies that it contains the boot block signature (55AAh), and then executes the boot program contained in the block. The boot program, in turn, begins reading the OS into memory.

buffer chaining. A DMA controller feature (e.g., in an EISA DMA controller) that facilitates "scatter," "gather" operations. This permits the DMA controller to read a contiguous block of data from a device and "scatter" it more than one memory buffer. Conversely, the DMA controller can read ("gather") a block of data spanning more than one memory buffer and pump it in a steady stream to an IO device.

bus enumerator. A bus-specific program that detects the presence of devices on its target bus (or buses), reads their required resource lists, and permits their configuration registers to be programmed.

card information structure (CIS). The resource requirement list supplied by a PCMCIA card.

card select number (CSN). The unique 8-bit number assigned to each PnP card by writing the value to the card's CSN configuration register. The configuration software can then wake a card up and gain access to its configuration registers it by writing its CSN into the wake command register.

Card Services. The PCMCIA program responsible for event notification, reading a card's resource requirements, and card configuration.

CardBus CIS pointer register. In the PCI revision 2.1 spec, a register that provides a pointer to a CardBus CIS.

CFG file. EISA configuration file. Contains the EISA card's resource requirements, and configuration register definition.

CIS. See "card information structure."

class code register. In PCI, the three-byte configuration register that defines the class, sub-class, and programming interface information about its device. PnP cards with PnP device ROMs also implement the class code (in ROM), but it is referred to as the device type code field. The configuration software can use the class and sub-class to locate a loadable device driver to use with the device.

CM. Refers to the Windows 95 Configuration Manager. The CM is the central entity that has responsibility for ascertaining the resource requirements of all system devices and ensuring that non-conflicting resources are allocated. In order to accomplish this task, the CM works with the various system bus enumerator programs (e.g., PCMCIA, PCI, PnP), the Device Installer, and loadable device drivers.

CMOS RAM. The non-volatile memory in which system configuration information is stored. This information is typically used to configure the machine on each re-start.

cold docking. Refers to the installation of a laptop into a docking station with the system powered off.

command register. Refers to the PCI configuration command register that is used to enable/disable various features of a PCI device.

Compatible device ID. A PnP logical device's resource requirement list can contain the EISA IDs of one or more devices that are register compatible with this logical device. This gives the OS the option of loading and using one of their device drivers if the one for this device cannot be located.

configuration address port. Refers to the PnP address port used to identify which configuration register acts as the target of reads and writes to the read and write data ports.

configuration command register. See "Command Register."

configuration control register. Refers to the PnP card's configuration control register. Used to: reset all CSNs to zero; to place the configuration logic on all PnP cards into the wait for key state; and to reset all logical devices and return all configuration registers to their default values.

configuration header space. Refers to the first 16 doublewords of a PCI device's configuration space. The registers that occupy this region are defined by the PCI specification.

Configuration Manager (CM). See "CM."

configuration mechanism #1. This is the preferred method of implementing a host/PCI bridge component to permit the processor to cause PCI bus configuration transactions.

configuration mechanism #2. This is the PCI configuration mechanism implemented in the earlier PCI chip sets. The 2.0 PCI spec says that configuration mechanism #1 must be used in all later chip sets.

configuration memory. The system non-volatile (NV) memory used to store configuration information for use on each power up.

configuration read data port. The IO port used to read data from the configuration registers on PnP cards. The data read is supplied by the configuration register pointed to by the configuration address port.

configuration register. A register used to select the resources (memory or IO space, interrupt lines, DMA channels) to be used by a device.

configuration write data port. The IO port used to write data to the configuration registers on PnP cards. The data is written to the configuration register pointed to by the configuration address port.

configure state. The state that a PnP card's configuration logic must be in to access its configuration registers.

control message. Using PnP BIOS function 04h, Send Message, the OS can issue a control message to the PnP BIOS instructing it to initiate an action (e.g., power the system down, undock, etc.).

CS. See "card services."

CS. Code Segment register. The x86 register that points to the start address of the area of memory that contains the currently executing program. Works in conjunction with the IP (instruction pointer) register, which identifies the location within the code segment from which the next instruction is to be fetched.

CSN register. Card select number register. Used by the PnP bus enumerator to assign a unique, non-zero, 8-bit card ID. When the configuration software wants to wake up the card and place into configuration mode, it writes this value into the wake command register. The card compares this value to that in the CSN register. If it matches, the card transitions to the configure state.

CSN. See "card select number."

DDI. See "DDIM."

DDIM. Device Driver Initialization Model. Refers to the manner in which PnP and PCI device ROMs are implemented. They are shadowed in system RAM and therefore have the ability to update internal data structures when their initialization code is executing. After initialization, the RAM is write-protected.

dependent function. Some devices (especially legacy devices) require the allocation of specific groups of related resources. A device describes related resource requirements using a dependent function structure in its resource requirement list. Assume that a device can be configured in any of the following manners:

- 16 contiguous IO ports starting at base IO address 01F0h, using IRQ10
- 16 contiguous IO ports starting at base IO address 02F0h, using IRQ11
- 16 contiguous IO ports starting at base IO address 03F0h, using IRQ15

In other words, the IRQ used is associated with a specific IO address range.

descriptors. Refers to the individual items (in a PnP device's resource requirement list) that define a particular resource required by the device (e.g., a block of memory space, an interrupt line, etc.).

device configuration registers. See "configuration registers."

device control registers. Refers to the following PnP card control registers: the activate, IO range check, reserved logical device control, and vendor-defined logical device control registers. Each logical device has its own set of device control registers.

device driver initialization, or DDI, model. See "DDIM."

device driver. The device-specific program that permits the OS to control a device. It receives requests from the OS to communicate with the device and converts the requests into the proper series of low-level IO operations to stimulate the device in the requested fashion. When the request has been processed, the results of the operation are passed back to the OS.

device ID. A unique ID that identifies a specific type of device. EISA and PnP device use EISA device IDs. The configuration software can use the ID to locate the device driver program associated with the device and load it into memory.

Device Installer. The Windows 95 program that interacts with the end user to handle the installation of new cards in the system. It creates an entry in the Registry for each device installed in the system, noting the name and location of its associated device driver and the recommended resources to be assigned to the device.

Device node attributes. This bit field in a device node provides information regarding the configurability of the device, as well as other device characteristics.

device node. A data structure maintained by the PnP BIOS that defines the resources used by a device embedded on the system board.

device ROM. A ROM (associated with a device) containing device-specific initialization code, interrupt service routine, BIOS routine, etc. In a sense, it's an extension of the system BIOS.

Device type code. A field located in the PnP device ROM header data structure. It contains the same information as the PCI class code register. The configuration software can use the device type code to locate a loadable device driver to use with the device.

device, static. A static device is one that is never installed or removed while power is applied to the machine.

disconnect vector. Points to the disconnect routine in a PnP device ROM. When executed, this routine restores any interrupt table entries that were hooked by the device's boot connection routine. If necessary, it restores any other information that was altered by the boot connection routine.

docking station. A home base into which a laptop can be installed to permit it access to more devices.

Dynamic Configuration. Each time that the machine is powered up, the BIOS can automatically scan each bus in the system to determine the machine's device population and the resource requirements of each device. It can then allocate non-conflicting resources to each device and activate them. This is referred to as dynamic resource allocation.

dynamic device. A dynamic device is one that can be installed or removed while power is applied to the machine. Some examples would be:
- Docking stations for laptop computers.
- PCMCIA cards (also referred to as PC cards).

EISA configuration file. See "CFG file."

EISA device ID. 32-bit device ID consisting of a three-character vendor ID (assigned by the administrator of the EISA spec, BCPR Services), a product ID, and a revision number.

EISA identifier. See "EISA device ID."

EISA product ID. See "EISA device ID."

EISA. Extension to Industry Standard Architecture.

Embedded System Board Devices. Devices that are permanently attached to the system board.

end of list tag. Special identifier that defines the end of a PnP card's resource requirement list.

enumerator. A bus-specific program responsible for detecting the presence of devices on its bus (or buses), reading their resource requirement lists, and writing to their configuration registers to assign non-conflicting resources to the devices. Windows 95's CM calls various system bus enumerators (e.g., PCMCIA, PnP) to manage the resources throughout the system.

event device driver. The driver routine that handles dynamic events (e.g., docking and undocking) when they occur.

Event Notification Flag. If the PnP BIOS uses polling as the event notification mechanism, this is the name of the memory location it uses to indicate that an event has been detected. It does this by setting bit 0 of the location to a one. The OS is responsible for periodically checking the bit. The OS determines the notification method and the flag location by reading the PnP BIOS installation check data structure from system ROM.

expansion ROM base address register. The PCI configuration register used to assign a start memory address to the device ROM and to enable its ROM address decoder.

far jump. An x86 instruction to jump to a location in another code segment.

frame buffer. The memory in which the video image is stored.

HAL. The Windows NT hardware abstraction layer. This code takes the place of the ROM BIOS, acting as the interface between the OS and the hardware platform.

handle. Used in the PnP BIOS spec as another name for a device node number. See "device node."

hardware abstraction layer. See "HAL."

hooking an interrupt. The act of placing the pointer to a device-specific interrupt service routine (or BIOS routine) into an entry in the interrupt table in memory. Prior to writing the pointer into memory, the current contents must be read and saved (this is the pointer to the service routine for the previous device that hooked the interrupt).

host/PCI bridge. The hardware component that acts as the bridge between the processor's bus and the PCI bus.

hot docking. Refers to the installation of a laptop into a docking station with the system fully powered on.

hot insertion and removal. Refers to the installation or removal of a device with the system fully powered on.

initial program load (IPL). The act of loading the OS into memory and passing control to it.

installation check structure. Short for the PnP BIOS installation check data structure. See "BIOS installation check structure."

INT 09h. This BIOS call invokes the keyboard interrupt handler. It could be hooked by another device to be used as the input device during the OS boot.

INT 10h. This BIOS call invokes the display BIOS routine. It could be hooked by another device to be used as the output device during the OS boot.

INT 13h. This BIOS call invokes the disk BIOS routine. It could be hooked by another device to be used as the IPL device during the OS boot.

INT 19h. This BIOS call invokes the bootstrap loader program that initiates the load of the OS into memory.

INT18h. In the original IBM PC, INT 18h was used to invoke ROM BASIC. Some machines, however, use this instruction to invoke an alternate OS boot loader program. The primary boot loader is invoked using INT 19h.

interrupt chaining. The process of creating a linked-list of interrupt handlers that share the same interrupt request signal line.

interrupt line register. This PCI configuration register is read/writable and is updated with the interrupt routing information by the system BIOS. The system BIOS detects that the device uses an interrupt output (INTA#, INTB#, INTC#, or INTD#) by reading from the device's interrupt pin register. It then programs the system board's interrupt router logic to route the device's PCI interrupt request line to a system IRQ line. The IRQ line number is then written into the device's interrupt line register. The device driver (or the OS) can read this register to determine which interrupt table entry to hook.

interrupt pin register. See "interrupt line register."

interrupt router. See "interrupt line register."

interrupt service routine. The device-specific program that is executed whenever its device generates an interrupt request. This routine services the device (in a device-specific manner) and then returns control to the interrupted program.

interrupt sharing. More than IO subsystem uses an interrupt request line to generate requests. This invokes the interrupt service routine associated with the device that last hooked the interrupt. It checks its device for an interrupt pending condition. If it exists, the body of the routine is executed to service the device. If, on the other hand, the device does not have an interrupt pending condition, its interrupt handler jumps to the service routine associated with the IO subsystem that hooked the interrupt just prior to this routine. It, in turn, polls its device.

interrupt table. The table in memory that contains the 256 pointers to the service routines associated with each possible interrupt level. Whenever a maskable interrupt occurs, the processor suspends the currently running program and marks its place (in stack memory). It then requests (from the interrupt controller) the interrupt level of the highest-priority device currently requesting service. This number is used to index into the interrupt table. The contents of the indicated entry supplies the start address of the service routine to jump to.

IO range check register. This register permits the programmer to verify that the IO range assigned to one of a logical device's IO address decoders does not conflict with any IO addresses used by any other device. The range check register resides at configuration location 31h.

IPL device. The initial program load device is the one selected by the BIOS to read the OS from.

IPL. See "initial program load."

ISA. Industry Standard Architecture. The IBM PC-AT architecture.

isolation state. The cards have been awakened and are competing to determine which will be chosen for configuration next. This is referred to as the **isolation state**.

Latency Timer. Also referred to as LT or MLT (master latency timer). Each PCI bus master must implement an LT register. The value assigned to this register by the configuration software defines how long a time slice (as a number of PCI bus clock periods) the master can own the bus each time that it successfully acquires ownership and initiates a transaction.

legacy ISA card. An ISA card that uses jumpers and/or switches to select the resources it uses. Alternately, its resource usage may be hardwired and not selectable at all.

logical device number register. The PnP device configuration register that is used to select the device on a PnP card to be configured. This register acts as a selector to enable access to the specified device's set of configuration registers.

logical device. Each PnP card may incorporate one or more devices (subsystems). Each is referred to as a logical device.

Master Latency Timer (MLT) register. See "latency timer."

MAX_LAT register. PCI maximum latency configuration register. The designer of a PCI bus master hardwires a value in this register indicating how quickly the device requires access to the PCI bus once it request bus ownership. This value is used by the PCI BIOS to choose what PCI bus arbitration priority to assign to the device.

MCA. Micro Channel Architecture. Bus/system architecture developed by IBM and used in the PS/2 and RS/6000 product lines. NCR also used this bus extensively.

memory-mapped IO. IO control, status, and data ports that respond to memory rather than IO accesses.

Message. In the context of the PnP BIOS, the OS and the PnP BIOS can exchange messages associated with events that occur during system operation.

Micro Channel Architecture. See "MCA."

MIN_GNT register. The PCI minimum grant configuration register. The designer of a PCI bus master hardwires a value in this register indicating the amount of time it would like to have guaranteed ownership of the PCI bus whenever it acquires bus ownership. The PCI BIOS uses this value to determine how big a value to program into the device's LT register. Also see "LT."

MLT. See "LT."

MPS. Multi-Processing Specification. The MPS 1.0 specification defines the architecture of an Intel x86-based platform that supports more than one processor and distributes interrupts evenly across the processors (i.e., symmetrical multiprocessing).

multi-function device. In PCI or PnP, a physical device package or card that incorporates more than one device on the same substrate or card. Each device is referred to as a logical device.

node list. A data structure maintained by the PnP BIOS that defines the resources used by all of the devices embedded on the system board. The PnP BIOS provides services for reading and updating the node list.

non-volatile (NV) memory. See "configuration memory."

NV memory. See "configuration memory."

OEM-defined message. In the context of the PnP BIOS, a message defined by the system PnP BIOS designer and sent to the BIOS by the OS using PnP BIOS function 04h, Send Message. The effect that the message has on the BIOS and/or the system is BIOS design-dependent.

PCI BIOS. The BIOS functions that permit the OS to access the PCI configuration register set for each PCI device.

PCI bus enumerator. The program that detects the presence of devices on the PCI bus (or buses), reads their required resource lists, and permits their configuration registers to be programmed.

PCI. Peripheral Component Interconnect bus.

PCI-to-PCI bridge. A hardware device that provides the bridge between two PCI buses. It permits bus masters on either side to converse with devices on the other side (if the target address is with the range assigned to a device on the other side).

PCMCIA. Personal Computer Memory Card International Association—the group that manages the PCMCIA and CardBus specs.

Plug and Play device driver. A Windows 95 device driver that obtains all configuration information from the CM, rather than by communicating directly with its device's configuration registers. It is also capable of exchanging messages with the OS (e.g., when a device is removed or installed during system operation).

PnP BIOS installation check structure. See "BIOS installation check structure."

PnP device ROM. See "DDIM."

PnP. Short for Plug and Play.

Polling. Checking for a condition (e.g., docking, undocking, data available, etc.) by periodically reading from a specific location (either memory or IO) and checking the condition of a bit.

POS register. Micro Channel programmable option select register. This is what MCA configuration registers are called.

Possible resource descriptor. Within a device node, this sub-structure defines the resource selections (e.g., the various IO ranges, memory ranges, interrupt lines, etc.) that can be made for the device.

POST. The power-on self-test program is the first program executed when the machine is powered up. It tests and initializes the system devices and then attempts to boot the OS into memory and pass control to it.

programmable option select (POS) registers. See "POS register."

PRSNT1# and PRSNT2#. The PCI add-in card present signals. When a PCI card is installed, it grounds one, the other, or both or these signals. The resultant pattern on these two signal lines indicates that a card is present and the maximum power requirements of the card (if it is subsequently configured and enabled).

range check register. See "IO range check register."

read data port. See "configuration read data port."

Registry. In Windows 95, the file that stores information regarding the configuration of the various devices and their associated device drivers.

resource data register. This PnP configuration register is used to read the resource requirement list from a PnP card.

resource data structure. The resource requirement list for a PnP card.

resource descriptors. The individual items that make up the resource data structure. Each one describes a resource required by a device on the card.

resource requirement list. The list of resources required by a PnP card.

resource. Any resource a device may require. Examples would be one or more blocks of IO or memory space, interrupt lines, DMA channels, etc.

response message. In response to an event message received from the BIOS, the OS issues a response message of OK or ABORT to the PnP BIOS (using function 04h, Send Message), instructing the BIOS whether to allow the reported event to proceed or to abort it.

RPL. Remote program load. The process of reading the OS into memory from a remote site (e.g., over the network).

serial identifier. Each PnP card must implement a 64-bit (eight-byte) unique serial identifier, followed by an 8-bit checksum byte. The first 32-bit field is a vendor ID in the form of an EISA device ID. The second 32-bit field of the serial identifier represents a manufacturer-supplied serial number unique to that card. In other words, if two or more cards of the same type from the same manufacturer were installed in the machine, the last 32-bit field of their serial identifiers are different and can be used by the configuration software to determine that there are multiple-instances of the same card present in the machine and to differentiate between them. It is the manufacturer's responsibility to ensure that this rule is adhered to. If a card manufacturer chooses not to support more than one instance of the card in a system, this value (the last 32-bits of the serial identifier) must be set to FFFFFFFFh

serial isolation register. The serial isolation register contains the serial identifier.

set read data port address register. Used to assign an IO address to the PnP configuration read data port on each PnP card. The assigned address is used to read data from the read data port.

setup mode. Another name for the configuration state wherein a PnP or a Micro Channel device's configuration registers can be accessed.

single-function device. An IC package or a card incorporating one device rather than multiple devices.

sleep state. The key has been received and the configuration logic on the community of PnP cards have entered the sleep state. They remain in this state until the configuration software awakens them to begin the process of assigning unique card select numbers (CSNs) to each of them.

small descriptors. A PnP card's resource requirement list is made of a series of descriptors. Some are large (consisting of eight or more bytes), while other types are small (consisting of up to seven bytes). See "descriptor."

Static Configuration. Each time that the machine is powered up, the BIOS uses the information contained in non-volatile(NV) memory to configure the machine. This is referred to as static configuration because the same, static resource image from non-volatile memory is used to configure the machine each time that it is powered on.

static device. A static device is one that is never installed or removed while power is applied to the machine.

Static resource information vector. Only used in a PnP device ROM associated with a non-PnP device. A PnP device must set this value to 0000h. If valid, this field points to a routine that reports the device's static resource usage when called. When called, ES:DI must point to a memory buffer at least 1KB in size. Upon completion, this routine has loaded the buffer with a data structure describing the fixed, non-configurable resources used by to the device.

status register. When reading data from a PnP card's resource requirement list, the programmer must check for bit 0 set to one in the status register before reading each byte from the resource data register. This bit indicates when the next byte is ready to be read.

subsystem ID. PCI configuration register, used in conjunction with the subsystem vendor ID to differentiate PCI devices based on the same core logic produced by another vendor (the vendor and device ID registers would have the core logic vendor's information).

subsystem vendor ID. See "subsystem ID."

symmetrical multiprocessing. See "APIC IO Module."

System Device Node. See "device node."

time slice. See "LT."

vendor ID. This PCI configuration register identifies the vendor of the PCI device.

wait for key state. The system has just been powered up. None of the PnP cards have been configured. The cards are all in a state awaiting a special key to enable their configuration logic. This is called the wait for key state.

wake command. A PnP card whose configuration logic is currently in the sleep state may be transitioned to the configure state by writing the card's assigned CSN to the wake command register. If the value in the wake command register matches that in the card's CSN register, the card enters the configure state. Its configuration registers can then be accessed.

warm docking. Refers to the installation of a laptop into a docking station with the system in suspend (sleep) mode.

write data port. See "configuration write data port."

Appendix D— References

The following is a list of recommended reference materials:

Title	Author	Publisher	ISBN #
ISA System Architecture	MindShare	Addison-Wesley	0-201-40996-8
EISA System Architecture	MindShare	Addison-Wesley	0-201-40995-X
PCMCIA System Architecture	MindShare	Addison-Wesley	0-201-40991-7
PCI System Architecture	MindShare	Addison-Wesley	0-201-40993-3
Hardware Design Guide for Microsoft Windows 95	Microsoft	Microsoft Press	1-55615-642-1
Plug and Play ISA Specification, version 1.0a	Available on Compuserve "PLUGPLAY" forum		
Plug and Play BIOS Specification, version 1.0A	Available on Compuserve "PLUGPLAY" forum		
Device Information Files and Microsoft Windows 95	Available on Compuserve "PLUGPLAY" forum		
PCI Design Issues for Windows 95 and Windows NT	Available on Compuserve "PLUGPLAY" forum		
Extended System Configuration Data Specification, version 1.03	Available on Compuserve "PLUGPLAY" forum		
Plug and Play SCSI Specification, version 1.0	Available on Compuserve "PLUGPLAY" forum		
Plug and Play SCSI, SCAM Level 1 Design Guide/Outline	Maxtor Corp. Available on Compuserve "PLUGPLAY" forum		

Title	Author	Publisher	ISBN #
PCMCIA Card Support in Windows "Chicago"	Microsoft Available on Compuserve "PLUGPLAY" forum		
Plug and Play Parallel Port Devices, version 1.0a	Available on Compuserve "PLUGPLAY" forum		
Plug and Play External COM Device Specification, version 0.99	Available on Compuserve "PLUGPLAY" forum		

Index

Index

Index

Index

Index

serial number 60, 73, 316
set read data port address configuration register 61
set read data port address register 81, 148
setup register 22
shadow RAM 198
shadowing of PCI device ROMs 187
signature, device ROM 193, 200
sleep 54
sleep state 65, 66, 74, 317
slot-specific IO space 24
slot-specific IO space, EISA 54
small descriptor 95
Socket Services 46, 50
Socket Services (SS) 44
SS 50
stack segment 222
start dependent function descriptor 96
state, configuration 66
state, isolation 65, 313
state, sleep 65, 317
state, wait for key 58, 65, 318
states, configuration 66, 68
static configuration 183, 231
static reconfiguration 226
static resource information vector 198
status register 82, 153
subsystem ID 15
subsystem ID register, Windows 95 and PCI 36
subsystem ID, PCI 31, 34
subsystem vendor ID 15, 34
subsystem vendor ID register, Windows 95 and PCI 36
subsystem vendor ID, PCI 31
system board ROM 184
system board timers 216
system device node 198, 216
system device node data structure 217

T

time slice, PCI bus master 31
timers 190
tuple 49
tuples used to form Windows 95 PCMCIA ID 49

U

undocking 227
Unicode identifier string descriptor format 100

V

vendor ID 9, 11, 15, 18, 30, 33
vendor ID register, Windows 95 and PCI 35
vendor ID, EISA 73
Vendor-defined card-level registers 83

Vendor-defined descriptor 96
vendor-defined descriptors 126
Vendor-defined logical device control registers 85
Vendor-defined resource descriptors 94
version number, Plug and Play 91
VGA display adapter 191
VGA-compatible controller 191
video frame buffer 40
virtual device drivers 47
VxD 47, 48

W

wait for key command 67, 92, 149
wait for key state 58, 65, 66, 318
wake command 61
wake command configuration register 61
wake command register 66, 71, 82, 151
warm docking 251, 257
Windows 95 13, 14, 30, 33, 34, 35, 36, 37, 38, 39, 40, 44, 48, 181
Windows 95 and interrupt-related problems 37
Windows 95 DDK 47
Windows 95 driver information file 47
Windows 95 inf file 47
Windows 95 PCI-related problems 34
Windows 95 PCMCIA bus enumerator 48
Windows NT 34, 35, 38
write data port 62, 66, 144
write data port, configuration 59
write-protection of shadow RAM 187

X

x86-based platforms 192

Technical Seminars

PCI System Architecture
PCI Software Environment
PCMCIA System Architecture
486 System Architecture
EISA System Architecture
CardBus System Architecture
Pentium System Architecture
Plug and Play System Architecture
ISA System Architecture
PowerPC Hardware Architecture
PowerPC Software Architecture

MindShare courses are presented at your site and are tailored to suit the needs of the audience.

To Contact MindShare

Internet: mindshar@interserv.com
Compuserve: 72507,1054
Phone: (214) 231-2216
Fax: (214) 783-4715

MindShare, Inc.
2202 Buttercup Drive
Richardson, TX 75082

Note: New courses are constantly under development. Please contact MindShare for the latest course offerings.